Star Trek:
Discovering the TV Series

Also by Tom Salinsky

Books

The Improv Handbook
with Deborah Frances-White, 2008

Best Pick: A Journey through Film History and the Academy Awards
with John Dorney and Jessica Regan, 2022

Star Trek: Discovering the TV Series
The Original Series, The Animated Series and The Next Generation
White Owl, 2024

Red Dwarf: Discovering the TV Series
Volume I: 1988–1993
White Owl, 2024

Plays

Coalition
with Robert Khan, 2013

Brexit
with Robert Khan, 2018

Star Trek:
Discovering the TV Series

Deep Space Nine and Voyager

Tom Salinsky

WHITE OWL

First published in Great Britain in 2024 by
White Owl
An imprint of Pen & Sword Books Limited
Yorkshire – Philadelphia

ISBN 978 1 39903 499 9

A CIP catalogue record for this book is
available from the British Library.

Typeset by Mac Style
Printed in the UK by CPI Group (UK) Ltd, Croydon, CR0 4YY.

MIX
Paper | Supporting
responsible forestry
FSC
www.fsc.org
FSC® C013604

The Publisher's authorised representative in the EU for product
safety is Authorised Rep Compliance Ltd., Ground Floor,
71 Lower Baggot Street, Dublin D02 P593, Ireland.
www.arccompliance.com

For a complete list of Pen & Sword titles please contact

PEN & SWORD BOOKS LIMITED
47 Church Street, Barnsley, South Yorkshire, S70 2AS, England
E-mail: enquiries@pen-and-sword.co.uk
Website: www.pen-and-sword.co.uk
or
PEN AND SWORD BOOKS
1950 Lawrence Road, Havertown, PA 19083, USA
E-mail: uspen-and-sword@casematepublishers.com
Website: www.penandswordbooks.com

For Gene, who started it all. For Rick, who kept it going.

And for Deborah. I hope I never have reason to write a book that isn't dedicated to you.

Disclaimer

This book is not authorised or endorsed by Paramount or anyone else associated with the production of **Star Trek** at any time. No infringement of any copyrights or trademarks is intended.

Contents

Notes   viii
Introduction   ix

Deep Space Nine – Season 1   1

Deep Space Nine – Season 2   19

Deep Space Nine – Season 3   43

Deep Space Nine – Season 4   65

Deep Space Nine – Season 5   86

Deep Space Nine – Season 6   112

Deep Space Nine – Season 7   136

The TNG Movies – Part One   159

Star Trek: Voyager – Season 1   167

Star Trek: Voyager – Season 2   186

Afterword   208
Appendix: Episodes by Rating   209
Index   215

Notes

Titles of series, and the words 'Star Trek' referring to the franchise as a whole, are shown in **bold**.

Titles of individual episodes are shown in *italics*, as are the names of other shows, movies, franchises or publications.

The six series dealt with in these three volumes are also sometimes known by the following abbreviations. What was retrospectively dubbed **The Original Series** is abbreviated to **TOS**. Following the same principle, **The Animated Series** is **TAS**.

Star Trek: The Next Generation is abbreviated to **TNG**. **Star Trek: Deep Space Nine** is abbreviated to **DS9**. People who want three-letter abbreviations for everything have also used **VOY** for **Star Trek: Voyager** and **ENT** for **Star: Trek Enterprise** but I won't be using those in the text, only for the episode headings.

Episodes and movies were watched on official DVD and Blu-ray releases, where commentaries, documentaries and subtitle trivia tracks were often helpful in providing additional context. I also consulted Peter Holmstrom's *The Center Seat: 55 Years of Trek* and Edward Gross and Mark Altman's *The Fifty-Year Mission*.

Although actor Alexander Siddig was generally credited under a different name for early seasons of **DS9**, I have assumed that the name he now uses is the name he prefers and so I have used it throughout this work.

Introduction

As I'm typing these words, *Volume I* hasn't been released yet. Publishing is slow and I'm in a weird limbo. I have no idea whether *Volume I* disappeared without trace or whether it's become a publishing phenomenon – the telefantasy tie-in non-fiction equivalent of *Harry Potter*. Nevertheless, the plan always was to cover everything from Kirk to Archer in two books and my daily viewing schedule has continued uninterrupted. Here's a quick recap for anyone who – for some reason – is reading these words and doesn't have a copy of *Volume I*.

I've always been interested in science fiction, since childhood, but although a scarily detailed expert on *Doctor Who* and *The Hitchhiker's Guide to the Galaxy*, I was only vaguely interested in **Star Trek**, with **The Next Generation** and the movies being what I knew best. So, at the end of 2021 I drew up a spreadsheet which demonstrated that everything from the first episode of **The Original Series** to the last episode of **Enterprise** could be watched at the rate of one episode a day and completed in two years. This project became a blog, and the blog became a book – or rather two books. And now, three books. While at first glance, it makes sense to tackle the first three TV series in *Volume I* and the second three TV series in *Volume II*, this overlooks that those first three series comprise 279 episodes and the other three comprise 446. That meant further decisions had to be taken about what material went where.

Once the decision had been taken to split the book at all, it made sense to save **Deep Space Nine** for *Volume II*, and that meant that although I was watching in strict release order, I had to postpone discussion of Sisko, Odo and the rest. So one option for book two would be to present the episodes reviewed here in release order, **Voyager** episodes interleaving with **Deep Space Nine**, but I've decided not to, for a couple of reasons.

One is consistency: the first volume established that this material will be presented series by series and season by season. That also makes the book easier to navigate. Then there's the fact that the two series that really share storytelling material are **TNG** and **DS9**, which were going to have to be split across two books in any case. The whole point of **Voyager** was that it was going to have to find new stories in the Delta quadrant. They have no idea what's happening to the rest of the Federation. They don't even get the new uniforms. Balancing the remaining material also means that we'll only get to Season 2 of **Voyager** this time around, with the back five covered in *Volume III*.

That just leaves the remaining **TNG** movies that weren't in *Volume I* (I really didn't want to end that book with *Nemesis*). That gives me two options: I make the arbitrary choice to drop the **TNG** movies into the narrative of either **Deep Space Nine** or **Voyager** (I did consider dropping the later **Original Series** movies into the narrative of **TNG** in *Volume I*) or I use the **TNG** movies to create breaks in the narrative between **DS9** and **Voyager** in *Volume II* and between **Voyager** and **Enterprise** in *Volume III* – and that's what I've decided to do. If we aren't going to go chronologically, then let's at least make the contents page look tidy. So here, you'll get seven seasons of **Deep Space Nine**, the first two **TNG** movies, and the first two seasons of **Voyager**. And if you still want more, *Volume III* will contain the remaining **Voyager** episodes, the last two **TNG** movies, and then four seasons of **Enterprise** – and we're done.

As with last time, you'll get some basic, factual information about each episode, but less than you'd find in Wikipedia or IMDb (which are still there, if you want them). Each story has a star rating out of five, with five being a near-perfect piece of work, four being very good but either less ambitious or flawed in some way, three being average but unremarkable, two being disappointing, and one being dreadful, with half-stars as the subtle gradations in between. Then there's a pithy, one-or-two sentence summation, followed by a longer analysis. This will range from a single paragraph to a long essay depending on the significance of the story or the complexity of my feelings about it – and these will be my personal, subjective feelings: I make no more grandiose claims for them than that.

Once again, I have lots of people to thank: Victoria and Jess at AM Heath, Jonathan and Charlotte and everyone at Pen & Sword, the forensic Linne Matthews, all of the friends and friends of friends who contributed their own thoughts about various episodes, and of course, Deborah, who put up with all of this for two years.

Lastly, thanks to you for buying this book (and, I can only assume, its predecessor). I hope you found it fun to come on this journey with me. Now, if you're ready, let's see what's out there.

Deep Space Nine
Season 1

Starring: Avery Brooks, René Auberjonois, Terry Farrell, Cirroc Lofton, Colm Meaney, Nana Visitor, Alexander Siddig, Armin Shimerman. Featuring: Aron Eisenberg, Max Grodénchik, Rosalind Chao. Executive producers: Rick Berman, Michael Piller. Supervising producers: Ira Steven Behr, David Livingston. Producer: Peter Lauritson. Co-producer: Peter Allan Fields. Associate producer: Steve Oster.

DS9 S01E01 Emissary ★★★☆☆

Story by Rick Berman and Michael Piller, teleplay by Michael Piller. Directed by David Carson. TX: 3 January 1993. Featuring: Patrick Stewart, Camille Saviola, Felecia M. Bell, Marc Alaimo, Joel Swetow.

Uncertain, the way that very many pilots are, but Kira, Quark and Odo make a great first impression and the setting is fresh and fun.

Paramount wanted a new show, and Berman and company didn't want to send another ship with another crew out exploring. If the original series had been Wagon Train to the Stars, the new show would be Border Town in Space. Various tendrils connect the old show to the new show, although not quite as many as hoped. Michelle Forbes was asked to return as Ro Laren. When she declined, I think I read somewhere that the part of Kira was offered to Suzie Plakson. In the end, it went to Nana Visitor. Colm Meaney turns up as Chief O'Brien and Captain Picard passes the baton in early scenes.

The big question mark hanging over **TNG** was: could they get lightning to strike again when it came to the regular cast? And it took a while. By the time **DS9** was being planned, the **TNG** core characters had been thinned out to just seven. I rate these actors as world class (Stewart), excellent (Spiner, Dorn, Burton) and very good (Frakes, McFadden, Sirtis) and by now all seven of these characters have become fan favourites. That's not a bad track record. This first episode of the new show counts eight actors in its titles. None of them can hold a candle to Stewart, but at least four of them can easily take that 'excellent' tag (Auberjonois, Meaney, Shimerman, Visitor) and Farrell, Siddig and Lofton will get better as the series continues.

Avery Brooks I find a bit of a mystery. Many fans think he's wonderful, but his style of delivery never strikes me as entirely natural, and I feel he's stuck between wanting to emulate what worked so well for Stewart and the need to create a new character. The scenes between him and Picard want to be able to distinguish between two equally capable yet profoundly different leaders. In fact, all they do is distinguish between a supremely able actor who's incredibly comfortable in his role with one who is still feeling his way.

The other contrast is in their uniforms. The *Enterprise* crew stick in the same togs until *Generations* (and more on that wardrobe catastrophe when the time comes) but Starfleet officers on the space station wear all black with coloured shoulders and a purple undergarment peeking through a small V-neck. I've really enjoyed watching **TNG**'s colourful episodes, the images beautifully restored from the original 35mm film elements. Watching **DS9** means watching smeary NTSC video, which even modern AI algorithms can't do much to clean up, and so it really doesn't help that almost everyone is inky black from the collarbone down, without even a proper belt to break up the monotony. And those coloured V-necks flop about in a very unmilitary way. Alas, **Voyager** will inherit the same look (and not get the upgrade that comes around the time of *First Contact*).

What is welcome is an even greater commitment to diversity and complexity. Of those eight regulars (and the cast of recurring characters will grow and grow) only four are Starfleet. The others are a Bajoran major, a Changeling security guard, a human child and a Ferengi bartender. This widening of the number of viewpoints is crucial to what makes this series work, and one of the reasons why it's so many people's favourite. It's also the only show never to have the airwaves to itself. These four episodes were shown in January 1993, after **TNG** went off the air for Christmas (following the mic drop of *Chain of Command*). Thereafter, both shows aired new episodes until **TNG** wrapped up its seventh season, whereupon **Voyager** kicked off. So, **DS9** became the 'deep cut' show that marked out the connoisseur fan from the casual viewer.

I don't remember when I saw these episodes for the first time. I think **DS9** was first shown in the UK on Sky. Possibly I watched it there, or maybe I caught up with it when the BBC was finally allowed to air it. I remember trying to follow it, and admiring it greatly, but now I can only call to mind a very few episodes, mainly concerned with key events in the war. Wanting to watch the whole show through from the beginning was one of my main motivations for starting this project and I'm thrilled that the moment has finally arrived.

We open with the Borg attack on Wolf 359, referred to but never depicted in *The Best of Both Worlds*, and now seen from Sisko's perspective. This is followed in short order by the fridging of Sisko's wife Jennifer. Most of this I think is model work, but the wormhole, which is the main MacGuffin of these early episodes, is primitive but effective CGI. That's why the overall image quality of these episodes is so poor compared to **TNG**. Everything in the earlier show was shot on film, even the spaceships. But so much of **DS9** was created digitally, and at 1990s TV resolution, it would all have to be redone from scratch to create a Blu-ray master. The relatively poor sales of the **TNG** remasters didn't inspire Paramount to spend even more money on a less popular series. The titles are only so-so as well. Visually, it's just a montage of shots of the space station for the most part, and the title music keeps threatening to arrive at a really good melody and never quite gets there.

What's far more effective is Sisko's initial tour of the space station. After the gleaming newness of the *Enterprise* for more than five years, the grime and disrepair of this environment is quite a tonic. We're also introduced to our regulars more smoothly than we were all those years ago in *Encounter at Farpoint*. Familiar Miles O'Brien shows Sisko (and us) around and introduces him to Major Kira. Nana Visitor makes an instant impression, immediately dispelling any regrets about Michelle Forbes. Visitor is electric and her character is fascinating. However, O'Brien later gets a whole scene in which he formally leaves the *Enterprise*, which feels unnecessary and poorly placed.

Acting royalty René Auberjonois is next, his highly impressive Odo taking on a small gang of bandits including Nog – a series regular in all but name – who in turn brings us to Quark, already spouting aphorisms but these are not yet dubbed 'rules of acquisition'. In amongst all this, there isn't much room for a story. When we first meet him, Sisko seems just as fed up with his job as Pike was in *The Cage* – but he rapidly ends up more like Picard than anyone else: pragmatic, compassionate, prone to giving inspirational speeches. He also comes up against a Bajoran high priest who recognises him as The Emissary of their legends. So, he's either Diet Coke Picard or The Second Coming of Space Jesus – take your pick. He gets the chance to revisit his first meeting with Jennifer (so this is the kind of fridging where you're really saving something for later).

Sisko, having been charged with keeping the peace by Picard, is now charged by Kai Opaka with finding Bajor's Celestial Table. Big day for Sisko, who takes the flashback machine with him for safekeeping (and the supplying of backstories). As noted when I wrote about *The Host* in *Volume I*, the Trill get reinvented here. Jadzia Dax is still the same old Dax, more or less, unlike Odan, who was exactly the same mind but in a different body. Terry Farrell doesn't get much to do, but seems happy enough to do it. Dr Bashir is keen as mustard, which is something we haven't seen much of in adult **Star Trek** characters, but the actor seems a little uncertain at this early stage.

It's also in this first episode that we meet recurring villain Gul Dukat. Marc Alaimo was the original Cardassian, but following David Warner is no easy task, especially when he's given the series-sell speech in the middle of the episode. Like so many others, he'll grow into the role as time goes on. Before long, Dax and Sisko find themselves on Planet Blue Screen in the centre of the wormhole. The trippy visuals here are quite a treat, but the concept of non-linear time is one of those things that you really don't want to interrogate too closely. Why do beings that exist in all points in time fear their own demise? And why don't they know that the Federation is coming? At one point, one of the wormhole dwellers pretty much says, 'What is this thing you call love?' for crying out loud.

Moving the station to the edge of the wormhole is a great sequence for O'Brien (virtually mirroring the saucer-separation procedure from *Farpoint*) but not many of the other characters get moments as revealing as this. Kira pops, Odo is fun, Quark shows promise but (despite getting the lion's share of the screen time) Sisko is all backstory and no personality so far, and the others just get **TNG** Season 1-style functional dialogue.

Compared to the **TNG** pilot, this has the advantage of taking place in a universe that's already five years old, and all of the additions to the lore work well. Ultimately, though, this is trying to keep too many balls in the air to be truly satisfying as ninety minutes of television drama. It's an overly complex guided tour of a place stories will take place in, rather than a narrative in its own right, but never dull for all that. Just as with **TNG, Deep Space Nine** was distributed in 'first-run syndication', Paramount doing deals with dozens of individual local stations. But the previous spin-off had been such a ratings smash that there was no difficulty persuading them to take the new show. Indeed, it debuted to an incredible 18 million viewers.

DS9 S01E03 Past Prologue ★★★☆☆

Written by Katharyn Powers. Directed by Winrich Kolbe.
TX: 10 January 1993. Featuring: Jeffrey Nordling, Andrew Robinson, Gwynyth Walsh, Barbara March, Susan Bay, Vaughn Armstrong.

The addition of Andrew Robinson as Garak is hugely welcome but much of this is just 'a day in the life of DS9*' and, like the pilot, it's all Kira and Sisko.*

Virtually the first thing we see in this episode is Garak the Cardassian 'tailor', who will prove to be one of the most fascinating and enduring members of the supporting cast. Meanwhile, Sisko and Kira are in (whisper it) conflict once more as she attempts to go over his head regarding his dealings with a Bajoran 'freedom fighter'. And – hey! – it's the Kleavage Sisters again, being made to surrender their weapons to Odo. Speaking of which, he seems to be able to morph into the shape *and size* of a rat, which either means that that's an incredibly heavy rat, which would probably overstrain the floor structures, or that his shapeshifting is little more than magic and he doesn't have to maintain the same mass.

The Klingons are in league with the freedom fighter, who isn't nearly as reformed a character as he maintained, so the Federation is proven right and the Bajoran liaison proven wrong, which is probably inevitable, but does make the balance of power on the station a little more stable and thus a little less interesting. This episode doesn't screw anything up but it isn't terribly interesting on either a plot or a character level. It feels like more table setting, a continuation of the pilot rather than a bold new leap into a fresh world of storytelling possibilities. In the pilot, I'm pretty sure people called the Ferengi bartender 'Quark' to rhyme with bark, lark, stark, park, hark and – as the word's inventor James Joyce had it – 'Muster Mark'. Now people are starting to rhyme it with pork, dork, fork, cork and so on. This is going to grate after a while. Speaking of Quark, this is the first mention of gold-pressed latinum, needed to solve the problem of a profit-oriented culture in a post-currency society.

DS9 S01E04 A Man Alone ★★☆☆☆

Story by Gerald Sanford and Michael Piller, teleplay by Michael Piller. Directed by Paul Lynch. TX: 17 January 1993. Featuring: Edward Laurence Albert, Stephen James Carver, Tom Klunis.

Fairly thin murder-mystery, plus Keiko starts a school. All fairly soapy and mundane and the main cast still aren't progressing much beyond the pilot.

Oh lord. This episode opens with the limpest, most nothing-burger of a teaser we've seen in ages, with the two least-well-defined characters playing a video game for a while before deciding not to. SMASH CUT TO TITLES. The interplay between Odo and Sisko is more interesting. The most senior authority figure and the head of security and they – gasp! – don't trust each other, or at least not yet. While Gene Roddenberry gets over his attack of the vapours, there's yet another shady Bajoran dude sneaking around the station while Nog and Jake are making friends and the O'Briens are doing their best to stay married. So, again, this feels low-key, soapy and I'm still waiting for the show to earn its keep as a syndicated science fiction adventure series, since the characters aren't nearly well defined enough or being put through enough for this to qualify as prestige drama. First appearance of Morn, whose presence will soon become a very funny running joke.

DS9 S01E05 Babel ★★★☆☆

Story by Sally Caves & Ira Steven Behr, teleplay by Michael McGreevey & Naren Shankar. Directed by Paul Lynch. TX: 24 January 1993.
Featuring: Jack Kehler, Matthew Faison, Ann Gillespie, Geraldine Farrell, Joe Zenga.

A mysterious virus sweeps the station and renders everyone on board mission system bucket torpedo basin. Biscuit dogma futile plasma evergreen window window window.

Hey! An actual science fiction plot with the potential to deeply affect our characters. Some kind of bug is going around and first O'Brien and then Dax lose the ability to process language, which results in their speech coming out as word salad – a challenge that the actors rise to very impressively. Odo tries to organise a lockdown, but you know how well that kind of thing goes down. So, although the symptoms are frighteningly novel, this is that familiar **Star Trek** cliché, the virus on the loose, complete with mutating strains, the regular cast dropping one by one and a last-minute cure that works almost instantaneously and leaves zero ill-effects. But it is at least exciting, which is more than can be said for the last couple of episodes, although the most exciting moment – the ship trying to pull away from the docking clamps – barely registers because the budget can't stretch far enough to show us what's physically happening.

DS9 S01E06 Captive Pursuit ★★★★☆

Story by Jill Sherman Donner, teleplay by Jill Sherman Donner and Michael Piller. Directed by Corey Allen. TX: 31 January 1993.
Featuring: Scott MacDonald, Gerrit Graham, Kelly Curtis.

O'Brien-centred episode with some bright spots, but seems stuck in the mode of alien-of-the-week-comes-through-the-wormhole.

O'Brien saves the life of a nervy-looking fellow who comes careering through the wormhole and won't say what he's there for. The resolution presents a fairly standard-issue Prime Directive moral dilemma, resolved with a little more insouciance than is typical for **Trek** of any kind. There's some decent Quark and Odo stuff here as well, but Dax and Bashir remain stubbornly bland for now. So, after four regular episodes, what's the engine for this new series? If we're just going to sit and wait for another alien-of-the-week to drop in with the kind of ethical conundrum you can solve in forty-five minutes, then how is this different from the shows it spun off from? What benefit are we getting from being stuck on a space station? This is a fine enough hour of television, but it still doesn't indicate the onward course in any meaningful way.

DS9 S01E07 Q-Less ★★☆☆☆

Story by Hannah Louise Shearer, teleplay by Robert Hewitt Wolfe. Directed by Paul Lynch. TX: 7 February 1993. Featuring: John de Lancie, Jennifer Hetrick.

'What I was hoping for was some witty repartee.' You and me both, buddy.

One way to discover what makes this show different from its progenitor is to make a direct comparison. We haven't reprised *The Naked Time* (at least not yet) but we can send Q over to the wormhole to see how this crew responds to his smug provocations. His arrival is foreshadowed by the reappearance of Vash, trapped in a stricken shuttle when the docking doors won't open. (Did no one think to beam her off?) It turns out that even Vash finds Q irritating given enough time, and now she wants to be shot of him. Last time we saw these two, Vash and Picard were attempting to replicate screwball comedy dialogue and falling a long way short. This time round, no one can be bothered even to make the attempt.

Meanwhile, Bashir is given Geordi's role of unlucky in love, which does little to further define his character. And 'My God, you're an impertinent waiter' is the kind of line that makes me want to never see him again. That's the dialogue you'd give to the bad guy in an eighties family comedy to make sure we all hated him and would enjoy seeing him humiliated. Meanwhile, in a direct comparison with Picard, Sisko looks childish and petulant – much easier to provoke, as Q astutely determines.

DS9 S01E08 Dax ★★★☆☆

Story by Peter Allan Fields, teleplay by D.C. Fontana and Peter Allan Fields. Directed by David Carson. TX: 14 February 1993. Featuring: Gregory Itzin, Anne Haney, Richard Lineback, Fionnula Flanagan.

That old stand-by, the courtroom drama, is used to deliver much-needed Trill exposition, but – in an episode named after her – we learn very little about who Jadzia Dax is, which is disappointing.

Anyone with an interest in criminology, true crime or murder mysteries will have heard of DNA identification and may have heard of chimeric DNA. A very few individuals whose conception involved the fusing of two different zygotes may have cells containing two different sets of DNA in their bodies. This can result in all sorts of shenanigans with crime scene investigations, but – crucially – a person with chimeric DNA typically doesn't know they've got it. So having chimeric DNA doesn't make your experience of being you any different than anyone else's. In a nutshell, that's what's wrong with this episode. These reinvented Trill live enormously long lives, upgrading their hosts every so often, and merging the memories and personality traits of the old with the new. And old lag D.C. Fontana (writing with Peter Allan Fields) works through the process with her customary rigour. But this episode treats Dax's symbiosis as little more than chimeric DNA, a technical detail that creates a legal problem. The far more interesting question of 'What is it like to be a symbiont?' which has much deeper ramifications, goes essentially unexplored here. In fact, we learn more about Curzon Dax than Jadzia Dax.

The story starts with Dax being abducted. Bashir witnesses this because he's sharking after her – that being the extent of their relationship. Seeing the crew scramble to prevent the abduction from taking place is a satisfying show of competency and teamwork. And also in the plus column, the chief baddie is Gregory Itzin, and the arbiter trying to decide the case is Anne Haney, both of whom do much to elevate the material, which is all basically courtroom drama, complete with surprise last-minute witness. Again, although it's all well-enough handled, there's little here that I can't imagine occurring on the *Enterprise*, with a more comfortable cast and nicer costumes. Auberjonois, Shimerman and Visitor continue to impress, even when given little to work with. But when is this new series going to emerge from the parent show's shadow?

DS9 S01E09 The Passenger ★★☆☆☆

Story by Morgan Gendel, teleplay by Morgan Gendel, Robert Hewitt Wolfe and Michael Piller. Directed by Paul Lynch. TX: 21 February 1993. Featuring: Caitlin Brown, James Lashly, Christopher Collins, James Harper.

Fairly dreary body swap intrigue with good stuff for Odo, but little else of interest.

Bashir continues to be given the most obnoxious and unlikeable lines imaginable. It's a good job that Alexander Siddig is as charming as he is, or this character would be irredeemable. As it is, he's still fairly punchable (Kira does well to restrain herself) and when a dangerous prisoner tries to strangle him, I'm not sure whose side I'm on. Speaking of unacceptable behaviour – in the minds of this writing team, Dax seems to exist only for male cast members to lust over, Bashir in earlier episodes and now Quark. A Lieutenant Primmin from Starfleet security turns up and he's now in the space station uniform, which suggests that these are being rolled out to all personnel, although news of the change doesn't reach the *Enterprise* while **TNG** is on television. I'm still distracted by the floppy necklines. Are they always like that and I just never noticed or were they stiffened and starched in later episodes, and on **Voyager**?

Much is made of just how different security is on a space station than it is on a starship, but this still feels like alien-of-the-week stuff to me and not all the cast are growing on me equally quickly. As a sort of space procedural, it's fine enough and there is good stuff for Odo, but I was told this was the best and most complex **Trek** there is. How long do I have to wait? As well as Quork/Quark we also have a mix of VAN-tika and Van-TEE-ka this week for the name of the resurrecting murderer/thief, which is annoying. The twist is pretty poorly concealed too, with the only question being, which body will the villain use? Sadly, it isn't much of an acting showcase for Siddig, who doesn't have anything like the required swagger.

DS9 S01E10 Move Along Home ★☆☆☆☆

Story by Michael Piller, teleplay by Frederick Rappaport, Lisa Rich and Jeanne Carrigan-Fauci. Directed by David Carson. TX: 14 March 1993. Featuring: Joel Brooks, James Lashly, Clara Bryant.

Oh. Oh dear. Oh no. No. No, no, no.

I've been waiting for **DS9** to get good for nine episodes now. I remembered the pilot quite clearly, but no other episodes have stirred my memory. I do remember this one, though, and I don't remember liking it. Continuing the theme of 'Let's just pretend we're on the *Enterprise* and not on a space station', we're on a first contact mission. The Wadi at least know how to pronounce 'Quark' but what they want is to play games. What follows is incredibly dumb and astonishingly tedious as Sisko, Dax, Bashir and Kira find themselves reduced to tokens in a seemingly lethal board game being played by the Ferengi barkeep. What this actually means is a lot of walking through identical corridors solving sub-'Pyramids of Mars' puzzles. It's paralysingly dull.

Quark, who has been clearly established as not giving a damn about anything except making a profit from his casino, looks deathly concerned when he figures out (from the flimsiest of clues) that his game pieces are the station's senior staff. He thus always chooses 'the safer path', which means that the stakes are as low as they can be. Wouldn't keeping him in the dark, gleefully sending our heroes into more and more peril, have been far more effective? In a frankly embarrassing scene (and there's no shortage of those here) he panics and wets himself when asked to choose a piece to sacrifice, which is exactly what you'd expect from an arch-capitalist like him, who barely knows these 'hu-mans'. At the end, in an astonishing 'screw you', it turns out that the game is only a game, and the crew were never in any real danger. The space station replicators can't make dress uniforms, for some unaccountable reason.

DS9 S01E11 The Nagus ★★★★☆

Story by David Livingston, teleplay by Ira Steven Behr. Directed by David Livingston. TX: 21 March 1993. Featuring: Wallace Shawn, Tiny Ron, Lee Arenberg, Lou Wagner, Barry Gordon.

Great stuff for Quark, but Jake and Nog's plot line is considerably less interesting.

A decrepit Ferengi known as the Grand Nagus Zek visits the station and we delve a little more into Ferengi lore as a result. Just because of that, this does start to feel a tiny bit like a story that this show could do, and which other **Star Trek** shows could not. To tell this story in **Next Gen** you'd have to have O'Brien stuck on the Ferengi homeworld, or La Forge as part of an officer exchange programme or some such. Here, it's Quark who's our point-of-view character, not a friendly human. Adding to the fun, that's none other than Wallace Shawn under all that foam rubber – maybe the best **Star Trek** guest star since Jean Simmons. Sadly, he spends most of the middle of the story presumed dead. With or without him, all of this double-dealing and the many reversals of fortune are highly entertaining. Sure, most plot developments required Quark to be something of a doofus, but that's more or less in character and Shimerman manages not to make any of it embarrassing (this time).

Rather sweetly, it's Odo who comes to Quark's rescue. One thing that no earlier version of **Star Trek** pulled off is that most adorable of long-form storytelling tropes, the traditional enemies who end up as friends. It's the one major thing that I think Peter Jackson fumbles in *The Lord of the Rings* (Legolas and Gimli, the details of whose relationship get rather lost in the shuffle) and it's an undoubted highlight of *Babylon 5* (G'Kar and Londo). I'd rather forgotten that it would be played out here between Odo and Quark, and how marvellous that it's maybe the two best actors on the show who get to go on this journey.

Elsewhere, however, things are duller. Apparently, Sisko has a son. Cirroc Lofton's name has been in the opening titles every single week, but apart from a couple of brief scenes here and there, he's hardly been in the actual show, and he certainly hasn't influenced any plots. Here, not for the last time, he's paired up with Quark's nephew Nog, who can't produce his homework because (he claims) Vulcans stole his PADD. Should have backed it up to the cloud, Nog. Jake's stuff with Nog and his dad is frustratingly generic and almost completely devoid of interest. Luckily, it's less than a quarter of the run time, so let's gloss over it. The first Rule of Acquisition is quoted here (which is also the First Rule of Acquisition, if you see what I mean) to whit: once you have their money, you never give it back. Rom returned a lost purse intact because he was dazzled by a customer's beauty, a cardinal sin in Quark's eyes.

DS9 S01E12 Vortex ★★★☆☆

Written by Sam Rolfe. Directed by Winrich Kolbe. TX: 18 April 1993.
Featuring: Cliff DeYoung, Randy Oglesby, Gordon Clapp.

Too many ideas for one episode, but some of the elements – especially those surrounding Odo's origins – are fascinating.

More good Quark and Odo stuff. I don't know whether to be frustrated that the show is doing so little to beef up the weaker characters or pleased to be spending so much time with the stronger ones. Some nifty effects allow one actor to play both Miradorn twins, although only one of them survives to the first ad break. The killer (with some of Michael Westmore's least convincing bumpy-forehead latex) has heard of shapeshifters before, which is of great interest to the station's constable. Despite the poor make-up appliance, I rather like Cliff DeYoung's casual delivery, which avoids that sub-Shakespearean thing that so many actors in sci-fi and fantasy productions seem to do as standard.

Odo has to escort this knowledgeable fellow back through the wormhole while avoiding the surviving twin, bent on vengeance. Meanwhile, Quark sics the Miradorn on Odo. There are probably too many moving parts here, and the chase-adventure-revenge plot gets in the way of the Odo-finds-out-about-his-origins plot, but that latter element is fascinating and Auberjonois is rapidly becoming the MVP of this show, able to make silly stories work and good stories approach greatness.

Also – I know this is becoming a bit of a silly obsession, but the necklines on the uniforms are still flapping about untidily, and Sisko's has now been cut very low, almost to his collarbone, to expose several inches of purple undershirt around his neck and throat, instead of the usual narrow strip. It's not particularly an improvement.

DS9 S01E13 Battle Lines ★★☆☆☆

Story by Hilary J. Bader, teleplay by Richard Danus and Evan Carlos
Somers. Directed by Paul Lynch. TX: 25 April 1993.
Featuring: Camille Saviola, Paul Collins, Jonathan Banks.

*Dull outing through the wormhole, which never amounts to more than a lot of talk
about conflicts we can't see and people we've never met.*

Of all the elements set up in the pilot, the one I was least excited about was
all the religious mumbo-jumbo with Sisko and the Gewgaw Of Hallucinatory
Flashbacks, so I wasn't thrilled to hear that the Kai Opaka was cashing in
the promise Sisko made to give her a tour of the station. Meanwhile, and
amusingly, Kira is dismayed to learn that her enemies didn't hold her in
particularly high regard. On an outing through the wormhole, the runabout
receives a distress signal and is then forced to crash-land – the Kai dying in
the process, which was a big surprise to me. Nana Visitor is remarkable here,
keening over the body of her spiritual leader. But, lo! Mike Ehrmantraut (in
standard-issue *Mad Max*-style eighties sci-fi togs) soon has her, Sisko and
Bashir at gunpoint – paranoid because they are a people at war. So, this is the
Federation (kinda) getting involved with a Zagbars vs Zoobles conflict again:
lots of backstory, lots of people we've never met before and will never meet
again but who we're supposed suddenly to care about. And none of this feels
like it means anything. It's just people in silly clothes talking nonsense on an
unconvincing planet set.

DS9 S01E14 The Storyteller ★☆☆☆☆

Story by Kurt Michael Bensmiller, teleplay by Kurt Michael Bensmiller and
Ira Steven Behr. Directed by David Livingston. TX: 2 May 1993.
Featuring: Kay E. Kuter, Lawrence Monoson, Gina Philips.

*Bedtime stories are great if you can't sleep. Also recommended: this episode of **Deep
Space Nine**.*

Sisko is overseeing treaty negotiations between squabbling Bajoran factions
– you know, like Picard does. Meanwhile, Bashir and O'Brien are witnessing
the death of a Bajoran elder who held his people together by telling stories.
Meanwhile – again – Jake and Nog are clumsily sharking after the seemingly
teenage girl who is leading one side of the negotiations. Berman-**Trek** would
love to believe that it takes place in a post-racism, post-sexism universe, but
countless episodes are mired in patriarchal BS and the presentation of Gina

Philips as Varis Sul is toe-curlingly embarrassing. Pairing Bashir and O'Brien makes more sense – it's a chance to use the character we've been getting to know for nearly six years to bring a newer, and so far rather ill-defined, character into focus.

But it's O'Brien's story, not Bashir's – he's just along for the ride. The chief of operations feels utterly unable to take over from the beloved leader who hands the baton over to him with his dying breath. (And also filed under patriarchal BS, O'Brien is presented with a trio of teenage girls offering him sexual services as thanks for assuming the role of storyteller.) Luckily, someone else is ready, willing and able to take over for him, so he's rapidly and easily off the hook, and the border dispute fizzles out in much the same ho-hum, low-stakes way. Even by the fairly feeble standards set by this new series so far, this is almost entirely free of incident, excitement or interest. Why are we watching Jake and Nog throw porridge over each other? Why, to be blunt, are we watching at all?

DS9 S01E15 Progress ★★★☆☆

Written by Peter Allan Fields. Directed by Les Landau. TX: 9 May 1993. Featuring: Brian Keith, Michael Bofshever, Terrence Evans, Annie O'Donnell.

And it is, kinda. Kira's strand on the doomed colony is deathly dull to start but gets better, and Jake and Nog's adventures in under-the-counter dealing are actually amusing.

Well, that's at least an aspirational title, and we start with a card game, which has historically been a good omen. Alas, we also start with Jake and Nog, probably the most generic and least interesting characters in the series. And yet, as Nog tells Jake he's got a lot to learn about opportunity, there's a glimmer of something with a little more depth and texture. Kira, meanwhile, is dealing with that hoary old **Trek** cliché, the stubborn evacuees who won't leave as ordered. And, because this is nineties **Trek**, the chief evacuee (and the only one to speak) is a sexist old dinosaur who calls Kira 'girlie' and 'dear' – and after a while, Kira gets to like it. This Federation vs the natives stuff is pretty routine, with only Nana Visitor's megawatt charisma keeping me watching. And it's that committed playing that makes the truly shocking ending work, but it's a bit of a slog getting there. Entirely to my surprise, I was actually rather caught up in Jake and Nog cos-playing as Del Boy and Rodney. It's not deep, it's not high stakes, it's not even particularly new. But it is fun, and that counts for something. Their trade involves a prodigious quantity of 'self-sealing stem bolts', gizmos whose functions is never revealed, and which turns into a running gag, still running in the last season of **Enterprise** over a decade later.

With the fantastic resolution down on the planet and the entertaining wheeling-and-dealing on the station, this approaches a four-star rating but doesn't quite make the grade. It is promising, though. Now even Morn is sharking after Dax. Jeebus.

DS9 S01E16 If Wishes Were Horses ★☆☆☆☆

Story by Nell McCue Crawford & William L. Crawford, teleplay by Nell McCue Crawford, William L. Crawford and Michael Piller. Directed by Robert Legato. TX: 16 May 1993. Featuring: Keone Young, Hana Hatae, Michael J. Anderson.

I wished for a less familiar, less skeezy, more thoughtful episode, but I didn't get what I wanted.

As usual, rather than a tense, attention-grabbing teaser, we just check in with various characters until O'Brien's storybooks start coming to life. This is scarcely a new idea – in **Trek** it goes back to Season 1's *Shore Leave* and I'm certain it has a far longer pedigree than that – but **Discovery** recently showed how to do it with flair. Here it's just dull, when it isn't being sleazy. It strikes me that, as diverse as the **DS9** regular cast is (it's the first **Trek** show with no white human Americans among its main characters, and that's still quite rare), it's a very male environment, and while Kira ain't taking none of your nonsense, it's depressing that Dax is so often portrayed as little more than an object of male lust.

What is refreshing, and does feel a) twenty-fourth century and b) in keeping with Dax's personal history, is that she's actually very sympathetic when confronted with Bashir's nympho sex doll version of her, telling him that she feels it's *his* privacy that has been invaded, rather than hers. Perhaps now these two can start to build a relationship as colleagues, rather than the *Confessions of a Starfleet Doctor* stuff we've been subjected to so far. There's a glimmer of interest in seeing the situation from the point of view of the fantasies, but the explanation at the end is pure nonsense and there's no resonance or depth to any of this silliness.

DS9 S01E17 The Forsaken ★★★☆☆

Story by Jim Trombetta, teleplay by Don Carlos Dunaway and Michael Piller. Directed by Les Landau. TX: 23 May 1993. Featuring: Majel Barrett, Constance Towers, Michael Ensign, Jack Shearer, Benita Andre.

Routine episode with some good Odo material albeit generated by a very tired plot device – and it's always nice to see Majel.

A trio of Federation ambassadors is touring the station, and their low-level squabbling is not nearly as diverting as we're supposed to think. Wait, it's a quartet, the fourth being Lwaxana, livening the place up considerably. As usual, she's shopping for a husband (because this-is-the-story-we-tell-with-this-character) but the choice of Odo as her latest intended is marvellous and Barrett and Auberjonois find a sparky chemistry very quickly. Sadly, the show can't think of anything more inventive to do with them than trap them in a (turbo) lift together. Meanwhile, O'Brien is fighting a losing battle with the fussy Cardassian computer controlling the station, in a throwback to some of the anti-technology sentiment we used to see on the sixties show. All of this is pretty low-stakes but when Lwaxana takes her wig off to reassure Odo, it is rather touching. Weirdly, a similar bonding apparently takes place with Bashir and the other delegates, but this one happens entirely off-screen.

DS9 S01E18 Dramatis Personae ★★☆☆☆

Written by Joe Menosky. Directed by Cliff Bole. TX: 30 May 1993. Featuring: Jeff Pruitt, Tom Towles, Stephen Parr.

The Naked Time again, a bit late in the day, but less interesting than usual because everyone goes nuts in the same way.

Both **The Original Series** and **The Next Generation** made the curious choice of having the crew we'd only just met start going bananas. Normally it would be ineffective to show a group we didn't know very well acting out of character, because we don't know what they're like when they act in character. In fact, it works just fine, because when some of their deeper personality traits are revealed and they stop acting like their job descriptions, we see more of who they really are. Here, near the end of Season 1, **DS9** tries the same trick, but this time everybody becomes the same sort of pantomime villain, so this doesn't tell us anything about who they really are, is very silly in its presentation and still manages to feel like a hand-me-down. It's just hard to get invested in either the intrigue or the fault lines opening up between the characters when it's so obvious that none of it is real. The cast has fun, though, and we're getting to know the actors as much as their characters, so that helps.

DS9 S01E19 Duet ★★★★☆

Story by Lisa Rich & Jeanne Carrigan-Fauci, teleplay by Peter Allan Fields. Directed by James L. Conway. TX: June 13, 1993. Featuring: Harris Yulin, Marc Alaimo, Ted Sorel, Tony Rizzoli, Norman Large, Robin Christopher.

Finally, the spin-off finds another gear. This is very strong stuff and Nana Visitor is revelatory.

Right from the earliest episodes, Kira and Odo have been among the most interesting characters in the regular cast. Quark is developing nicely, but brings a lot of Ferengi baggage with him. Odo has had a couple of great moments, but Kira's best episode so far was mired in a lot of other over-familiar material. The main conflict here is certainly not novel – it's a riff on Nazi war criminals trying to evade justice after the Second World War, among other things – but it's paying off one of the promises of the set-up and brings us excellent character actor Harris Yulin as the genial yet shifty Marritza, who may or may not have served at the labour camp liberated by Kira some years ago. Nana Visitor is just superb here, playing all of the layers of her internal conflict, torn between her duty to Starfleet, her personal loyalty to Sisko and her fiery need for Bajoran justice. It's enough to make you glad Michelle Forbes said no. And she's matched by Yulin, who manages to make his early avuncular evasion and his later maniacal boasting both equally convincing. We also get Marc Alaimo back as Gul Dukat (where's Garak, now I come to think of it?) trying to paint Kira as a 'Bajoran hatemonger' in Sisko's eyes.

It's all gripping, powerful stuff and (along with *Progress*) feels like the kind of story that is worth telling but wouldn't fit on **TNG**, because the way to do this on the *Enterprise* is to give the key conflict to a guest star, and we had enough of that in Seasons 1 and 2. Here, it's one of our main characters who's having to deal with uncertainty, justice, revenge and duty. Towards the end, it all gets a bit convoluted and further clichés (like the villain having had plastic surgery to disguise his identity) fog the fascinating moral issues, but these flaws can't eclipse the wonderful work done earlier in the story – and the very end is a final bracing shot of vinegar. Bravo.

> **JOHN PEEL, writer of original *Doctor Who* and *Star Trek* novels and much else besides**
> *Duet* is a powerful and disturbing story that gave Nana Visitor a chance to really shine as Kira suspects a visiting Cardassian is actually a war criminal. Always wonderful, Harris Yulin steals the show as a man consumed by his own guilt. The story is filled with sharp interplay as the two characters duel with one another and both characters have to come to terms with their feelings in the aftermath of the Cardassian occupation. And then, of course, we discovered that the story was ripped off from a famous play. Sigh.

DS9 S01E20 In the Hands of the Prophets ★★★☆☆

Written by Robert Hewitt Wolfe. Directed by David Livingston.
TX: 20 June 1993. Featuring: Louise Fletcher, Philip Anglim, Robin Christopher.

Keiko vs the Bajoran creationists doesn't have the power of Kira vs the concentration camps, but this is decent stuff.

I'm not especially interested in Bajoran mysticism and I imagine I would respond to Vedek Winn pretty much the same way that Keiko O'Brien does. Viewing their debates as a third party, the script seems to be bending over backwards to make Keiko combative and Winn generous, but it is still Winn who wants to dictate what Keiko can and can't teach whereas Keiko has no problem with Bajoran kids receiving religious instruction from Winn. Sisko's position is nuanced but the debate doesn't get under the skin the way that Kira vs Marritza did last time, despite a classy bit of casting for Winn (Oscar winner Louise Fletcher). O'Brien's strand is less interesting, with the bad guy pretty much obvious from very early on. Once again, though, we do get something more than an alien-of-the-week coming through the wormhole. This feels like a story this show could tell and **TNG** couldn't. It's just surprising that it's taken this long for that to feel in any way routine.

DS9 Season 1 wrap-up

- It's striking to compare **TNG** Season 1 with these episodes. **TNG** was a colossal punt. Nobody had any idea if it would work, if it could be done, and if anyone would watch. **DS9** began with a ready-made, loyal audience, built up over five years, and they could start telling stories within a detailed world that already existed. They did pretty well with the regular cast – in fact, it's probably the most accomplished team of actors to appear in any **Star Trek** pilot, with only Alexander Siddig and Cirroc Lofton looking at all uncertain by this stage (Terry Farrell seems relaxed but is getting very little to work with). René Auberjonois, Colm Meaney, Armin Shimerman and especially Nana Visitor are all doing wonderful work and Avery Brooks is at least providing a solid centre to anchor the others.

- But it's taken the new series more episodes to figure out how to tell stories in this setting. Early **TNG** tended to emphasise the wrong things, only belatedly figuring out that it was the 'family' of regular characters who would keep the audience coming back for more. But plenty of early **TNG** stories are built on strong science fiction ideas that make the most of the concept of a spaceship exploring the unknown. **DS9** does a better job of setting up its core cast and has the benefit of a more diverse group of characters with more conflict to mine, but far too many episodes feel like **TNG** hand-me-downs and when that's combined with the usual year one uncertainties, that makes a lot of the episodes feel less than thrilling.

- We've kind of got used to the idea that these shows take a year or two to find their feet. But it's not entirely clear why that should be. Very few long-running shows do their very best work in year one, it's true, but **TOS** hit the ground running and the first years of shows like *MASH*, or *LA Law* or *Frasier* or *ER* while they might not be top-notch aren't anything like as poor as the first years of **TNG** or **DS9** (or **Voyager**, if memory serves).

- So, tales of **DS9** being the high-water mark of Berman-**Trek** have not so far been proven to be true, although there is bags of promise here. But we need more complexity, more serialisation and much, much less of Bashir and Quark objectifying Dax. Average score for **DS9** Season 1 is a fairly poor 2.76, a bit worse than **The Animated Series** and about the same as **TNG** Season 2. *Duet* is hands-down the best episode of the season and *Progress* and *In the Hands of the Prophets* are both decent. Worst episodes include the silly *Move Along Home*, the witless *Q-Less* and the nonsensical *The Storyteller*.

Deep Space Nine
Season 2

Starring: Avery Brooks, René Auberjonois, Terry Farrell, Cirroc Lofton, Colm Meaney, Nana Visitor, Alexander Siddig, Armin Shimerman. Featuring: Aron Eisenberg, Max Grodénchik, Rosalind Chao. Executive producers: Rick Berman, Michael Piller. Co-executive producer: Ira Steven Behr. Supervising producers: James Crocker, David Livingston. Story editor: Robert Hewitt Wolfe. Producers: Peter Allan Fields, Peter Lauritson. Associate producer: Steve Oster.

DS9 S02E01 The Homecoming ★★★★☆

Story by Jeri Taylor and Ira Steven Behr, teleplay by Ira Steven Behr. Directed by Winrich Kolbe. TX: 26 September. Featuring: Richard Beymer, Michael Bell, Marc Alaimo, Frank Langella (uncredited).

Thoughtful and compelling investigation into the nature of hero-worship and leadership. To be continued... Wait – what?

The first episode of Season 2 basically picks up where Season 1 left off – the sets look the same, nobody has grown a beard or left the show, the uniforms are unchanged, the titles are identical, and the Siskos' father–son bonding is as generic as ever. Kira's mission of mercy is kicked off by an earring turning up at Quark's. As if to try to warm up the tepid drama, people keep portentously saying 'I need to speak with you' or 'There's something you should see', rather than just saying what's on their minds. It's a television writer's tic that would be better eliminated.

Last year, we heard about labour camps and Bajoran prisoners (in the excellent *Duet*). This time, we join Kira and O'Brien on a raid to one such in order to retrieve freedom fighter Nalas (played by Richard Beymer, familiar as Tony from the movie version of *West Side Story*). In a delicious twist, when the prison camp is liberated, silver-tongued Gul Dukat issues a smooth apology for its very existence. Continuing the high-class casting, here's Nixon himself, Frank Langella (uncredited for some reason) as a Bajoran minister. And complicating everything is a splinter group called The Circle who are carving their logo into the space station's walls (and bartenders).

As noted, there's nothing here that makes this feel like a different show – until the very end. Suddenly, Kira's out, and we end our first episode back on an explicitly unresolved note. A two-parter? At the beginning of the season? Spicy.

DS9 S02E02 The Circle ★★★★☆

Written by Peter Allan Fields. Directed by Corey Allen. TX: 3 October 1993. Featuring: Richard Beymer, Stephen Macht, Bruce Gray, Philip Anglim, Louise Fletcher, Frank Langella (uncredited).

More strong work in what turns out not to be the conclusion of a two-parter, but the second in a multi-part narrative.

We pick up, as expected, with 'Last time on **Deep Space Nine**...' but this is followed not by 'And now the conclusion...' but 'And now the continuation...' Whuh? Are we not going to be done with this story in forty-five minutes' time? And the story continues to engross. Highlights include Odo recruiting Quark as his deputy and Sisko's interaction with General Krim, when he doesn't attempt to bargain with the information he has. Krim is played with smooth authority by Stephen Macht (who was Roddenberry's first choice for Captain Picard, fact-fans).

On Bajor, Kira (with a fringe) is building a water feature, but Vedek Bareil shows her the flashback box from the pilot, and suddenly she's not sure if she wants to stay or go – until Sisko mounts a rescue mission that is as exciting as it is perfunctory and gets her the hell out of there. Frank Langella's torture of her is pretty grim – and the make-up on Nana Visitor is shocking – but the wounds are easily mended by Bashir. That's my only problem with this episode: it's shooting for the moon and some of the revelations are jaw-dropping – the whole premise of the show is being called into question and there's no sign of a major reset button – but several small things are being reset very quickly, so I'm still suspicious that the status quo might return in part three. Jake is still playing the 'I really think you oughta come down, Dad' game instead of just coming out and saying what he needs to say. Stop it.

Bruce Gray appears as 'Admiral Chekote'. That's a name we'll hear again soon, although with a different spelling. Also – the Prime Directive applies. Does it? I thought it applied only to pre-Warp civilisations.

DS9 S02E03 The Siege ★★★★☆

Written by Michael Piller. Directed by Winrich Kolbe. TX: 10 October 1993.
Featuring: Steven Weber, Richard Beymer, Stephen Macht, Philip Anglim,
Louise Fletcher, Frank Langella (uncredited).

A rousing conclusion to an epic adventure which, yes, leaves us back where we started, but with many more questions raised about where we go next.

Ah, so this is the conclusion. Okay. Evacuating the station feels very real, very significant, almost apocalyptic, but Sisko's plan is delicious, and it's great fun watching it unfurl. Like the best villains, Stephen Macht's General Krim is one step ahead of our heroes and isn't easily fooled. Meanwhile, Kira and Dax's adventures in a beaten-up old shuttle are very enjoyable and do much to shore up Dax's character – her world-weary acceptance of the ludicrous risks she's forced to take are new, but make sense of her long life.

In terms of plot, concepts and characterisation, this is probably another four. Nixon and Ratched are rather simple moustache-twirling villains, the Cardassians who are actually pulling the strings are never seen, Li Nalas's death feels a bit perfunctory (although it helps that the victory comes at a price) and Kira's PADD is the golden snitch of plot devices, resolving everything the moment it is presented to the right person on Bajor.

But I'm going to bump it up by an extra half a star because overall the story has had an epic scope which feels very fresh and exciting, with great material for Kira, good stuff for Quark, Odo, Dax and Sisko and a much greater appreciation for the kind of political stories that this set-up lends itself to. The supporting cast are getting stronger all the time and the regulars are coming into focus. We just need to figure out what to do with this doctor, who hasn't even risen to the level of this-is-the-story-we-do-with-this-character yet (although he has stopped turning into the Tex Avery wolf whenever Dax walks by, thank goodness). For the first time, the spin-off is doing better work than the parent show, which is flailing about a bit as it enters its seventh year.

Some of the Starfleet staff during the early briefing scenes are wearing weird uniforms with the lilac undershirt visible around their necks, but no vees in the outer garment.

DS9 S02E04 Invasive Procedures ★★★☆

Story by John Whelpley, teleplay by John Whelpley and Robert Hewitt Wolfe. Directed by Les Landau. TX: 17 October 1993.
Featuring: John Glover, Megan Gallagher, Tim Russ, Steve Rankin.

Decent race-against-time stuff with good material for all the regulars, especially Terry Farrell, but nothing like as ambitious as last time.

Following the epic three-parter which saw the situation become so untenable that the whole station has to be evacuated, here we have an ordinary one-off episode in which... the whole station has to be evacuated. Quark, who last time found himself left behind because he couldn't get his suitcase of latinum on board the shuttle, in a novel twist this time has stayed behind because he couldn't get his suitcase of latinum on board the shuttle. Seriously?

While the station is on lockdown, O'Brien and Odo encounter Klingon and Trill raiders who are after Dax. Odo having been neutralised, and with O'Brien's life on the line, Bashir is forced to remove Dax's symbiont and implant it into Verad (played with nervy relish by John Glover). Terry Farrell, who seemed a little unsure in Season 1, has really found a groove now. With very little help from the scripts, she's begun to create a completely rounded old-head-on-young-shoulders characterisation, which is quite fascinating and makes her frailty when she's deprived of her symbiont all the more affecting. Alexander Siddig still doesn't get much on the page and hasn't found any depth to Bashir yet, alas.

It's also fairly easy to see how this is going to go – Verad will eventually be made to put Dax back into Jadzia – but the journey is worthwhile and this is decent tense-hostage-situation stuff with hissable villains and noble heroes, albeit it's a step back from the complexity and scope of the opening trilogy. Almost unrecognisable under Michael Westmore's Klingon latex is Tim Russ, whom we'll be seeing more of (and seeing more of) quite soon now.

DS9 S02E05 Cardassians ★★★★☆

Story by Gene Wolande & John Wright, teleplay by James Crocker. Directed by Cliff Bole. TX: 24 October 1993. Featuring: Andrew Robinson, Marc Alaimo, Robert Mandan, Terrence Evans, Vidal Peterson.

Expert blending of the personal and political with excellent guest stars who don't detract from the regulars.

Garak is back!! And bitten on the hand by a Cardassian boy brought on board the station by his Bajoran adoptive father. Gul Dukat wants to use the incident to repatriate the abandoned kids – and we can only hope that Sisko figures out how adoption works a little faster than Picard. Other sources, though, say that the boy is mistreated by other Bajorans who see in him the face of the enemy.

It's a good showing for Bashir, verbally fencing with Dukat, and even if we aren't learning much about the character, Siddig, given something to play, seizes the opportunity and begins to shade in some of the Doctor's idealistic impulsiveness. He's never going to be the most complex character on the show, but if we get him up to, say, Geordi's level, I'll be quite satisfied. Showing more layers, at first O'Brien is openly racist against Cardassians (recalling his attitude in *The Wounded*), but he and the tug-of-love boy Rugal bond over their dislike of Cardassian food. He's also seen at one point, truculently playing on his phone, like a Zoomer.

Complicating everything is the arrival of Rugal's biological father Kotan Pa'Dar, played by Robert Mandan with enough exaggeration to get through the latex, but enough subtlety to make the dilemma I dismissed so easily suddenly seem much more complicated. At the end of the episode, following some shockingly speedy detective work by Garak, Rugal is sent home to start a new life on Cardassia, against his stated wishes. Not what I would have done, but the episode does such a good job of showing the situation from all sides that I can no longer condemn it outright. Maybe he will be happier among his own people, eventually.

Not much from Dax, Odo, Kira or Quark this week, but great to see a proper vehicle for Bashir and there's good stuff for O'Brien, Keiko and Sisko, and for the first time I'm watching **TNG** impatiently waiting for the episode to be over so I can get back to this show.

It's worth noting at this point that Andrew Robinson had a very clear idea of what was going on between Garak and Bashir when he accepted the part. His reading of the script was that the Cardassian's interest in the dashing young doctor was mainly carnal, and he played the lines with that intention. After several of Garak's return appearances, Alexander Siddig picked up on this too, and then the writers, who had tried and failed to get gay characters past Rick Berman, also noticed and began giving the two men even more to play with. Then – finally – Berman noticed and shut the whole thing down. But 'Little Achievements', a delightful piece of fan fiction written by Elmie K-E and performed by Robinson and Siddig over Zoom during the 2020 lockdown, did see them established not just as a couple but actually married. If you share my frustration that Berman thought the risk to the franchise wasn't worth acknowledging **Star Trek**'s legions of gay fans, then this may provide a crumb of comfort.

DS9 S02E06 Melora ★★☆☆☆

Story by Evan Carlos Somers, teleplay by Evan Carlos Somers and Steven Baum and Michael Piller & James Crocker. Directed by Winrich Kolbe. TX: 31 October 1993. Featuring: Daphne Ashbrook, Peter Crombie.

Earnest and well-meaning treatment of disability without much texture or insight.

The space station plays host to a wheelchair-bound alien. Again, I have very little confidence that the series is going to have the slightest idea how to handle this. As soon as she's mentioned, Bashir is fangirling like crazy (because this is the story we tell with this character). She's played by *Doctor Who*'s Daphne Ashbrook (no, of course they didn't cast a disabled actor, don't be ridiculous). Again, we have a low-key character-focused teaser, which doesn't promise a lot of high-stakes jeopardy, and that's pretty much what the episode delivers.

Attempting to raise the stakes mildly, we have Quark's strand in which an old 'friend' comes to call and gives the Ferengi plenty of notice that his life is in danger. But why doesn't he just kill Quark if that's what he wants? The Quark/Odo stuff is fine, but nothing we haven't seen before. In fact, very little of this works. Bashir is sharking after Melora, because of course he is. It's a tiny bit more subtle than it was in Season 1, but it's still clumsy. Effects-wise, the flying stuff is pretty good for TV, but it doesn't really make sense on a plot level: 'This is astonishing!' cries a weightless Bashir, who has spent his whole career in space. Melora's condition is scientifically dubious as well and Bashir's magic make-you-walk-again gizmo is months of patient research achieved in twenty minutes.

DS9 S02E07 Rules of Acquisition ★★★☆☆

Story by Hilary J. Bader, teleplay by Ira Steven Behr. Directed by David Livingston. TX: 8 November 1993. Featuring: Wallace Shawn, Helene Udy, Tiny Ron, Brian Thompson.

Feminist Ferengi. Not a very appealing prospect, but a moderately amusing episode.

A youth disguised as a boy is a venerable old plot device but that's no doubt because it works. Here the Ferengi make-up aids the deception considerably, meaning that it's just possible to watch this episode and not be ahead of the revelation, despite the fairly heavy-handed foreshadowing as Quark and Rom (but mainly Quark) drool over Dax. In more good news, Wallace Shawn is back as the Grand Nagus so the stage is set for one of the funny episodes of the 'dark' incarnation of **Star Trek**. I don't think I mentioned it last time, but

Michael Westmore's make-up here is tremendous, and the combination of Shawn's weaselly performance and Westmore's crenelated latex is very, very effective. On the other hand, the wine merchants from the Gamma Quadrant look more like kids at a face-painting party than a hitherto unknown alien race.

After a strong opening, Pel's relationship with Quark is not really developed much more than if it had been a Brian Rix farce, all unconvincing lies, homosexual anxiety and close calls. Waiting for the other shoe to drop is frustrating and the script seems not to know whether Pel's predicament or Quark's business deal is more interesting – it's Pel's predicament, which makes it all the more disappointing that it's handled so poorly. The showdown between Quark, Zek and Pel is more satisfying, but it's a long time coming. We're still in adventure-of-the-week territory so the episode ends with Quark, Pel, Zek and Rom all reset to their starting positions. Once again, Armin Shimerman demonstrates why he's such an asset to this show, making even the silliest moments breathe and feel real.

Instead of Dabo, the game of choice this week is Tongo, which the writers do a good job of making sound like a real game – not a trivial task. First mention of the Dominion.

DS9 S02E08 Necessary Evil ★★★★☆

Written by Peter Allan Fields. Directed by James L. Conway.
TX: 14 November 1993. Featuring: Marc Alaimo, Katherine Moffat, Robert MacKenzie.

Moody, almost melodramatic, tale of murder, intrigue and lies. Bizarre, but highly entertaining.

The opening of this episode is so melodramatic and over the top that I initially assumed that we were in a holosuite. The odd tonal shifts continue with Odo's misanthropic personal log creating a further film noir feel. To be honest, most of the Quark/Rom/Odo stuff seemed pretty dull – until suddenly we were back on the station when the Cardassians were in charge and Odo was chatting to Gul Dukat. René Auberjonois is amazing here – head bowed in humiliation and defeat – and Marc Alaimo modulates his smooth villainy as well, adopting a much more front-foot energy than when he's playing at diplomat. Odo's flashback murder investigation leads him to Kira, and then this starts to get a bit too convoluted for its own good, but Odo remains the MVP of this show and his scene at the end with Kira is tremendous. He even gets to do the *Columbo* 'One more thing' trick. Someone should let Sisko know that his son is no longer on the station. We haven't seen him except in the opening credits for most of the season so far.

DS9 S02E09 Second Sight ★★★☆☆

Story by Mark Gehred-O'Connell, teleplay by Mark Gehred-O'Connell, Ira Steven Behr and Robert Hewitt Wolfe. Directed by Alexander Singer. TX: 21 November 1993. Featuring: Salli Elise Richardson, Richard Kiley.

Sisko's new girlfriend is a sort of mind-ghost-leech-fantasy, and the story is as awkwardly convoluted as that sounds, but with some bright spots here and there.

Jake's back! Cirroc Lofton's actually really good here, I just don't know what the purpose of the character is, or what makes him different from any other teenage American boy, let alone why he gets to be in the opening titles and Rom, Nog, Dukat and so on don't. Grieving for Jake's mother, Sisko starts a weirdly intense conversation with a random on the promenade – who proceeds to vanish into thin air.

Next day, Sisko switches up his morning brew and Kira – who knows she's in a science fiction show – gives it this whole 'Who are you, and what have you done with Sisko?' but actually he just fancied a change, and he has his hands full with the latest in a series of **Star Trek** crackpot engineers. This one plans to jumpstart a star, and is brimming with jovial confidence, whereupon up pops the Commander's imaginary friend again. I wonder if these two plot strands are connected? Lo! The mad scientist's wife turns out to be Sisko's dream girl. The interplay between Sisko and Dax here is fun, doing much to shore up their relationship, and the mad scientist is veteran American actor Richard Kiley, who knows how to fill a set with his ebullient personality.

It transpires that the two identical women are aspects of the same person: one is a sort of parasitical psychic projection of the other. This is all a bit too complicated to feel resonant in any interesting way. It's also the kind of thing that could have easily happened on the *Enterprise* – and it's been a while since I had that complaint. So, this is a serviceable bit of space-problem-solving but fairly thin compared to some earlier episodes this season, and all of the intrigue fogs up the Sisko-in-love strand, which is then rushed through without the time it needs to really register.

Oddly, faced with a medical crisis, Dax proclaims that there's nothing to be done and nobody even thinks to call actual doctor Julian Bashir. The crew of the ship carrying out the experiment are all in the old uniforms. Starfleet really needs to invest in some remote-controlled shuttles.

DS9 S02E10 Sanctuary ★★☆☆☆

Story by Gabe Essoe & Kelley Miles, teleplay by Frederick Rappaport.
Directed by Les Landau. TX: 28 November 1993. Featuring: Deborah May,
William Schallert, Andrew Koenig, Michael Durrell.

*Gibberish-talking matriarchs want to settle on Bajor. Displaying little subtlety or
complexity, this is poorly paced and slightly ridiculous.*

Kira has installed a Bajoran musician in Quark's who sounds like he's playing
the **Deep Space Nine** theme, an in-joke on the level of the Indian flute player
in *Octopussy*. That doesn't get us off to a great start and – oh joy! – this is
Berman-**Trek** examining gender roles again. To pad out an episode that clearly
doesn't have enough story, the matriarchal Skrreeans (who have stupid hair
and stupider spelling) fox the universal translator for the first fifteen minutes,
after which they don't and the issue never comes up again. Naturally, instead
of the cold, desolate planet that the Federation has picked out for them, they
want to settle on Bajor, and eventually a problem regarding where to home
millions of refugees collapses down to one joyriding kid who isn't allowed to
land. This episode is likely to be remembered as the one with Andrew Koenig
(son of Walter) in it, or possibly the one where we started paying attention to
these tricky-sounding 'Dominion' coves, but it's all a bit silly and overwrought
and the gender politics is high school stuff, when it isn't actually *The Two
Ronnies* and 'The Worm That Turned'. Elsewhere, Jake is getting it on with a
Dabo girl. You go, Jake.

DS9 S02E11 Rivals ★☆☆☆☆

Story by Jim Trombetta and Michael Piller, teleplay by Joe Menosky.
Directed by David Livingston. TX: 2 January 1994. Featuring: Chris
Sarandon, Barbara Bosson as Roana.

Two silly sitcom plots braided together, neither of which is particularly compelling.

Quark is basically a slightly more successful version of Space Arthur Daley, not
that I imagine Michael Piller ever watched even a second of *Minder*, but that
show worked by taking a ripe performance of a sitcom plot and giving it a bit
of Thames TV drama production value. That could have worked here as well,
but the sitcom plot needed to be a good deal more inventive, and the guest
cast a lot more on their toes. A conman needs to be smoothly convincing and
charismatic, but Chris Sarandon – whom I've seen be excellent in other things
– looks stiff and awkward throughout. Elsewhere on the station, Bashir and

O'Brien are playing space squash, at which Bashir is an expert and O'Brien a beginner. Bashir trying to let O'Brien win doesn't work, and so what we have here are Space Competitive Dads, a plot line that neither fills out the Doctor's thin characterisation nor allows Colm Meaney to show his class. When the two plots converge, the machine that produces statistical flukes puts me in mind of another sitcom, this time the long-running British comedy *Red Dwarf,* which features a luck virus in one of its best episodes. That kind of silliness works there, but feels completely at odds with this show, making this awkward instalment one of my least favourites in quite a while.

DS9 S02E12 The Alternate ★★★☆☆

Story by Jim Trombetta and Bill Dial, teleplay by Bill Dial. Directed by David Carson. TX: 9 January 1994. Featuring: James Sloyan, Matt McKenzie.

Digging into Odo's backstory should be fascinating, but this is a bit of a slog, with the emphasis on all the wrong things.

There's a risk inherent in setting up a character whose backstory is a mystery, because backstories are empathy-generation devices and if you make a character's backstory mysterious, you make it harder to get to know them. The benefit is that you create a mystery to be unravelled, and you also keep your options open as the series progresses. And it makes a difference whether the backstory is a mystery to everyone or only to the audience. We didn't know much about Worf at first, but gradually we pieced together how a Klingon came to be serving on the bridge of the Federation's flagship. Data's backstory was a mystery to the characters as well as the audience, but again, the writing team on **TNG** did pull off a coherent explanation of how he came to be – just about.

This is the first time we've looked deeply into Odo's history, much of which is not clear to him either. The vehicle for this is a reunion with his 'dad', James Sloyan as Dr Mora Pol, who mentored Odo when he was first discovered. But a lot of this is just fairly standard issue uh-oh-we-brought-something-nasty-back-from-the-away-mission-and-now-it's-trying-to-kill-us plotting, when actually it's the relationship between Mora and Odo that's of interest to me. When Odo seemingly goes rogue and has to be hunted down, that's exciting, but I can't help thinking that the point of view is off. We aren't with Odo and don't know what he's going through – and he's the one we care about. We're with Dr Mora, whom we don't know, don't really trust, and don't care about. There are other stumbles as well – Mora actually says 'Dear god, what have I done?' at one point.

There's also some stuff about Jake (hello Jake!) studying Klingon opera for homework. Sure. Whatever. And I'm struck by the revelation that Ferengi chop up their dead and sell the bits, which makes much more sense than the nonsense about death rituals that we were spun in *Suspicions* over on **TNG**. Lastly, when the transporter was first mooted for **Star Trek**, several writers feared that being able to operate the device at will and be instantly whisked out of danger would make creating high-jeopardy plots almost impossible. Hence, the need to have a bloke operating the controls, who has to hear your request for transport over the radio, lock on to your co-ordinates and so on (not to mention all the episodes in which one or other of those things doesn't work for some technobabblish reason or another). Here, Odo just announces 'Computer, energise' and off they go. How long have they been able to do that, then?

DS9 S02E13 Armageddon Game ★★★★☆

Written by Morgan Gendel. Directed by Winrich Kolbe. TX: 30 January 1994. Featuring: Darleen Carr, Peter White, Larry Cedar.

Standard-issue bonding-in-the-face-of-adversity storyline but well done and with a couple of nice twists.

We're pairing Bashir and O'Brien again, in the hope that some kind of *Odd Couple* rapprochement can be achieved, or at least we'll start to shade in a bit more dimension in especially the Doctor's character. Putting them in a life-or-death situation works rather better than having them playing space squash, even if that's quite a well-worn trope. In other well-worn-trope news, the Zagbars and the Zoobles have buried the hatchet but need Federation help to destroy their stock of biological weapons. These one-time-only alien cultures are always tricky to pull off, and the details are barely sketched in here, which is why it is a relief that the majority of the run time is spent with characters we do know and do care about.

There's also some nifty plotting here. It's hard to be terribly caught up in anyone's grief when we know that our heroes are alive and well, but it's cool that it's Keiko who spots the clue that leads to the deception being uncovered, and *very* cool that the supposed clue was not a clue at all, and she just doesn't know her husband as well as she thinks she does. This episode is really only worth three and a half, but I bumped it up a whole extra half star because I liked that detail so much.

The rest of it is competent, well played by Siddig and Meaney especially, if slightly prone to cliché ('Tell my wife...' 'You'll tell her yourself' and 'It's been an honour serving with you') but the stakes are well ramped up, Sisko's trick with the runabout at the end is fun and there's some decent Dax material.

DS9 S02E14 Whispers ★★★☆☆

Written by Paul Robert Coyle. Directed by Les Landau. TX: 6 February 1994. Featuring: Susan Bay, Todd Waring.

'Who am I, and what have I done with O'Brien?' It's a novel twist and well played by the always-excellent Colm Meaney.

In an unusual framing sequence, O'Brien, alone on a shuttle, needs to set the record straight about the last fifty-two hours – a very exact figure, following which he muses, 'I'm trying to remember the first time I noticed things were wrong...' Keiko and Molly are being off with him over breakfast. He's been researching a people called the Paradas (who have an emotion-related odour) but when he gets back, Sisko keeps giving him busywork to do. Convinced that he's the victim of an *Invasion of the Body Snatchers*-style conspiracy, O'Brien ends up fighting his way out, and it's always fun to watch this kind of human-vs-the-automated-systems adventures.

A bit like *The Alternate*, this is partly an exercise in playing the story from the wrong, or at least an unusual, perspective – and here it works rather better because we're with O'Brien and we know and care about him. As with those silly M. Night Shyamalan films, though, it means we're denied access to the agonising decision-making process that led to letting the deception play out. But as a way of ringing the changes in a forty-five-minute TV episode, it's a worthwhile experiment and a fun mystery as it unfolds. It also works better in the gritty **DS9** context than it would in the optimistic **TNG** environment. You wouldn't believe for a second that Picard or Geordi or Troi had actually turned to the dark side – but Odo or Quark? Or even Sisko? Sure.

DS9 S02E15 Paradise ★★★☆☆

Story by Jim Trombetta and James Crocker, teleplay by Jeff King, Richard Manning and Hans Beimler. Directed by Corey Allen. TX: 13 February 1994. Featuring: Gail Strickland, Julia Nickson, Steve Vinovich, Michael Buchman Silver.

Thin story with a one-sided Federation vs Luddites debate failing to generate much interest, but there's good material for Kira and Dax.

O'Brien and Sisko are surveying the Gamma Quadrant and find a nice-looking planet. But when they beam down, none of their gadgets are working. I note that they've arrived in a runabout of which they were the only occupants, so beaming back again is going to be an automated process. Okay, so that's a thing in **Star Trek** now. How come I never noticed this before? 'Joseph' recognises the Starfleet uniforms. He and his mates have been living in a technology-free utopia for ten years. This is a real throwback to **TOS** episodes, such as the similarly named *The Paradise Syndrome* from Season 3, complete with anti-technology sentiment.

The problem here is a tricky one. It's basically planetary quicksand. Anyone who beams down will find it impossible to communicate with anyone in orbit. How can they get off the surface if they can't send a signal? It turns out, of course, that as well as being Luddite farmers, the isolated group of farmers are also vicious disciplinarians whose punishment for trivial crimes is being shut up in a *River Kwai*-style cage. That combined with the one-dimensional zealotry of Gail Strickland's Alixus makes this episode a good deal less nuanced than it thinks it is. Sisko and O'Brien just stiffly glower their way through, while Kira and Dax on the rescue runabout are rather more fun, but this is pretty thin stuff all round. There's also something rather sinister about O'Brien saying 'I can do it so it won't hurt at all' before concussing poor Joseph.

Last week, Jake's grades were stellar. Now he needs tutoring from O'Brien to get out of the bottom third.

DS9 S02E16 Shadowplay ★★★★☆

Written by Robert Hewitt Wolfe. Directed by Robert Scheerer.
TX: 20 February 1994. Featuring: Philip Anglim, Noley Thornton,
Kenneth Mars, Kenneth Tobey.

Triple-stranded character piece with little drama but some nice character beats for Kira, O'Brien and Odo.

Even at this stage, over halfway through Season 2, **DS9** is still largely stuck telling stories in which Starfleet types in a runabout go through the wormhole and find the planet of the Zagbars or those in which a delegation of Zoobles turns up on the station, bringing a plot with them. Or, in other words, stories in which an away team beams down from the *Enterprise* to a strange planet, or those in which a bunch of people in foam latex beam on board the *Enterprise*. I thought the whole point of this 'frontier town' set-up was that we would be telling different kinds of stories, stories that we can't warp away from at the end of the episode. That hasn't been reliably the case so far.

It's Dax's turn for a field trip through the wormhole. Odo doesn't understand the point of gossip (or romantic coupling). Even after seven lifetimes, Dax can't conceive of anyone other than a woman fancying Odo, who isn't even humanoid, let alone male. Once they beam down, Odo and Dax end up tangling with, of all people, Kenneth Mars (Franz Liebkind in *The Producers*), underplaying by his standards but still giving much more of a sitcom performance than anyone on this show since Wallace Shawn. The mystery they're there to solve only takes about twenty minutes of airtime, and doesn't need any more than that. It turns out that the huge machine giving off strange readings and the odd disappearances are – would you believe it? – related. The rest is all standard-issue *Blade Runner* can-a-machine-feel? stuff.

Hey, everyone, Jake is on the station! And at 15, he's in need of a job (something that everyone needs in a post-scarcity economy). In three episodes we've gone from his grades are excellent but he needs some advice from O'Brien, to he's failing his exams and needs tutoring from O'Brien, to he knows nothing about engineering so it's silly to suggest that he be apprenticed to O'Brien. I'm not saying the writers aren't particularly interested in Jake as a character, but it does seem as if not everyone is paying very close attention. Cirroc Lofton's inexperience is still showing, but Colm Meaney makes him look good, like all really fine actors are capable of doing.

In a third strand, Vedek Bareil from the opening three-parter is on the station. This I do like – filling out the universe of the show by creating a deeper bench of recurring characters, and not letting us forget about past conflicts, hard-won victories, or unresolved grudges. His scenes with Kira are, again, not very rich in drama, but I do appreciate the detailed character work. This is a sit-back-and-let-it-happen episode, rather than an oh-no-what's-going-to-happen one, but that's okay once in a while, and this cast is really growing on me now. Shame that Dax was just along for the ride, otherwise this might have tipped over into four-star territory.

Garak is referred to but does not appear. Odo has himself beamed up by computer once more. He doesn't even stand up to do it.

DS9 S02E17 **Playing God** ★★★★☆

Story by Jim Trombetta, teleplay by Jim Trombetta and Michael Piller.
Directed by David Livingston. TX: 27 February 1994.
Featuring: Geoffrey Blake, Ron Taylor, Richard Poe.

A slightly over-stuffed episode with extraneous protouniverses, space seaweed and persistent voles drawing attention away from Dax's fascinating relationship with a hopeful host.

A potential new Trill host is on the station, anxiously babbling exposition at Bashir, and trembling in anticipation of meeting feared mentor Dax, who is renowned for rejecting hopefuls from the programme. As is so often the case, at this stage, at any rate, the script doesn't serve anyone other than Quark with any particularly characterful dialogue in the rather low-key teaser, but Terry Farrell is really growing on me now, and is managing to imbue even these bland lines with a charmingly world-weary swagger. Given that her character is basically a one-line description of her species, that's quite an achievement. Geoffrey Blake as Arjin is rather stiffer, and it's hard to tell to what extent that's deliberate.

On a sightseeing tour of the Gamma Quadrant, Dax and her charge bring back some 'subspace seaweed', which they then forget about while having an awkward lunch. In this B-plot, the seaweed turns out to be a 'protouniverse', which is a fairly ridiculous idea that doesn't really create the kind of scientific wonder or fascinating moral dilemma that I assume was hoped for. This is only required to create a means by which Arjin can show Dax what he's made of, and you can see the rivets where the two stories have been hammered together. That A-plot is really good, though, and makes a much better job of using the unique symbiotic properties of the Trill to tell a good story about this Trill, her baggage, and her issues.

The C-plot deals with, of all things, voles infesting the station. Even when centred on O'Brien and Kira (and who doesn't want to see more of Nana Visitor and Colm Meaney?), this doesn't generate much in the way of interest.

DS9 S02E18 Profit and Loss ★★★★☆

Written by Flip Kobler and Cindy Marcus. Directed by Robert Wiemer. TX: 20 March 1994. Featuring: Mary Crosby, Andrew Robinson, Michael Reilly Burke, Heidi Swedberg, Edward Wiley.

Of all the bars, in all the space stations, in all the galaxies, your ship conks out at mine… Quark in love is a tough sell, but they make it work.

One of the things you can do with an ensemble cast is pick one of them and push them through a familiar plot, in the hope that the combination of two known quantities will result in something fresh. On that basis, how does 'Quark's old Cardassian girlfriend drops by' sound as a pitch? That's the A-plot for this episode in which a trio of Cardassians run aground at the station and Sisko promises to get them on their way as soon as possible, but not before one of them belts the Ferengi bartender around the chops, saying, 'I told you never to speak to me again.' This is Mary Crosby, Denise's aunt, as Natima.

Much more excitingly – Garak is back! I remember this series fondly not least for the deep bench of secondary and tertiary characters, which we haven't seen all that much of in these first two years, but any time Andrew Robinson is on screen, I am a happy viewer. Even better, this isn't one of those two-or-three-plots-potter-along-in-parallel episodes of **DS9**. Garak's input into the agendas and safety of the visiting trio is crucial and his multi-layered conversation with Quark is fascinating and beautifully played by both actors.

It does seem weird to see Quark declaring his love for Natima, apparently with all sincerity, but we've seen enough of this character to know that there's more to him than a simple desire for latinum, and Armin Shimerman is such an excellent performer that this all works beautifully. What I'm less enamoured of is the *Casablanca* pastiche, which gets in the way more than it adds. It's the details of this conflict and these characters that I'm here for. Luckily, they're both very strong.

DS9 S02E19 Blood Oath ★★☆☆☆

Written by Peter Allan Fields. Directed by Winrich Kolbe. TX: 27 March 1994. Featuring: John Colicos, William Campbell, Michael Ansara.

Nostalgia-fest, which perhaps hoped to establish the new show as part of the fabric of the franchise, but it's a bit of a slog.

Three **Original Series** Klingons swing by the station with the new bumpy-forehead make-up ('We do not discuss it with outsiders'). Turns out that they palled around with Curzon Dax, eighty-odd years ago. Now they're back to wreak revenge on 'The Albino'. Trouble is, this all rests on events and relationships established off-screen and generations in the past, so all we have to connect us to the present is Terry Farrell and she isn't given a whole hell of a lot to work with here. She gets a nice scene with Nana Visitor, which explores their different takes on the nasty business of killing. But we awkwardly cut away from that to the sight of a jovial Klingon cackling in Quark's. That's this episode all over. It grapples with some big themes, but it doesn't quite seem to know what to do with them. It just hopes that the barely recognisable sight of three actors from **The Old Show** will be enough. It isn't really.

DS9 S02E20 The Maquis, Part I ★★★★☆

Story by Rick Berman & Michael Piller & Jeri Taylor and James Crocker, teleplay by James Crocker. Directed by David Livingston. TX: 24 April 1994. Featuring: Bernie Casey, Marc Alaimo, Tony Plana, Bertila Damas, Richard Poe, Michael A. Krawic, Amanda Carlin.

Subtle and powerful tale of intrigue and politicking, which feels thrillingly pulpy and deeply grown-up at the same time.

Well, here's something that would have caused the Great Bird to choke on his millet – terrorists in Starfleet uniforms blowing up innocent Cardassians. It's a strong opening to an episode with a title that means more now than it would have done in 1994. The Maquis are going to feature in **DS9** and **TNG** and (sort-of) become important for the premise of **Voyager**. It's also the first part of a two-parter, this time acknowledged as such on-screen, as opposed to the trilogy that opened the season. As befits such a key episode, all of the top brass get their names on the 'story by' credit.

Meanwhile, ~~Felix Leiter~~ Cal Hudson (in the old uniform) pays a call. In something that helps this all to feel like one big universe, he's overseeing the demilitarised zone established over on **TNG** last week, and dealing with the same colonists that Picard tangled with. Also making a welcome return appearance is Gul Dukat, as smoothly evasive as ever, hiding in the shadows while professing to be Sisko's friend. This kind of double-dealing and subtle politicking is rapidly becoming my favourite thing about this series, and one of the things that I can't readily get on sunny, optimistic **TNG**. Cardassians and Federation colonists are scrapping (the budget only allows us to the see the ships as icons on a scanner screen) to Dukat's evident frustration, and there's a real sense through the middle of this episode of a diplomatic solution falling apart.

Quark, meanwhile, is forging a meaningful business relationship with a Vulcan gunrunner, further adding to the general atmosphere of distrust, unease and peace balanced on a knife-edge. And when Sisko gets back to the station, he finds a fiery Major Kira waiting for him. This is amazing stuff, where everyone has a point of view, where we care about the characters and the relationships, where it isn't even clear what the right thing to do might be. Bashir wants to know if Sisko is prepared to fire on Starfleet vessels. Sisko doesn't respond. Wow.

There are 285 Ferengi Rules of Acquisition. Cardassians are famous for their photographic memories. Gul Dukat has seven children.

DS9 S02E21 The Maquis, Part II ★★★★☆

Story by Rick Berman & Michael Piller & Jeri Taylor and Ira Steven Behr, teleplay by Ira Steven Behr. Directed by Corey Allen. TX: 1 May 1994. Featuring: Bernie Casey, Marc Alaimo, Tony Plana, John Schuck, Natalija Nogulich, Bertila Damas, Michael Bell, Amanda Carlin.

If you can get past the steel-plated plot armour, this is every bit as good as Part I, but the writers need to be careful about painting their heroes into corners.

And of course, it's Felix who's the traitor – pretty much following the **Star Trek** movie rules – which makes Sisko even more conflicted. His uniform's been feeling a little tight lately, but nobody wants peace more than the Maquis. Sisko isn't convinced, and so because Felix is a sensible insurrectionist, he phasers all three Starfleet snoopers to death on the spot. Roll credits.

When we rejoin the action, it becomes apparent that murderous, death-procuring Felix is actually an old softie, with phasers set to stun, because Sisko, Kira and Bashir just stroll back onto the station as if nothing had happened. That's a remarkably sloppy start to the second part of what was such a fantastic opener. Continuing the cross-fertilisation between this show and **TNG**, Admiral Nechayev is on the station, looking askance at Odo, and letting slip that she knows all about the Maquis and their blood-soaked ways.

'It's easy to be a saint in paradise,' observes Sisko, 'but the Maquis do not live in paradise.' It's a strong speech – on the nose, sure, but clear-eyed and passionate. In a fascinating twist, Sisko now comes riding to the rescue of Gul Dukat, even as John Schuck's Legate Parn tries to throw him under the bus. When we check in with the Cardassian politician, the Vulcan Maquis is trying to mind-rape him – without success. Marc Alaimo is superb here, managing that excellent trick of gnawing on the scenery without sacrificing subtlety. In my enthusiasm for seeing as much of Andrew Robinson as possible, I'd quite forgotten this amazing addition to the wider world of the show. In barely forty episodes, this show has made Federation space feel vastly more familiar, richer, more complicated.

Apart from that stumble at the beginning, this is a very fine story. It's got great material for Quark, Odo and Kira and series-best stuff for Sisko, and while it resolves its main conflicts, it leaves us in a far more fraught situation than we were two weeks ago. Even Felix leaves to Maquis another day (although that's the last we see of Bernie Casey).

Vulcans are a species that appreciates good ears.

DS9 S02E22 The Wire ★★★★☆

Written by Robert Hewitt Wolfe. Directed by Kim Friedman.
TX: 8 May 1994. Featuring: Andrew J. Robinson, Paul Dooley.

***Star Trek** does* Trainspotting *with Garak and Bashir. I'd watch that in a heartbeat, and this is very, very strong stuff.*

More Garak action, and he's in need of medical attention, which he declines to accept from his best bud Bashir. They've been having weekly lunches for a year now. Eventually he collapses and Bashir discovers a doohickey in his head. The Obsidian Order is taking an interest in the situation – even the Romulan Tal Shiar can't compete with them for intelligence gathering. His skull whoosit makes him immune to torture by flooding his system with endorphins (nasty) and before he lets Bashir help him, Garak insists on filling in some of his backstory. Surprise, surprise, he isn't just a simple tailor. This is beautifully played by both actors – Alexander Siddig keeps getting better, and Andrew Robinson is superb. I also appreciate that there's no music over this conversation, just the low hum of the space station. The words are enough.

One individual helping another through withdrawal isn't terribly new, but previous attempts to tackle drug use in this franchise have been simplistic and naive. This feels real and specific, and it's harrowing stuff. Peeling back the layers of a secretive character like this is always a risk – often mysteries are far more interesting than answers – but the revelations are so shocking, the emotional arc so well charted, and the reset button so delicately deployed, that not only do we not feel that we've learned more than we wanted, we can't even be sure by the end that we learned anything at all. 'They're all true, especially the lies.'

What's missing is an equivalent arc for Bashir, who remains the principled Starfleet officer, prioritising patient care, that he's always been. Also worth mentioning is the other guest star – Andrew Robinson is almost matched by the excellent Paul Dooley as the retired head of the Obsidian Order, who has his own line in avuncular psychopathy.

The story in the classic Cardassian novel *The Neverending Sacrifice* gets a little redundant after a while – but, ugh, that's the point, you philistine. Bashir gets to say, 'I'm a doctor, not a botanist.'

DS9 S02E23 Crossover ★★★★★

Story by Peter Allan Fields, teleplay by Peter Allan Fields and Michael Piller. Directed by David Livingston. TX: 15 May 1994.
Featuring: Andrew J. Robinson.

A love letter to the original series as well as a thrilling adventure and detailed character study in its own right. Tremendous stuff.

Bashir is continuing his mission to annoy everyone on the station into being his friend, and today it's poor Kira's turn to listen to him prattle on about music, do drama school breathing exercises and mansplain English idioms. Suddenly, everything goes skew-whiff and they find themselves in the Mirror Universe.

I have two things to say about the Mirror Universe. The first thing is that it makes no sense whatsoever. The Mirror Universe, with the precise and limited differences from the one we know, which we saw in **TOS**, would have given rise to a far more divergent one than the one we get here. Certainly, none of the Earth people we're familiar with would ever have been born. However, that's a very dull thing to worry about. The fun of a mirror universe is seeing our regular characters all with goatees and eyepatches.

The other thing to say is that – especially in a post-**Discovery** landscape – it's slightly amazing that we never travelled to the Mirror Universe in **TNG** and that we almost got to the end of Season 2 of **DS9** before we saw it again. Anyway, now it's here and it's glorious. Nana Visitor slinks over to her other self in a uniform that's painted on, and sinks her teeth into the scenery. She gets to lay out the plot, which connects directly to Kirk's adventures in *Mirror Mirror*. Spock's mission of peace led to an alliance of Cardassians, Bajorans and Klingons taking over this part of the galaxy and subjugating the humans. The delicious twist here is that Mirror Kira is a pacifist (at least by the standards of this world) and our Kira hopes to learn her warlike ways. Nana Visitor does a wonderful job of sustaining the scenes with herself and the video effects are top-notch, as is the wonderfully gory death of Mirror Odo at Bashir's enthusiastic hands.

Mirror O'Brien tries to jump universes too, and with memories of Thomas Riker, I wondered if he might succeed. Actually, it's Mirror Sisko who turns out to hold the key to their return, and he promises to look after Mirror O'Brien. This is a brilliant continuation of what **TOS** began, a wonderful showcase for the cast, and if I know **DS9**, it's the beginning, not the end.

Those Mirror Universe Klingon goons have auto-transporters too.

DS9 S02E24 The Collaborator ★★★☆☆

Story by Gary Holland, teleplay by Gary Holland, Ira Steven Behr and Robert Hewitt Wolfe. Directed by Cliff Bole. TX: 22 May 1994.
Featuring: Philip Anglim, Louise Fletcher, Camille Saviola, Bert Remsen.

Overly dense episode with strong themes but not enough character stuff, even though Nana Visitor is never less than compelling.

It's Vedek Bareil's turn to look into the Flashback Box of Dutch Angled Dream Imagery and he sees a vision of his hanged body cut down by Major Kira. During some post-coital exposition, it transpires that he is in the running to be the new Bajoran Kai and that Kira has a vote, even though if he wins, she'll see a lot less of him.

Smarming around the station is the deliciously malevolent Louise Fletcher as Vedek Winn. She doesn't seem certain of the difference between 'infer' and 'imply' so you know she's a wrong-un. Pretty soon, she's buttering up Sisko and seems mysteriously open to Bajor joining to the Federation – if that's the will of the prophets. A public appearance of the two of them would not be appropriate until the vote for Kai is concluded, of course, since Winn is Bareil's chief competition.

Elsewhere, a Bajoran collaborator turns up on the station and is promptly arrested by Odo. Kubus Oak wants to end his exile and return to Bajor, which Kira denies but which is approved by Winn. This is pretty dense politicking, and it needs to tap into our core characters and their relationships more than it does early on, if it's to be truly engaging. Too much of this is people with latex heads telling each other stories about people we've never met who have silly names. We never saw the Kendra Massacre that everyone is referring to, so we have to take the characters' word for it that it matters.

Winn's plan is to use Kubus's testimony to smear Bareil and take the Kai-ship for herself, and she recruits Kira to find out the truth about who was responsible for what. One problem is that this one is all Kira, Odo and then tertiary characters like Winn and Bareil. I appreciate the depth of **DS9**'s bench of personalities, but that doesn't mean I don't want to check in with the regular cast once in a while. There are fleeting scenes with Quark and O'Brien, but there's next to nothing for Dax or Bashir or even Sisko. Jake is still MIA, of course.

The best episodes of **DS9** use the ever-present political situation to examine our characters and put them under unique pressures, but without sacrificing strong adventure storytelling. This isn't one of the worst episodes by any means, but a lot of it feels like 'Last time on **Deep Space Nine**' rather than a story unfolding in front of us right now. Because this is **Deep Space Nine**, Winn – who'd certainly twirl a moustache if she had one – is the one who comes out on top. It is the will of the prophets. I just hope next time they will give us a more exciting story.

DS9 S02E25 Tribunal ★★★★☆

Written by Bill Dial. Directed by Avery Brooks. TX: 5 June 1994.
Featuring: Richard Poe, Caroline Lagerfelt, John Beck.

Odo gets to play Rumpole of the Station in this fun episode pitting O'Brien against the Cardassian justice system.

O'Brien is off on his hols, and good thing too – he seems to have body swapped with Dr Bashir, or at least he's been taking how-to-be-annoying lessons from him. A chance meeting with an old friend on his way out the airlock leads to him being framed for gunrunning.

As I've observed before, the benefit of a flexible format is that you can take a story with a familiar shape and feed it through the meat-grinder of your setting and your people and hopefully get something unique. Here it's the courtroom drama, and more than that it's the falsely-accused-innocent flavour of courtroom drama. **Deep Space Nine** has always had a nuanced take on the Cardassians, with characters like Garak and Dukat showing the shades of grey in their black hearts, but they're still the series' main 'heavies' (at least for now), so it's intriguing to see their idea of a fair trial, especially when we remember Gul Madred's treatment of Picard.

As there, so here – O'Brien is stripped naked, given drugs and Cardassians clip off any bits of him they like the look of. (Other fans have noted that most seasons contain one or two episodes in the sub-genre of O'Brien Must Suffer, and this is one such.) The verdict, of course, has already been determined, and his execution has been scheduled. The purpose of the trial is merely to establish how the crime was committed. The plot runs on rails from this point on, but there's loads of fun to be had in the ripe guest performances, Colm Meaney's impassioned ranting, the Kafkaesque Cardassian jurisprudence and the frantic scrambling of his friends on the station.

The *Enterprise* gets a name check. Avery Brooks is behind the camera for this one. He wasn't going to make Gates McFadden's mistake and wait until Season 7.

DS9 S02E26 The Jem'Hadar ★★★★☆

Written by Ira Steven Behr. Directed by Kim Friedman. TX: 12 June 1994. Featuring: Alan Oppenheimer, Molly Hagan, Cress Williams.

Awkwardly structured introduction to the Big Bads that are coming to get us, but the last act is thrilling stuff.

Jake exists. And he's doing generic kid thing number five – a science project for school. He twists his old man's arm and scores a trip to the Gamma Quadrant, with Quark and Nog along for the ride. It's kind of a low-stakes and domestic way to kick-off a season finale and it quickly morphs into generic kid thing number six – the family camping trip.

As well as being an outsider in a way that no regular cast member of any previous **Star Trek** series was, Quark is also unique thus far in being deployed principally for comic relief. Early attempts to give him dramatic material foundered – who can forget his absurd hysterics in *Move Along Home*? But

Armin Shimerman is such a skilled performer that given an even half-decent script he can make it sing, and there are layers to this avaricious creature that keep revealing themselves. It does help, though, that when his purpose is to be amusing, he reliably is – such as here, where he declares himself allergic to nature and starts putting aluminium sunblock on his ears.

This is all just softening us up, however, as the true threat, for most of the rest of the series, is coming – and they're named in the title. The Jem'Hadar don't quite have the charisma of the Borg, or the complexity of the Cardassians, but they're going to prove to be quite intractable foes. Before then, please enjoy this backstory.

Having detained Sisko, Quark and a Dominion woman called Eris, the Jem'Hadar saunter onto the station, sabres rattling, and pretty soon Starfleet's all in a paddy. Since the first episode, the fabled wormhole has been little more than a hyperspace bypass to novel races, whom one hopes will bring interesting plots with them. Now, we turn a major corner as it turns out that a far more deadly enemy is lurking there – one that doesn't take kindly to strangers.

Jake and Nog's adventures on the runabout are only busywork, although Sisko and Quark end up making quite a formidable team – and it's nice to see a galaxy-class ship and my preferred uniforms once more. But Captain Keogh on the *Odyssey* struggles to hold his own once the Jem'Hadar forces close in. Really, it isn't since the Borg that we've seen anything close to this kind of existential threat to the Federation and our guys. In fact, this is essentially *Q Who* but without John de Lancie – establishing a major new threat and not resolving it. The difference is that on **TNG**, the *Odyssey* would never have been taken out by a suicide run as it was retreating. Golly.

DS9 Season 2 wrap-up

- A big jump in quality from Season 1. As we might expect, the characters are stronger, the actors are more comfortable, the writing is surer. But more than that, the true personality of the show is coming through. This is going to be about long arcs, dealing with consequences, and an end to the comfortable complacency that we sometimes saw on **TNG**.
- To make that work, the darkness is going to need to be balanced with some fun. Too much O'Brien Must Suffer and The Dominion Kills Everybody and we're going to be wrung out. That doesn't mean I want more episodes like *Leprechauns on the Station* or *Space Monopoly of Doom*, however.
- The Dominion is going to shape the next several years of the show. One fair question would be – did we need to wait two years to get here? After all, **TNG** had already spent five years creating the twenty-fourth century. But even though Season 1 in particular was a rough ride, the big strength of this

show is the secondary/tertiary cast, so the time taken to establish characters like Kai Winn, Gul Dukat, The Grand Nagus and especially Garak is time very well spent.

• This season also sees **TNG** winding up, which means that **Deep Space Nine** is now the established show and no longer the new upstart. **Voyager** will kick off during Season 3, but not in syndication.

• Average score for Season 2 is a very impressive 3.62, nudging ahead of **TNG** Seasons 3–5, but not quite exceeding **TNG** Season 6 or **TOS** Season 1 – still the high-water marks for the franchise in my view.

Deep Space Nine
Season 3

Starring: Avery Brooks, René Auberjonois, Terry Farrell, Cirroc Lofton, Colm Meaney, Nana Visitor, Alexander Siddig, Armin Shimerman. Featuring: Aron Eisenberg, Max Grodénchik, Rosalind Chao, Andrew J. Robinson. Executive producers: Rick Berman, Michael Piller. Producers: René Echevarria, Peter Lauritson. Co-executive producer: Ira Steven Behr. Supervising producers: Ronald D. Moore, David Livingston.

DS9 S03E01 The Search, Part I ★★★★☆

Story by Ira Steven Behr & Robert Hewitt Wolfe, teleplay by Ronald D. Moore. Directed by Kim Friedman. TX: 26 September 1994. Featuring: Salome Jens, Martha Hackett, John Fleck, Kenneth Marshall.

Sisko takes the new car out for a spin. Odo has dinner with his family. Game-changing stuff, setting up a whole new set of conflicts and intrigues.

After a little over three months off the air – but without the prior episode ending 'To be continued…' – we're back with quite a detailed recap. This is called 'Part I' but really it's part two of *The Jem'Hadar Trilogy*. However, things have happened while we've been away. Sisko's gone and got a new motor, Dax is doing her hair like Betty Grable, and I think finally the coloured uniform lapels have been given a bit of starch, so they aren't flopping about in that aggravating fashion.

The news is grim. Seven simulations give the station two hours to hold off the Jem'Hadar once they start coming through the wormhole. The *Defiant* was supposed to be the solution to the Borg threat – a new fighting-class runabout. Yep, Starfleet is building warships, with – pointedly – no families and no science labs on board. All available space is used for weapons, which means that the damn thing doesn't work properly. But Benjamin 'Take the Fight to Them' Sisko has a sabre and he's going to rattle it. The new warp-powered H-bomb even has a cloaking device, courtesy of visiting Romulan T'Rul, played by Martha Hackett, shortly to be seen again in another role in **Voyager.**

And as this is the 'all change' episode, Odo is being stood down. He now has to report to Starfleet's Lieutenant Eddington, which leads to his resignation. Kira, knowing that he's contracted for six seasons, tries to reinvent him as a diplomat. And Sisko is trying to do the same with Quark, who suggests his brother instead, since 'Rom only has a son to think about, I have a business.' Hah!

The other change is that, after two years, Sisko has finally unpacked his stuff. Once again, Jake doesn't get anything resembling an actual storyline of his own, but having Sisko discuss his personal life with his offspring is more believable than him discussing it with the crew (even Dax) and more elegant than having him growl his way through a voice-over or give himself a pep talk in the mirror.

Off we go then, to try to bring about peace through superior firepower. It doesn't work, but nor do we see much of the action. The *Defiant* is presumed destroyed and we discover that Odo and Kira have escaped in a shuttlecraft. After a tense and thrillingly doom-laden episode, this feels like a bit of a cheat, but the final scene with Odo gives us our proper cliffhanger into the next episode. He's home.

DS9 S03E02 The Search, Part II ★★★☆☆

Story by Ira Steven Behr and Robert Hewitt Wolfe, teleplay by Ira Steven Behr. Directed by Jonathan Frakes. TX: 3 October 1994. Featuring: Salome Jens, Natalija Nogulich, Martha Hackett, Kenneth Marshall, William Frankfather, Dennis Christopher.

A sort of sneak preview at what the next five years might include. Thrilling while it's on, but it's hard not to feel betrayed by the rug-pull of an ending.

René Auberjonois is superb, creating a genuinely touching portrait of a lost man trying to find his way home. However, some of the information given in past episodes is contradicted here: Odo based his human form on the Bajoran who found him, Dr Mora, but all of the other Changelings greet him looking similar. This is an acceptable visual shorthand, of course, but it feels sloppy. (Let's not stop and explain it, though; I'd prefer to accept the ret-con and move on.)

Oddly, Kira seems more concerned that Odo observes social niceties with the other Changelings than she does about the high probability that Sisko, Bashir and the rest are floating like cinders in space and she'll never see them again. We quickly establish that they're fine and have made it back to the station, so we can stop worrying, but I don't think Kira should.

And, my, things move quickly back on the station. The Dominion start creating a formal alliance with the Federation and the Cardassians, but they insist on being a dick to the Romulans. When Sisko – a Starfleet commander who is able to summon an actual real-life admiral to a very brief face-to-face meeting! – can't talk his superiors round, he sets off on a mission to collapse the wormhole, which mission involves and costs the life of poor old Garak, who thinks the Dominion will be dangerous friends.

As the manic pace builds, and the small inconsistencies build up, eventually it's a mild relief to be told 'it was only a dream', as unsatisfying as that is. The real revelation here is that the Founders, the Changelings, the Dominion and the Jem'Hadar are all aspects of the same group. In other words, the implacable foe waiting on the other side of the wormhole is Odo's kith and kin. Wow.

The new-style combadge (designed for *Generations*) turns up here, and for the rest of the run. None other than Jonathan Frakes is credited as director, giving it lots of pace and energy. Also behind the scenes, Ron Moore has come on board from **TNG**, and a lot of the war stuff (and Klingon stuff) that's to come bears his stamp.

DS9 S03E03 The House of Quark ★★★★☆

Story by Tom Benko, teleplay by Ronald D. Moore. Directed by Les Landau. TX: 10 October 1994. Featuring: Mary Kay Adams, Robert O'Reilly.

Hugely entertaining episode focusing on one of the series' best actors. But the tonal whiplash after last week is a little disconcerting.

When Quark scuffles with an inebriated Klingon who ends up with a fatal dagger wound, the Ferengi sees no harm in taking credit for the murder. It's excellent PR. But pretty soon, family members are crawling out of the woodwork and Quark is not initially able to successfully navigate these waters. That's the one false note in this very entertaining episode. I can't help feeling that Quark should've known more about Klingons. As an experienced bartender, and an excellent businessman, it's his job to know about the peoples and races who frequent his establishment. But, I suppose, he needs to explain Klingon honour codes to us, the audience. Later in the episode, it turns out that Quark's expertise in bookkeeping is quite the asset, and there's always fun to be had in finding loopholes, even in made-up statutes. His final confrontation, refusing to give his Klingon foe an honourable kill, is a big moment for him too.

My only real complaint about this episode is that this is not the show I was watching last time. *Babylon 5*, which had a full five-year plan mapped out before show one went on the air, used to include a variety of 'arc' and 'non-arc' episodes over the course of a given season. I guess this is a 'non-arc' episode, and it's a very high quality one. But there are loose ends from last week. Such as – when did Odo get his job back?

DS9 S03E04 Equilibrium ★★★☆☆

Story by Christopher Teague, teleplay by René Echevarria. Directed by Cliff Bole. TX: 17 October 1994. Featuring: Lisa Banes, Jeff Magnus McBride, Nicholas Cascone, Harvey Vernon.

Decent non-arc episode with Dax needing medical attention on the homeworld, but still more interested in Trill biology than Jadzia as a person.

Cooking With Sisko is going to be a thing, it seems. Bashir is being a dick as usual – in this case to beets – but I suppose this is the **DS9** version of the **TNG** poker game. We also recently saw Captain Pike pulling the same trick over on **Strange New Worlds**. There's a family feeling to the senior staff now, which wasn't present before. I think I like it. Bashir and Dax swapping childhood stories about doctors, for example, does a lot to build a bit more empathy for his character. But it's Dax who's at the centre of this story, and again, this is more about Trills in general than her in particular, which is frustrating. Key to the resolution is the discovery that there is a lie at the heart of Trill society. Rather like that silly **TNG** episode *Dark Page* in which Lwaxana's family history nearly does her in, the problem is that I wasn't heavily invested in this fact before this episode, and so being told that reality is different is only of passing academic interest. Unlike *Dark Page*, though, this is very dramatic and there is some striking imagery in some of the dream sequences: characters who take off their masks revealing further masks underneath is a very nifty bit of filmmaking.

DS9 S03E05 Second Skin ★★★★☆

Written by Robert Hewitt Wolfe. Directed by Les Landau.
TX: 24 October 1994. Featuring: Gregory Sierra, Lawrence Pressman, Tony Papenfuss, Cindy Katz.

Delicious mind-swap fantasy makes for a great showcase for Nana Visitor.

Now, stop me if you've heard this one. Kira awakes and sees her reflection in the mirror – and she's a Cardassian. Yep, it's *Face of the Enemy*, but with a bit of Patrick McGoohan's seminal sixties television show *The Prisoner* stirred in too. Friendly Cardassians – one of them claiming to be her father – tell her she has been undercover for ten years and that it will take a while for her memory to return. What's fantastic about this is that Kira doesn't believe a word of it – she's seen *Face of the Enemy* as well! True, this is another story asking: what really happened in a place we've never seen, years before the show started? That's potentially a weak structure, but the drama of this episode isn't rooted in the details of the historical Cardassian/Bajoran conflict, it's Kira's refusal to submit and it's the relationship between her and Lawrence Pressman's Ghemor, hoping to see his daughter again.

Also adding to the fun – it's Garak who helps Sisko come riding to the rescue. Sisko has had the *Defiant* upgraded with Zoom filters, but when his deception seems to be foundering, Garak reels off a string of threats and code words, all of which he claims to have overheard while hemming somebody's trousers. He's brilliant. But don't trust him – he's a dangerous man, according to some of his fellows. Of course, this is also an opportunity to see the world of the show from the point of view of the bad guys. The Cardassians love their children too (as Sting might put it) and to put Kira so close to one of the bastards who massacred so many she was close to is very affecting.

This really is top-drawer stuff: exciting, funny, moving, unpredictable and brilliantly played, especially by the always excellent Nana Visitor who looks amazing in Cardassian make-up. The only thing stopping from awarding this the full five stars is that I've already seen *Face of the Enemy*. I also can't tell you how pleased I am that they finally got those Starfleet uniforms sorted out.

DS9 S03E06 The Abandoned ★★★☆☆

Written by D. Thomas Maio & Steve Warnek. Directed by Avery Brooks. TX: 31 October 1994. Featuring: Bumper Robinson, Jill Sayre.

Thoughtful but low-key episode with good stuff for Odo, and the usual rather generic stuff for Jake and his dad.

Quark gets more than he negotiated for when a consignment of junk turns out to include a fast-growing infant, who ages to seemingly 8 or 9 in twenty-four hours, and then starts talking. This is all kinds of nonsense, having nothing whatever to do with how language acquisition really works. Moses turns out to be a young Jem'Hadar warrior and Starfleet Command wants to run tests on him. Odo, usually pragmatic and hard-headed (if you see what I mean), suddenly has an attack of conscience and wants to protect and nurture the boy, and not see him treated as a lab rat. But then, this is personal for him. This is not inconsistent characterisation, it's layering.

The attempt to socialise the Jem'Hadar infant is doomed, which is obvious from the beginning. There's a certain amount of tragic power in this, but I was never hugely invested in the fate of the boy, and the stakes felt low. This is mainly because the ending was all too predictable. I mean, did anyone watching this really think we were going to add a Jem'Hadar to the crew roster? (But then again, wait till we get to **Voyager**.)

Meanwhile, Sisko is dealing with his actual son growing up faster than he anticipated. Yes, everyone, Jake exists! He's seeing a Dabo Girl. You go, Jake. Sadly, Sisko's dinner with Jake and Mardah is equally generic and predictable. Avery Brooks directs smoothly.

DS9 S03E07 Civil Defense ★★★★☆

Written by Mike Krohn. Directed by Reza Badiyi. TX: 7 November 1994. Featuring: Marc Alaimo, Danny Goldring.

Fine and fast-moving thrilling-escape-from-death storyline with good character beats.

Sisko, Jake and O'Brien are trapped when an old Cardassian security device is triggered. Skinny Jake has to crawl through an ore pipe to get them out. But everything they do makes matters worse as the station AI believes that it's under threat from rebelling Bajoran workers and continues to implement counter-measures including flooding the habitation areas with nerve gas and then beginning a countdown to self-destruct.

While I have to question the wisdom and/or competency of the Bajoran and Federation operatives who took over the station but who left the tanks of nerve gas hooked up to the ventilation system, this is a fun mechanism for putting our characters into jeopardy and creating some unlikely alliances – between Odo and Quark, Garak and Kira, Jake and O'Brien. The situation is seemingly resolved by a swaggering Gul Dukat taking gleeful advantage of the hazardous situation. Marc Alaimo is a fabulous actor and a huge asset to this series, making this *Deus Ex Cardassia* ending far more satisfactory than it might have been – especially as he then screws it up. Lovely stuff.

DS9 S03E08 Meridian ★☆☆☆☆

Story by Hilary J. Bader and Evan Carlos Somers, teleplay by Mark Gehred-O'Connell. Directed by Jonathan Frakes. TX: 14 November 1994. Featuring: Brett Cullen, Christine Healy, Jeffrey Combs.

Deep Space Nine does Brigadoon. *Twee, maddening and incredibly dull.*

Despite the continuing threat posed by the Dominion, Sisko has convinced Starfleet that this is a non-arc episode, so off the *Defiant* goes on another sightseeing tour of the Gamma Quadrant. We have here two competing storylines with varying levels of dullness. This here-today-gone-tomorrow planet doesn't connect deeply to any of our people, making the question of whether it can be made to endure rather a theoretical one. Quark pimping out holo-Kira is just ick (plus homosexual anxiety gags, yay) and not nearly funny enough, despite the welcome presence of Jeffrey Combs – who will have a much more interesting role in future stories. Oh, and someone is sharking after Dax again, this time in a particularly cloying and doe-eyed fashion. The trouble is, even in this new long-form, serialised show, I know the relationship is doomed. Deral absolutely for sure will not be living happily ever after with Dax, counting her spots as they grow old together. And their dreadful flirting makes me want to claw my eyes out of my head.

Jonathan Frakes directs in what was presumably punishment for some past misdeed. Kira, who as far as I know has never been to Earth, has strong feelings about how to drink coffee.

DS9 S03E09 Defiant ★★★★☆

Written by Ronald D. Moore. Directed by Cliff Bole. TX: 21 November 1994. Featuring: Jonathan Frakes, Shannon Cochran, Marc Alaimo, Tricia O'Neil.

Thrilling space adventure with great character beats and fascinating political machinations. This is classy stuff, but the ending is a little muted.

Kira is struggling with scheduling, logistics and resources and she's taking it out on Bashir, who prescribes a vacation. She's just coming to terms with that when Riker smarms into view, in what I believe is known as cross-franchise-corporate-synergy (*Generations* was in theatres). He likewise has been prescribed downtime by Dr Crusher, he claims, and he's in the old-style uniform (but with the new-style combadge).

Kira is caught off-guard when he asks for a tour of the *Defiant* and makes off with it – for this is not Will Riker, loyal number one on the *Enterprise*. This is transporter clone Tom Riker, who has now thrown his lot in with the Maquis. In order to avoid a war, Sisko agrees to return to Cardassia Prime with Gul Dukat and help him to hunt down the rogue ship and – if Dukat has his way – destroy it. It's a wonderful set-up.

And the story doesn't squander all this promise. We get to see another side of Riker, who does his best to get Kira onside, and who can't completely stop being a Starfleet officer. Then we have Sisko and Dukat trying to outwit Tom and his cronies, and fencing with the Obsidian order, who seem to have their own secret ships in operation. And it's very hard to guess the outcome – Tom is deliciously killable. In the end, it comes down to diplomacy, which gives the final act a slightly low-key feel compared to the sky-high stakes in the middle – Tom's offered a decent deal, and he takes it. And I note that Kira hightails it back to Federation space at Warp 8, so I trust that silly business about space having an eco-friendly speed limit (as established in the fairly recent **TNG** episode *Force of Nature*) is something we can all forget about now.

Of course, this is all a set-up for the upcoming **Star Trek: Voyager** (in what I believe is known as cross-franchise etc. etc.).

DS9 S03E10 Fascination ★☆☆☆☆

Story by Ira Steven Behr and James Crocker, teleplay by Philip LaZebnik. Directed by Avery Brooks. TX: 28 November 1994. Featuring: Majel Barrett, Philip Anglim.

Dismal love potion nonsense riffing on Shakespeare, which is a very poor fit for this setting.

In yet more cross-franchise etc., Lwaxana is on the station and hoping to pick up where she left off with Odo – and she helpfully supplies a recap for new viewers. Kira is enjoying time with Bareil and trying to fit in preparations for a Bajoran festival. An exhausted Keiko is reunited with O'Brien. It's all a bit domestic, dull and laborious – the exact details of the Bajoran ceremony are of scant interest to me, for example. When Jake starts cracking on to Kira, I can only assume that some kind of mind-altering love potion is in the air. That would be clichéd – but if that isn't what's happening, then it would actually be ludicrous. When Bareil does the same to Dax, it becomes clear that that is indeed the story we're to be subjected to. Presumably, Lwaxana's doing. Oh, I see. It's *A Midsummer Night's Dream*. Thanks, I hate it. Make it stop.

DS9 S03E11 Past Tense, Part I ★★★★☆

Story by Ira Steven Behr & Robert Hewitt Wolfe, teleplay by Robert Hewitt Wolfe. Directed by Reza Badiyi. TX: 2 January 1995. Featuring: Jim Metzler, Frank Military, Dick Miller, Al Rodrigo, Tina Lifford, Bill Smitrovich.

Satisfyingly ludicrous time-travel shenanigans with a sheen of social commentary but not enough to frighten the horses.

Sisko and team are returning to Earth for a jolly when – whoopsie – a transporter glitch sends Sisko, Dax and Bashir back in time to space year 2024 where some kind of fascist regime wants to see their IDs. It's a nifty premise. Rather than have them come back to the time the show was made, or back to a familiar period of history, we visit a time period significant to the Federation but where the writers can make up the details (for more examples, see **Picard** Season 2 or *Star Trek: First Contact*).

Separated from Dax, Bashir and Sisko are in a Sanctuary District – something that keen history student Sisko knows all about – and are interrogated by none other than that guy from that cult film you like, Dick Miller. Dax, meanwhile, is hacking herself some ID, courtesy of a blandly good-looking local media mogul. This is a lovely, intractable problem, ripe for a two-parter, so I can forgive it for being another non-arc episode, although I assume that the Dominion aren't going to wait forever before making their move.

Naturally, it turns out that a few days from now, Sisko and Bashir will be caught up in historic riots, which will see hundreds of deaths at the hands of government troops – and time travel is sufficiently commonplace that Bashir was taught not to interfere in key events while at the Academy. One Gabriel Bell will become a national hero and martyr, which will lead to the end of the Sanctuaries and put the USA on the path to Federation-style peace and harmony. That hints at America's racist past (and present) but neither of these two non-white men encounters any explicit racism. What they do encounter is that same Gabriel Bell – and they get him killed.

On the *Defiant*, O'Brien thinks he knows when the others are (or has narrowed it down to half a dozen different time periods) and Kira proposes sending a series of search parties. Using the transporter and some handy 'chronoton particles' we handwave how to send people through time from the ship. No thought is given at this stage as to how to get a *Defiant*-less party back to the twenty-fourth century. For no very clear reason, at this exact moment, the Federation winks out of existence and only Kira, O'Brien and Odo are unaffected. Roll credits!

DS9 S03E12 Past Tense, Part II ★★★☆☆

Story by Ira Steven Behr & Robert Hewitt Wolfe, teleplay by Ira Steven Behr & René Echevarria. Directed by Jonathan Frakes. TX: 9 January 1995. Featuring: Jim Metzler, Frank Military, Dick Miller, Deborah van Valkenburgh, Clint Howard, Richard Lee Jackson, Tina Lifford, Bill Smitrovich.

Slightly less compelling conclusion, but entertaining enough and boasting series-best stuff from Avery Brooks.

Sisko's plan has a notable flaw. In order to take the place of Gabriel Bell, he's going to have to give his own life. Freed from his Starfleet uniform and the constraints of command, Avery Brooks loosens up considerably, and begins to demonstrate the charisma that a major historical figure like Bell will need. The building-under-siege situation helps build the tension and there are nice moments with some of the hostages and hostage-takers. Bashir, frustratingly, remains as bland as ever. Alexander Siddig is settling into the part, but there's still nothing to the character except his job description.

Odo (who can assume any form he wishes) sends O'Brien and Kira (who needs to wear a Band-Aid on her nose to avoid drawing attention to herself) into the past. They turn up in the roaring twenties and can't pick up the trail. Then they try the flower-power sixties and dematerialise in front of some whacked-out hippies. These jolly japes sit oddly with the life-or-death-intensity of the siege stuff. Travelling to later time periods gives O'Brien a clue about when his crewmates might be – and they have three candidate timelines left to choose from, but only one more shot. O'Brien doesn't use the clue he got, though; he just makes a blind guess and gets lucky. That's pretty poor scriptwriting, but this whole section has just been about keeping Kira and O'Brien busy until the time is right for them to enter the story.

As usual in these time-travel stories, once our heroes take the action that their memory of history tells them they should take, the timelines are restored exactly as they were, with not a single glitch. It's a simplistic take on time travel from a show that is making its name as the part of the franchise that embraces complexity, nuance and grey areas. But the two-parter as a whole shows ambition and daring and kept me watching and guessing.

DS9 S03E13 Life Support ★★★★☆

Story by Christian Ford and Roger Soffer, teleplay by Ronald D. Moore. Directed by Reza Badiyi. TX: 31 January 1995. Featuring: Louise Fletcher, Philip Anglim, Aron Eisenberg, Lark Voorhies, Andrew Prine.

Part medical ethics drama, part teen romance, neither particularly compelling, but a perfectly fine use of forty-five minutes.

A ship docks with a busted blah-de-blah. Kai Winn and Vedek Bareil are on board and Bareil is stretchered out of there. Wearing the regulation *Dead Ringers* red gimp suits, Bashir operates on Bareil with the help of a Bajoran nurse, but all the saltshakers in the world aren't doing him any good. Which is a bummer because Winn and Bareil have been back-channelling peace talks with Cardassia for ages now. About to perform an autopsy, Bashir notices neurons still firing and is able to bring his patient back from the brink, but not without cost.

Bashir wants to put the Vedek back into stasis while he works the problem, but Bareil wants to get back to the negotiation table. Naturally, there's an experimental drug that could help, and equally naturally, Bashir capitulates to his patient's demands to be put on it. As ever, Bashir is a simple personification of medical ethics – it's striking that the Emergency Medical Hologram on **Voyager** has more personality than the completely human Julian Bashir, and it's due to the writing far more than the acting – Siddig does everything that's asked of him.

The medical ethics get increasingly absurd. Having heard Bashir talk about replacing damaged organs, Winn wants to know if he can replace damaged bits of his brain as well. Bashir puts up a decent fight against the nonsense but ends up giving his patient positronic implants, not knowing what the outcome will be, which does rather pose the question: for what purpose were these devices constructed, if no one can be certain of the extent of their efficacy? Essentially, Bashir ends up turning Bareil into Data – not an uninteresting storyline, but the path to this conclusion is paved with gibberish.

In a rather dull B-plot, Jake is on the station and he's a smoooooth operator, chatting comfortably with Leanne, a cute human girl he remembered eating Klingon food with. Nog expects this to be a double date, and he doesn't expect the 'females' to do any talking. It's pretty thin culture-clash stuff and Nog is at his most annoying. Mysteriously, Jake can only talk to Nog about how he's being a bit of a dick if they're both arrested.

Maybe it's been like that for ages and I haven't noticed, but Kira's hair, which used to be swept straight back, is now parted on one side and makes her look just a tiny bit like Harry Potter.

DS9 S03E14 Heart of Stone ★★★★☆

Written by Ira Steven Behr and Robert Hewitt Wolfe.
Directed by Alexander Singer. TX: 6 February 1995. Featuring: Salome Jens.

Kira and Odo's relationship is tested when Kira is trapped in amber. Nog wants to join Starfleet. Neither plot line delivers everything it promises, but both are engrossing.

Kira and Odo return in a shuttlecraft, casually swapping exposition, before they pick up a Maquis ship, which they pursue to a moon in the Badlands. They begin exploring the cave system but no sooner than Odo's back is turned (why is Odo's back turned?) Kira's foot is trapped in crystalline quicksand.

Because Kira doesn't know *The Sorcerer's Apprentice*, she phasers the crystal, which doubles in size. Unable to contact the runabout, Odo returns to the surface, but he can't help from there either. On the one hand, this is a suitably intractable problem, and Nana Visitor and René Auberjonois sell it well. On the other hand, I super don't trust the way we got into this situation and it's hard to buy into the reality of her dilemma when I'm just waiting for the other shoe to drop. Would I have enjoyed this episode more if I hadn't seen the twist coming? Very probably, and I do think seeing twists coming is at least sometimes a matter of bad luck. Viewers are always asking 'Why did that happen?' 'What will happen next?' And if they aren't, it's because they aren't engaged. On Twitter, I gave this three and a half stars, but on reflection, the depth of Odo's feelings towards Kira are worth more, so I've bumped this up to four, and that's reflected in the season average too.

Back on the station, Nog has had his bar mitzvah and wants to become a Starfleet officer. This is pretty silly stuff, but Sisko's treatment of the young Ferengi is not without interest, and his clumsy insistence on shaking hands like a hu-man is funny enough. I actually hope they stick with this one. Why shouldn't there be a Ferengi in Starfleet and why shouldn't it be Nog?

Odo, who can assume any form he wishes, crouches down when trying to estimate Kira's assailant's height. Kira actually says 'There's one thing I still don't understand' at the end of the episode.

DS9 S03E15 Destiny ★★★★☆

Written by David S. Cohen and Martin A. Winer. Directed by Les Landau. TX: 13 February 1995. Featuring: Tracy Scoggins, Wendy Robie, Erick Avari, Jessica Hendra.

Standard-issue prophecies-are-open-to-interpretation stuff, with good stuff for Sisko and Kira and rather a silly subplot for O'Brien.

The new plan is to rig up a pair of tin cans and a length of twine through the wormhole, and to this end, there are Cardassian scientists coming to the station. But Vedek Yarka is here too with a warning from the prophets – Sisko will bring destruction on us all. When they arrive, the scientists are flighty, nervous things, hardly the harbingers of doom we expected. And, as the mission unfolds, aspects of the prediction start to come true, or so it seems. Kira is convinced that if they continue with the mission then disaster awaits, but hardheaded Sisko is equally sure that the prophecies are just vague stories.

Meanwhile, the Cardassian scientists are butting heads with O'Brien, who has been rebuilding and replacing aspects of the station. On Cardassia, women dominate the sciences and so O'Brien is thought to be ill-equipped to help. This worm-that-turned stuff is better by far than the blatant sexism of **TOS**, but it still feels dated and awkward in 2022, especially as Gilora (Tracy Scoggins) ends up doing a lovesick woman act that put me in mind of McGivers and Khan in *Space Seed*. The endless prophecies of Trakor are so tedious that we cut to titles as Vedek Yarka is in mid-sentence.

In a particularly nifty pair of Rules of Acquisition, we learn that peace is good for business. But then so is war.

DS9 S03E16 Prophet Motive ★★☆☆☆

Written by Ira Steven Behr & Robert Hewitt Wolfe. Directed by René Auberjonois. TX: 20 February 1995. Featuring: Wallace Shawn, Tiny Ron, Juliana Donald.

Low stakes and frequently very silly episode, which is only really entertaining when it's being completely ridiculous.

The Grand Nagus is back and cock-blocking Quark who might finally be able to get rid of those self-sealing stem bolts, but before he can sign the contract, he's kicked out of his apartment and forced to re-enact *The Odd Couple* with Rom. Worse is to come, as the Nagus appears to have taken leave of his avarice and is rewriting the Rules of Acquisition to focus on hugging and kittens instead of profit. His seeming insanity may be connected to one of those Bajoran flashback boxes.

In the B-plot, Bashir has been nominated for a medical prize, but his nomination appears to have nothing to do with all of the extraordinary feats he pulled off which resolved so many medical-ethics plots in past episodes. Instead, it's for biomolecular replication, whatever that may be. Bashir is more irritated than honoured, as the Carrington Award is usually seen as a lifetime achievement rather than something given to eager young bucks with their best work ahead of them.

Neither plot strand is particularly diverting, although any episode focusing on Quark and featuring Wallace Shawn is fine by me, and it's fun seeing the irreverent Ferengi pushed through the usually po-faced Bajoran mysticism. René Auberjonois directs, but I'd rather have him the other side of the camera.

DS9 S03E17 Visionary ★★☆☆☆

Story by Ethan H. Calk, teleplay by John Shirley. Directed by Reza Badiyi.
TX: 27 February 1995. Featuring: Jack Shearer, Annette Helde, Ray Young,
Bob Minor, Dennis Madalone.

*Spooky time-travel intrigue, which starts well but ends up rendering temporal
displacement mundane and trivial.*

Chief O'Brien has radiation poisoning and has to take it easy, so he's installing
a darts board at Quark's – and finds he's watching himself from across the
promenade. It's a very spooky and beguiling image, but as questions are replaced
with answers, what at first seemed shocking becomes increasingly ordinary
and even convenient. Adding to the general sense of trademarked **Deep Space
Nine** suspicion and unease, Klingons and Romulans are both on the station.
The Romulans have come for an intelligence briefing on the Dominion, and
accuse Odo of either being a spy or holding out on them. Meanwhile, O'Brien's
frequent trips through time turn out not to be an existential threat but a neat
get-out-of-jail-free card. Eventually, he stops fainting when he comes back
to the present, and greets his past self with a cheery 'Am I pleased to see you!'
Even the *Rick and Morty*-esque ending is treated with blasé indifference by
everyone except O'Brien, who therefore also shrugs it off. A good premise
rather thrown away.

DS9 S03E18 Distant Voices ★★☆☆☆

Story by Joe Menosky, teleplay by Ira Steven Behr & Robert Hewitt Wolfe.
Directed by Alexander Singer. TX: 10 April 1995. Featuring: Victor Rivers,
Ann H. Gillespie.

*Ploddingly obvious mystery built around the show's thinnest character who only
gains talcum powder in his hair and not any actual depth.*

We open with Garak and Bashir, which is usually a good sign. Bashir is fretting
about turning 30, which is scarcely the most eye-poppingly original bit of
character-building I've ever seen. Garak hands him an early birthday present
– a holosuite program adapted from a Cardassian mystery novel. Quark's
Lethean friend wants to buy some Biomimetic gel from Bashir but it's not
available at any price. Suddenly, Bashir awakes to find himself in a smashed-up
lab with a terrified Quark hiding under a table. Presumably, therefore, this is
either the holosuite program or the Lethean's doing, and the only real question
remaining is, which?

As well as being an obvious fantasy, the implementation doesn't make any sense. Having already figured out that everyone he's interacting with is a figment of his imagination, Bashir still marvels at 'Sisko's' medical expertise. Unconscious Bashir's mind can't magic up the kind of tricorder readings he's seen before and would expect to see, but is capable of showing him accurate medical data about his real body, which he can have absolutely no knowledge of.

Breaking a character down into component parts is the kind of thing *Red Dwarf* used to do brilliantly. Here, if Bashir didn't laboriously identify who was who, we'd have no clue as the regulars all come across as generically argumentative and petulant. In the final showdown, there's an attempt to ret-con the furiously tenacious Bashir as a quitter who could have been an awesome tennis player and who deliberately flunked his exams. As if this wasn't all clichéd enough, we're also giving the ageing-rapidly-to-death storyline another outing. Dear oh dear.

In Cardassian Enigma novels, all the suspects are always guilty. Cardassian hearing is not as acute as that of humans.

DS9 S03E19 Through the Looking Glass ★★★★☆

Written by Ira Steven Behr and Robert Hewitt Wolfe. Directed by Winrich Kolbe. TX: 17 April 1995. Featuring: Felecia M. Bell, Tim Russ.

DS9's second trip to the Mirror Universe isn't as bracing as the first but is still lots of moody fun.

I was knocked out by **DS9**'s first trip to the Mirror Universe and stunned to realise that it hadn't ever been revisited since it was first seen in **TOS** Season 2. The teaser wastes no time in having O'Brien bundle Sisko onto a transporter at gunpoint and take him to Looking Glass Land – seemingly the first time that anyone has made the trip purposefully.

Avery Brooks's swaggering portrayal of alt-Sisko was a huge highlight of *Crossover*, so on the one hand, it's disappointing that we won't be meeting him again. On the other hand, I'm waiting and waiting for Brooks to show what he can do, and playing 'our' Sisko pretending to be 'their' Sisko sounds like it could be great fun. 'Their' O'Brien is much like our O'Brien, but we also get to see omni-horny Intendant Kira again, which is a delight.

All the changes are rung deliciously well. Dax is Sisko's lover. Sisko's wife is a collaborator. Rom is a spy. Tim Russ appears as Tuvok in a neat bit of corporate-cross-franchise-synergistic-collaboration. But, if anything, Sisko finds the deception a bit too easy for it to be really fun.

Felecia M. Bell, who had a few brief scenes as Jennifer in the pilot, returns here, and is… fine. She sees through Sisko's pretence, when Kira doesn't, which is cool. There's nothing really wrong with this episode, it's salutary to see what the galaxy looks like without the benign influence of the Federation, and this is the series to do it. It just doesn't have the ice-water shock of *Crossover*, that's all.

DS9 S03E20 Improbable Cause ★★★★☆

Story by Robert Lederman & David R. Long, teleplay by René Echevarria. Directed by Avery Brooks. TX: 24 April 1995. Featuring: Paul Dooley, Carlos Lacámara, Joseph Ruskin, Darwyn Carson, Julianna McCarthy.

More delicious Obsidian Order skulduggery, although the terrain has been fairly thoroughly explored already.

Garak is tangling with Shakespeare and gets as little out of Earth literature as Bashir got out of Cardassian Enigma novels. But just as he's finished fuming that Caesar should have known that opposing forces were massing against him, somebody firebombs his shop with him inside. Pretty soon, he and Odo are joining forces to try to track down his would-be assassin. While Andrew Robinson is still a delight, the pattern of lies within lies and casual dissembling has started to become overfamiliar, and this doesn't have the high stakes of *The Wire*, which makes the fact that it's another stealth two-parter even more surprising. Let's have a fuller discussion of the overall plot when everything has been wrapped up (or as close as we ever get to that on this show).

DS9 S03E21 The Die is Cast ★★★★☆

Written by Ronald D. Moore. Directed by David Livingston. TX: 1 May 1995. Featuring: Paul Dooley, Kenneth Marshall, Leland Orser, Leon Russom.

Twisty-turny fun, centring minor characters and putting the Federation squarely in the Founders' cross-hairs.

Part one had plenty of good dialogue and a pleasantly unhurried pace, but a slight sense that there probably wasn't quite enough material for forty-five minutes. Its key purpose was to put Garak back by his old mentor's side with Odo bearing witness. Rather sweetly, Bashir is missing his friend (O'Brien makes a poor substitute). The other big plot element, which is played as shocking news at the top of part two, is that the Cardassian and the Romulan secret polices are joining forces to mount a pre-emptive attack on the Founders. It's a curious idea to try to wring tension out of – three of our traditional enemies are going to go toe-to-toe. Seems like whoever loses, we win. But this broader canvas is very much a part of **DS9**'s MO, and I suppose nobody wants war.

Part two continues the unhurried pace. The episode is almost a third over before we catch up with Odo, but any time we get to spend with Andrew Robinson and René Auberjonois trading bitter quips is time well spent. Sisko defies orders and plunges into the wormhole in the *Defiant*, looking for his head of security, who is the subject of a kind of tug-of-sadism between Garak and Tain, which results in a truly chilling scene where Odo is forced to remain humanoid as a form of torture. However, when the attack on the Founders goes south, Garak rescues the shapeshifter, and it quickly transpires that the Founders were pulling the strings all this time. This two-parter is probably more noteworthy for its arc-significance than for its pure entertainment value, but it is good stuff, and it's rare to see a part two that is better than part one. So let's give credit where it's due: to Ron Moore's script, which pays everything off, and to Avery Brooks, back in the director's chair, keeping it all moving.

Admiral Toddman is wearing the **TNG**-style uniform in gold with weird rank pips on both collars.

DS9 S03E22 Explorers ★★★☆☆

Story by Hilary J. Bader, teleplay by René Echevarria. Directed by Cliff Bole. TX: 8 May 1995. Featuring: Marc Alaimo, Bari Hochwald, Chase Masterson.

Sisko sets sail and Bashir flames out in this diverting but mundane episode.

When he took the part of Sisko, Avery Brooks wanted to play it as he had done in ABC's *Spenser for Hire* and its short-lived spin-off series *A Man Called Hawk*, i.e. with a shaved head and a goatee beard. He put this to the producers, who mused, 'No, then you'll look like your character Hawk from *Spenser for Hire* and *A Man Called Hawk*. You'd better do it clean-shaven and with short hair.' Finally, after sixty-seven episodes, Brooks has his beard back. The shaved head (and the promotion to captain) can't be far away.

Sisko's strand sees him building an ancient Bajoran solar sailing ship in order to demonstrate the plausibility of tales of Bajoran interstellar travel decades before the Cardassians ventured out of their solar system. Bajoran enthusiasm for their own ancient technology recalls Chekov's insistence that all the best things were invented in Russia in **TOS** but here, the attempt is baked into the ongoing political story, rather than just being the subject of interchangeable character gags.

This mission is interesting from a couple of perspectives. Is this something we imagined that Sisko would do? He drags Jake along, who continues to do Generic Teenage Boy things, rather than develop a real relationship or personality, but Sisko's determination a) to test an ancient legend and b) to doggedly pursue a dangerous hobby seem both to have dropped out of thin air slightly. On the other hand, I definitely can't imagine Janeway or Picard doing this (no, building ships in bottles isn't the same thing) but it feels like more the kind of *idée fixe* that would consume O'Brien, or possibly La Forge, rather than our steady-as-she-goes station commander.

The other thing it does is to massively expose the Key **Star Trek** Metaphor, which is so embedded into the series, and has been virtually since day one, that it usually goes unacknowledged, but all the talk of sailing forces us to confront it. Basically: space = oceans, planets = nation states, races = societies, Starfleet = navy, Federation = NATO. It's why so many alien races are so monolithic. They look to humans the way the French look to the British or the Swedish look to the Americans. And – wouldn't ya know it? – it turns out that the journey of the ancient Bajorans is highly plausible. While Dukat's smooth climb-down is as delicious as ever, I can't help thinking that 'Huh, the nice guys were right all along' is probably the least interesting way this strand could have ended. **DS9** has conditioned me to expect gloom, or certainly ambiguity, and so I really expected that the Sisko boys would need to be rescued, or that they would fluke their way to Cardassia in a way that didn't really support the ancient legend.

Elsewhere, Bashir's old college rival is on the station, but she walks right past him. There's probably something being said there about different perspectives on the same events, but it doesn't get the screen time it needs to be fully developed. I do treasure O'Brien telling the bouncy doctor: 'People either love you or they hate you. I hated you when we first met. And now…' (munches on peanuts). And the sight of them singing 'Jerusalem' together at the end is perfect.

Sisko comments that going home for lunch every day must have used up a lot of transporter credits, which is an odd thing to say in a post-scarcity society.

DS9 S03E23 Family Business ★★★★☆

Written by Ira Steven Behr and Robert Hewitt Wolfe. Directed by René Auberjonois. TX: 15 May 1995. Featuring: Jeffrey Combs, Andrea Martin, Penny Johnson.

Surprisingly convincing and affecting tale of Ferengi suffragettes, made more effective because of the family relationships it's built on.

This is another non-arc episode, and yet one that sets up three different future recurring characters. It occurs to me that whereas story-of-the-week shows have been with us forever, and now almost everything on TV is serialised, this semi-serialised pattern with arc and non-arc episodes was short-lived and feels odd today. Modern television almost always gives us either a movie cut into chunks, or an episode with an element of a self-contained story that nonetheless advances the season-long (or sometimes series-long) narrative as well. Here, nothing that happens touches on the Founders, the Cardassians, the Dominion − even the wormhole scarcely merits a mention. You could watch this one in complete isolation if you wanted a taste of what **Deep Space Nine** was all about. But at the same time, it's picking up threads from past episodes and will itself be returned to more than once.

Given very little time to make an impression is Penny Johnson, now more familiar to me as Dr Finn on *The Orville*, but debuting here as Sisko's love interest, the eccentrically spelled Kasidy Yates. Dominating the episode is the saga of Jeffrey Combs's Liquidator Brunt vs Quark vs the amazing Andrea Martin as Ishka, his mom, also known as 'Moogie'. As a one-off gag, 'You allow your women to wear clothes' is a bit silly and now feels a bit dated. The job of this story is to take that silly idea and make us buy it. It works, largely because Armin Shimerman and Andrea Martin are so good, and while Max Grodénchik isn't in quite the same league, he does well here (and his co-stars make him look good).

So, on the one hand, this is a bit of a reprise of *Rules of Acquisition* from Season 2, but this time we make it the planet Ferenginar and there are plenty of plot twists, choice gags and excellent character work to keep us interested. Both Ishka and Brunt will be back, and so will Combs in a variety of guises.

DS9 S03E24 Shakaar ★★☆☆☆

Written by Gordon Dawson. Directed by Jonathan West. TX: 22 May 1995. Featuring: Louise Fletcher, Duncan Regehr, Diane Salinger, William Lucking, Sherman Howard, John Doman.

Thin slice of unconvincing politicking, with a side order of darts. Tepid stuff, for the most part, marking time till the season finale.

Kai Winn is becoming one of the more nuanced villains we've seen in this franchise. Clearly, she's both in the grip of an ideology and seized with a lust for personal power, but she's not nuts, she has a point of view that extends beyond her zealotry, and she can be reasoned with. She is a nasty piece of work, though, no doubt about that, and having her heading up the Bajoran provisional government is not good news. It's typical of the complexity and pessimism of this show that the good guy Bajorans are being led by a hissable bad guy.

Alas, Winn's mission on the station isn't all that thrilling (or villainous). It seems as if some farmers have half-inched some agricultural doohickeys and Bajor's new number one wants Kira to go and ask if she can have her ball back. Naturally, their leader is someone that Kira counts as a friend, which is why this is now her problem, but it takes about a third of the episode to get this far, and I don't feel as if I've been promised a really juicy situation, only more people calmly talking in rooms.

Shakaar, the friend in question, is a kind of Diet Coke Kirk Douglas and his position is similarly underpowered. His reason for not sharing the equipment with the rest of the planet seems limited to 'finders keepers' and the whole dilemma seems to overlook the fact that if they asked nicely, the Federation would presumably replicate as many of the damn things as they wanted.

Things ramp up a little in the final act, which sees Winn overreaching and Kira forced to return to her life of guerrilla warfare, but it all feels a bit contrived and synthetic. The awkward peace-making at the end, while continuing the low-stakes feeling, has a little more nuance to it, and *The Wire*'s John Doman adds class, but none of this feels essential, neither thrillingly dark nor goofy fun.

In the even less interesting B-plot, O'Brien is in the zone, until he isn't.

DS9 S03E25 Facets ★★★☆☆

Written by René Echevarria. Directed by Cliff Bole. TX: 12 June 1995.
Featuring: Max Grodénchik, Aron Eisenberg, Chase Masterson.

Profoundly peculiar body swap introspection story with great material for Odo and Dax. Plus, Nog continues to pursue his Starfleet dream.

We haven't forgotten that Nog is attempting to become the first Ferengi in Starfleet, I'm pleased to see. It's a fascinating way of differentiating what could be a homogenous parade of big-eared space capitalists and it helps to stitch them further into the fabric of the show. Meanwhile, Dax summons the regular cast (plus additional Bajoran rando) and tells them she wants to borrow their bodies for a few hours. We take a brief pause for the opening titles and then the conversation continues. Normally this ceremony would be performed with other unjoined Trill, but they're thin on the ground right now. Everyone volunteers enthusiastically, even Sisko, who is due to embody the previous host who was a psychopathic murderer. Fun times.

This sounds like it should be right in my wheelhouse – character-based, and giving the rest of the cast a chance to show their range – but I have concerns, because Dax's previous hosts don't show themselves in Jadzia in any meaningful ways, and because those new personalities get imposed onto the host bodies. So, watching Nana Visitor as Lela or Colm Meaney as Tobin doesn't tell us much about Kira or O'Brien – as fun as it is watching them explore different ways of being. (Delightfully, Odo starts to look like Curzon, as well as behaving like him.) And I'm struck that Jadzia doesn't seem to remember basic information about her time in previous hosts. I thought the point was that she embodied everything that they were, as well as her own uniqueness. And that's nearly fatal to the big dramatic turn of this episode.

It seems at first as if it's Joran in the body of Sisko that is going to create all the problems. The issue of course is that while the Commander can take control anytime he wants to, there's no way to know for sure that it's really Sisko and not Joran pretending. But this is a feint. In fact, the story is about Odo and Curzon choosing to remain as two minds in one body, so this does end up shining a light on Odo in a fascinating way, but, as noted, how can Curzon reveal dark secrets to Jadzia when, until a few hours ago, Jadzia had access to all his memories and feelings?

DS9 S03E26 The Adversary ★★★★☆

Written by Ira Steven Behr and Robert Hewitt Wolfe. Directed by Alexander Singer. TX: 19 June 1995. Featuring: Lawrence Pressman, Kenneth Marshall, Jeff Austin.

Gripping slice of John Carpenter-style paranoia that triumphs over a few plot holes and points the way forward to an even grimmer Season 4.

Finally, our leading man has that fourth pip and can join the roster of Starfleet captains. He's also in a **TNG**-style dress uniform and even Jake is allowed a sip of vintage champagne. (That's enough.) His first task is to deal with a nearby coup d'état, which requires a show of strength from the *Defiant*.

In structure, this is a very **TNG**-feeling show. Our spaceship is despatched by higher powers to go and referee a power struggle, but – uh oh – looks like something's sneaked on board when we weren't looking. But because this is **DS9**, we have both a significant tertiary character given a chance to shine – Federation security officer Eddington – and some fairly serious inter-crew conflict as Bashir becomes accused of sabotage during the voyage.

Before long, the *Defiant* is under the control of one or more Founders who send the Federation's most warlike vessel on an attack vector, something that

Sisko fears will spark a war. His solution is to program the self-destruct while they try to track down the intruder and regain control of the ship. Some of the plotting here feels like it could have used another draft: since when does Starfleet take orders from passing random ambassadors, and was there really no way they could have made their intentions plain despite the sabotage? And, sure, this is nothing we haven't seen before (on this show, and on other shows, and in movies) but it's really hard to screw up the it-could-be-any-one-of-us device and it shines a strong clear light on the characters: always a strength of this show.

Eventually, they track down the miscreant and there's some heartbreaking stuff from Odo, who's forced to injure one of his own, having boasted about never firing a weapon or taking a life while acting as security chief. Despite some fairly basic direction, this is very strong stuff: tense, clammy, funny when it wants to be, and once again demonstrating that when the Founders do decide to act, the Federation are going to need to be ready.

DS9 Season 3 wrap-up

- There's a definite sense here of a show that's maturing, as was the way with **TNG** – it seems to take three or so years, so I'll need to be patient with **Voyager**. All of the regular cast are now well established, with Dax casting aside any initial worries I had, and Bashir settling in nicely. Only Jake is underserved, appearing in a handful of episodes, and stuck in generic teenager plots that give Cirroc Lofton no opportunity to demonstrate any abilities he might have.
- **DS9** is also goofier than I remembered. Yes, episodes like *Past Tense*, *Heart of Stone* and *The Adversary* are fan favourites but what other show could have attempted anything like *Prophet Motive*, or *Family Business*? The two strands come together in the Mirror Universe stories and if *Through the Looking Glass* wasn't quite as strong as *Crossover*, it still gives me something I can't get anywhere else in this era of the franchise.
- The supporting characters are also fantastic. My heart skips whenever Andrew Robinson or Marc Alaimo's names are in the credits, but we also have characters like Zek, Nog, and Kai Winn, and we can kill off people like Bareil, which makes the stakes soar without anyone having to renegotiate any contracts.
- Top episodes include: *Second Skin*, *Civil Defense* and *The Adversary*. No fives this year, and that's reflected in the slightly lower season average of 3.37 (down from Season 2's 3.62). Contributing to this were a couple of real stinkers early on: *Meridian* and *Fascination*, both about as dreadful as I can remember. But after that, there's nothing below a 2, and I think only one of those.

Deep Space Nine
Season 4

Starring: Avery Brooks, René Auberjonois, Michael Dorn, Terry Farrell, Cirroc Lofton, Colm Meaney, Nana Visitor, Alexander Siddig, Armin Shimerman. Featuring: Aron Eisenberg, Max Grodénchik, Rosalind Chao. Executive producers: Rick Berman, Michael Piller. Producers: René Echevarria, Peter Lauritson. Co-executive producer: Ira Steven Behr. Supervising producers: Ronald D. Moore, David Livingston.

DS9 S04E01-2 The Way of the Warrior ★★★★★

Written by Ira Steven Behr and Robert Hewitt Wolfe. Directed by James L. Conway. TX: 2 October 1995. Featuring: Andrew Robinson, Penny Johnson Jerald, Marc Alaimo, Robert O'Reilly, J.G. Hertzler, Obi Ndefo.

Fantastic storytelling on the biggest and smallest scales – plus Worf is here now.

In his ultimate configuration, with four pips, a goatee beard and now shaved head, Sisko is hunting a Changeling on board the station. He has Kira at his side, and she also has a new do, making her look a little less Daniel Radcliffe and a little more Farrah Fawcett. The hunt is a training exercise led by Odo. Finally, the big bad of the series feels a little more tangible. The titles and theme music have been refreshed, too.

There are a ton of Klingons on the station and among their number is Michael Dorn as Worf. His name appears in the opening credits before we see him – so we now have nine in our regular cast, including is-he-or-isn't-he Cirroc Lofton as Jake. Feels like a lot. Speaking of which, Dorn will appear in the show for the next four years, racking up around 280 episodes in the role, which is a **Star Trek** record. Does the show need him? Possibly not. Does it benefit from his presence? Assuredly. He makes quite an entrance, the camera travelling up from his boots, across his **TNG**-style uniform and baldric before revealing his face.

Comparisons with **Voyager** are very flattering to this show. The characters here are so much more individualised and rich. Odo and Garak can sit and talk and it's fascinating. Kira and Dax can sit and talk and it's fascinating. Sisko and Kasidy can have dinner and it's... but, Odo and Garak, right? And the big political story – the Klingons plan to attack Cardassia because they believe that the Dominion already has a toehold there, and they are willing to do this even if it means ending their allyship with the Federation – is refracted through the characters, particularly new arrival Worf, who has to figure out whether he is a Klingon first or a Starfleet officer first. It's rich, textured stuff.

It's taken a while, around a year longer than **TNG**, but this feels like a mature and confident series, ready to tell its own story, well clear of the shadow of its progenitor (and thus free to help itself to one of that progenitor's legendary characters). Klingon blood is much more red here than it was in *The Undiscovered Country* ('We do not discuss it with outsiders.').

DS9 S04E03 The Visitor ★★★★★

Written by Michael Taylor. Directed by David Livingston.
TX: 9 October 1995. Featuring: Tony Todd, Galyn Görg, Rachel Robinson.

Bonkers mash-up of It's A Wonderful Life *and* All Good Things *but it plays as a beautifully moving family drama, with an astounding guest performance from Tony Todd. Epic.*

Late at night, an old man who has pictures of Sisko and son on his desk receives a mysterious visitor. This is elderly Jake Sisko, a very good match for Cirroc Lofton. His teen ambition to become a writer, dismissed by me as being arbitrary and generic, is paying off in a small way. If this vision of the future is to be believed, Jake only wrote two books in his lifetime. He begins to tell us how his father died – when he was only 18!

Back in 'our' timeline, Sisko *père* is battling a warp core breach and it seems as if he has been successful but then he is seemingly vaporised. He's splintered through time, and the Klingons occupy the station, forcing Jake out. We see Jake's home on Earth, his wife, Nog as a Starfleet lieutenant. It's not the first time we've seen a vision of a possible future on this show, and the uniforms even recall *All Good Things*, but it's never been this emotional before. As with any event on this scale in an episode of a television show, let alone one predicated on time-travel shenanigans, a reset switch is coming, but it's almost unbearably emotional, as adult Jake sacrifices himself in order that his father can have a chance at life. Not only that, it seems clear from the final shots that although this version of Jake is erased from existence, Ben remembers everything. This is amazing, heart-stopping stuff.

DS9 S04E04 Hippocratic Oath ★★★★☆

Story by Nicholas Corea and Lisa Klink, teleplay by Lisa Klink. Directed by René Auberjonois. TX: 16 October 1995. Featuring: Scott MacDonald, Stephen Davies, Jeremy Roberts, Marshall Teague, Roderick Garr.

Echoes of **TNG***'s* Symbiosis *and* I, Borg *but this is as black as pitch compared to those.*

Not for the first time, O'Brien and Bashir are stuck in a runabout together on a fairly flimsy pretext (their mission sounds like it could be handed off to a couple of Starfleet grunts, rather than requiring two of the station's senior staff to take care of it). 'Why can't Keiko be more like a man?' fumes O'Brien, channelling Henry Higgins.

Despite there being no Dominion outposts for weeks, they crash-land and are immediately imprisoned by the Jem'Hadar. But these Jem'Hadar are keen to break away from the Dominion and they want Bashir's help to get them off the drug that they have been engineered to be dependent on. It's a typically murky and nuanced premise from this show, which keeps surprising me with its willingness to engage with the darker consequences of its concepts.

And while this doesn't reinvent Bashir or upend our idea of who the young doctor is, this is Siddig's best performance to date, free of a lot of the tics and puppyish jittering of Season 1. It is slightly surprising that initially Bashir is only focused on escape and doesn't immediately try to convince O'Brien that they should stay and help. When he does, and has to pull rank to get what he wants, a strong episode becomes a great one.

In the B-plot, Worf has it in for Quark and cannot understand why Odo doesn't have him behind bars. It's fascinating to see Worf, whose devotion to Picard I consistently found so touching, dealing with a more pragmatic, less by-the-book Starfleet captain in Sisko. It's also fascinating to see a 'new' character get introduced not as having uniquely valuable abilities but rather coming in and screwing up what's already there.

Most of the cast still pronounce the Ferengi's name to rhyme with 'fork', except Armin Shimerman, who pronounces it to rhyme with 'bark'. O'Brien's destruction of Bashir's experiment is a special effect almost unparalleled in its shoddy appearance.

DS9 S04E05 Indiscretion ★★★★☆

Story by Toni Marberry & Jack Treviño, teleplay by Nicholas Corea. Directed by LeVar Burton. TX: 23 October 1995. Featuring: Marc Alaimo, Penny Johnson, Roy Brocksmith, Cyia Batten.

Kira and Dukat join forces and dig up the past in a striking series of scenes, which enriches both characters. The same can't be said for the Ben/Kasidy stuff, which never sparks into life.

Back for more is Roy Brocksmith, this time as Bajoran smuggler Razka Khan. So is Hans Beimler, of all people. Once booted out of **TNG**, along with writing partner Richard Manning, as Michael Piller's new broom swept out the old staff, now he's back and will contribute more scripts as time goes on. In this one, Kira is searching for a ship, the *Ravinok*, missing, and thought destroyed. Since this was a Cardassian craft, the new civilian government wants to send an observer along with Kira's expedition. Delightfully, this observer is none other than Gul Dukat. The danger here is that this will be another episode in which we hear endless stories about people we've never met, doing things we don't care about, in places we've never been to. But the pairing of Dukat and Kira keeps the actual story where it belongs, between the on-screen characters, and these are two of the finest actors across the entire franchise. The combination of their fraught backstory and the skill of these two players makes a simple dialogue scene completely compelling.

When they find their quarry, director LeVar Burton makes the most of the location filming. The crashed ship looks very impressive. Even more impressive is the depth of feeling that Alaimo brings to the discovery that a Bajoran woman Dukat was in love with is among those buried near the wreckage. Humiliatingly, the Cardassian next gets a spine up his rear end and Kira has to hoik it out for him. They even end up laughing together. But the laughter sticks in Kira's throat when Dukat admits that to preserve his Cardassian family he will have to murder his half-Bajoran daughter.

While the Kira–Dukat stuff is all pretty great, Sisko being afraid of commitment and screwing up his nice dinner with Kasidy is far less interesting (although Dax and Bashir ganging up on their captain is good fun). How is it that, when dealing with the made-up conflicts of bumpy-headed space aliens, this series manages to be so detailed, specific and truthful, but when dealing with the personal lives of ordinary American humans like the Siskos, the writing degenerates into generic clichés?

It would dishonour Cardassian dead for Bajorans to see the remains.

DS9 S04E06 Rejoined ★★★★☆

Story by René Echevarria, teleplay by Ronald D. Moore and René Echevarria. Directed by Avery Brooks. TX: 30 October 1995.
Featuring: Susanna Thompson, Tim Ryan, James Noah, Kenneth Marshall.

Proper grown-up relationship drama, wonderfully played by Terry Farrell and Susanna Thompson, albeit not quite sure how to end.

Successfully exploiting the possibilities of the Trill lifestyle for the characters (as opposed to just rehashing the biological details), this story has Dax required to share the station with her ex, a scientist named Lenara Kahn. The incel narrative that **Discovery** is woke-ism newly run amok requires at the very least ignoring the fact that Jadzia is clearly a trans character, but the complicated history of the Dax symbiont allows this same-sex relationship to be explored without Rick Berman having an aneurysm, on the basis that when they were married, Dax and Kahn were a perfectly proper hetero couple as God and the FCC always intended.

While Kahn's team is here to create the galaxy's first artificial wormhole, the script is focused almost entirely on the relationship, and only cares about the technobabble a tiny bit more than I do. Rekindling past relationships is strictly taboo, something that it seems hard for Jadzia to keep in mind – she's rather sweetly bashful and awkward around Kahn when they meet at the buffet table. It's a new side of Dax, and Terry Farrell is more than able to rise to the challenge.

The Trill taboo makes it easy to read this as a depiction of homophobia, which is very clever, adding a real-world resonance to the made-up society, but what really makes this work is the strong playing of Farrell and Susanna Thompson as Kahn. The adventure genre reasserts itself towards the climax, and so this slightly dribbles away at the end, but it still feels like a real love story in a way that so often evades this franchise – and they even manage a proper kiss!

Worf's small talk and Quark's befuddlement at conjuring tricks are the source of some amusement. I don't know if the sleight of hand is a metaphor for Dax and Kahn's hidden feelings, or for the scriptwriters hiding a gay storyline in plain sight, or just there for a bit of extra colour, but it's fun whichever is the case.

DS9 S04E07 Starship Down ★★★★☆

Written by David Alan Mack and John J. Ordover. Directed by Alexander Singer. TX: 6 November 1995. Featuring: James Cromwell, F.J. Rio, Jay W. Baker, Sara Mornell.

Tense adventure with a submarine flavour and some wonderful stuff for the regulars.

Frequent guest star James Cromwell turns up again, grousing about Quark's various made-up tariffs and taxes. Before long, the Jem'Hadar are firing on the *Defiant*, which has to lurk in the atmosphere of a gas giant. Cue the kind of *Das Boot* claustrophobia we haven't seen perhaps since *The Immunity Syndrome* in **TOS**, complete with Dax and Bashir on the wrong side of an emergency bulkhead (and presumably no way to beam them back to safety), Worf clambering about through the guts of the *Defiant*, and Kira desperately trying to keep an injured Sisko conscious. This is a great lesson in how to write an episode of a case-of-the-week show for an ensemble. Here, pretty much every featured character gets a strong arc or relationship with another key cast member, and yet nothing feels like it's been discarded, upended or reinvented. Only Quark's subplot fails to live up to the promise. The 'Morn-is-a-chatterbox' running gag, which has been hinted at for some time, is now revealed in its full glory.

DS9 S04E08 Little Green Men ★★★★☆

Story by Toni Marberry & Jack Treviño, teleplay by Ira Steven Behr & Robert Hewitt Wolfe. Directed by James L. Conway. TX: 13 November 1995. Featuring: Megan Gallagher, Charles Napier, Conor O'Farrell, James G. MacDonald.

Hilarious blend of Cold War paranoia and Ferengi avariciousness. Another bonkers episode, which only this show could do.

Nog is off to Starfleet Academy and is selling off his personal possessions. Meanwhile, Quark has come into possession of a shiny new ship, dubbed *Quark's Treasure*, and is turning Nog's trip to Earth into a smuggling operation. But the craft has been sabotaged and Rom's efforts to avoid disaster send them hurtling back in time – all three Ferengi wake up in an army base in post-war America, where talk of Roswell is already circulating. That's an absolutely delightful premise for an episode. This is the 'grim' **Star Trek** at its goofiest, but also its most entertaining. They even remember that all aliens speak English only because a universal translator is in operation. Although I could have sworn that this technology was built into their combadges, rather than being buried in the ear canal.

Once communications are established, the Ferengi counter the American Army's wonderment at this world-altering event with a sleazy desire to flog off Federation tech for as much gold as they can carry. Only Nog is worried about damage to the timelines. Further complicating matters is the presence of Odo, who snuck on board the ship. He and Rom hatch a plan that owes more than a little to an early draft of *Back to the Future* wherein Marty had to drive the DeLorean into ground zero of an atomic blast. Eventually, the

Ferengi, and even the friendly humans, are forced to make up pulp science fiction nonsense involving mind control powers, death rays and the like. It's a remarkable blend of influences that never fails to entertain.

There's a nice nod to *Past Tense* (Gabriel Bell looks like Sisko). When Ferengi die, they go to the Divine Treasury.

DS9 S04E09 The Sword of Kahless ★★☆☆☆

Story by Richard Danus, teleplay by Hans Beimler. Directed by LeVar Burton. TX: 20 November 1995. Featuring: John Colicos, Rick Pasqualone, Tom Morga.

Dull treasure hunt story, which takes three fabulous actors and only lets them bicker like infants.

I really should try to get over my dislike of Klingon mythology episodes. Actually, when I sat down and watched **TNG** from the beginning, very few of them were as dull as I feared. But my efforts to try to engage are not helped when the cast themselves can hardly bear listening to this gasbag warrior banging on about glorious battles and famous victories. Worse, the gasbag Klingon is toting a treasure map as if we didn't have clichés enough to deal with. Elevating this slightly is the fact that the gasbag in question is the returning John Colicos as Kor, but it's still hard for me to be super-invested.

Dax, Worf and Kor follow the trail and (having reversed the polarity), like a triple-headed Indiana Jones, they come across the sacred bat'leth of legend, just as they hoped. Something about the lighting or the composition or the sound effects contrives to make the prop seem particularly plasticky and flimsy, which is a shame after all the build-up. Despite this, there's plenty of double-crossing and malice between the two Klingons as we transition from *Raiders* to *The Treasure of the Sierra Madre*. But none of this really means anything, and despite excellent work from all three leads, the final act only reminds me of squabbling children.

Shaving technology appears not to have moved on much in the intervening centuries. Fair enough, I suppose. All these caves look the same to me.

DS9 S04E10 Our Man Bashir ★★★★★

Story by Robert Gillan, teleplay by Ronald D. Moore. Directed by Winrich Kolbe. TX: 27 November 1995. Featuring: Andrew J. Robinson, Kenneth Marshall.

Cheerful fantasy, which is almost unparalleled in its freewheeling absurdity. A quite delightful hour of television.

Jay Chattaway's music is a pitch-perfect pastiche of mid-sixties John Barry, as Bashir indulges his adolescent Ian Fleming fantasies on a holosuite, whereupon Garak intrudes, eyes ablaze with curiosity. Knowing now what I do about the behind-the-scenes debates regarding the Garak/Bashir relationship, it's easy to surmise that this was the production team's effort to de-queer the good doctor by casting him as the red-blooded star of a thoroughly butch spy adventure. The only problem is that the *James Bond* films are so ludicrously camp that the attempt is doomed to fail.

Dependable Eddington has to perform an emergency beam-out to save Sisko and much of the senior staff from a sabotaged shuttle and the crew ends up 'stored' in Bashir's recreation of silly spy movies. This is a fabulous opportunity for the cast to play new versions of their characters, something I always appreciate. Kira becomes a Russian femme fatale, Dax is a kidnapped scientist, O'Brien an eye-patch-wearing henchman, Worf a white jacket-wearing casino owner, and Sisko is the big bad Dr Noah.

Some of the satire here is spot on – the costumes are wonderful. Some is rather sub-*Austin Powers* (the name 'Mona Luvsitt' almost caused me to chuck the remote control across the living room). But then again, *Austin Powers* was still two years away. The name of the episode is a nod to James Coburn's wannabe *Bond* flick *Our Man Flint*. Meanwhile, Rom is quickly proving himself to be O'Brien's (or La Forge's) equal when it comes to jury-rigging get-out-of-jail-free devices. His lash-up to connect the holosuite to the *Defiant* looks like something out of *Apollo 13*.

In a complete reversal of *Distant Voices*, Bashir is incensed when Garak suggests that they should quit while they're ahead. And it's that not-quite-climactic scene that pushes this delectable nonsense firmly into the five-star league. Everybody mispronounces 'valet' but that's so typical now that the wrong pronunciation is virtually correct.

DS9 S04E11 Homefront ★★★★☆

Written by Ira Steven Behr and Robert Hewitt Wolfe. Directed by David Livingston. TX: 1 January 1996. Featuring: Brock Peters, Susan Gibney, Robert Foxworth.

The Changelings have reached Earth. Slightly awkward mix of domesticity and intrigue, but a very engrossing curtain-raiser.

Nothing's quite right on the station. The wormhole has the jitters. Someone has moved Odo's chair 3cm to the left. But this pales in comparison to the massacre committed during a peace conference on Earth – a bomb that left twenty-seven people dead, and it looks like the work of the Changelings. Sisko's family has always been a bigger feature of his life than Picard's was for him. We were introduced to him with a wife and son. Now we meet Brock Peters as Sisko's dad, who's keen for him to spend time in New Orleans. It's a slightly odd mix. Ben is at pains to point out that this trip is not a vacation, but his later conversation with Jake is all about domestic chores, and there's scarcely a mention of the galaxy-spanning crisis he's actually there to deal with. This tone of cheerful levity is maintained when O'Brien and Bashir visit Quark's, straight from cos-playing as the Dambusters (complete with full costumes and funny voices).

The two strands collide when Sisko's dad refuses to submit to Changeling-testing, and before long there's an unexplained planet-wide power outage, and Sisko insists to the Federation president that Earth be put under martial law. The question here is a pertinent one – how much freedom are you prepared to surrender in order to preserve your way of life? The trip home also makes possible a reunion between Jake and Starfleet Cadet Nog, who has belatedly discovered that 'Academy' is another word for 'School' and is having trouble fitting in. This doesn't really go anywhere, but I'm prepared to be patient during what is part one of two.

On Earth, Sisko is back in his **TNG**-style uniform, which makes **Voyager's** use of the **DS9** look for everyone even more confounding. And not for the first time, a potential job change for a member of the regular cast is played as a doom-laden act-out. Susan 'Leah Brahms' Gibney returns as new character Benteen. Klingon gods were more trouble than they were worth, and so the Klingons had them all executed.

DS9 S04E12 Paradise Lost ★★★★☆

Story by Ronald D. Moore, teleplay by Ira Steven Behr and Robert Hewitt Wolfe. Directed by Reza Badiyi. TX: 8 January 1996. Featuring: Brock Peters, Robert Foxworth, Herschel Sparber, Susan Gibney.

Remember Conspiracy *from* **TNG**? *This is basically the same plot, but this time it's got over three years of backstory to set it up, and that makes a huge difference.*

Now the 'Red Squad' storyline set up by Nog last week takes centre stage. Far from being a Dominion vs Earth narrative, this is actually Starfleet vs the Federation, which is pretty dark and nihilistic, even for this show. Worse is to come, as Sisko is removed as Acting Head of Earth Security, fails to get the Federation president onside, and is taunted by an O'Brien Changeling who tells him that the humans' fear is what will defeat them. Admiral Leyton

– latest in an implausibly long line of corrupt, misguided or compromised Starfleet top brass – manages to frame Sisko as a shapeshifter, and with his old friend out of the way, he looks forward to essentially installing himself as dictator. Like I said, this is dark stuff. And that's before we get to the Admiral ordering his ships to destroy the *Defiant*. The climax is hurried, though, with the major plot-resolving decision being taken off-screen by someone we barely know – due to budget limitations, perhaps?

DS9 S04E13 Crossfire ★★★★☆

Written by René Echevarria. Directed by Les Landau. TX: 29 January 1996. Featuring: Duncan Regehr, Bruce Wright.

Odo gets comprehensively friend-zoned and it's a bitch, especially when his competition for Kira's affections is such a blank.

Everyone's in their dress blues to welcome First Minister Shakaar, whom we first met at the end of the last season, but he made so little of an impression that everybody spends half the teaser reciting his backstory at each other. He's played by the ghost that bothered Crusher in the idiotic TNG episode *Sub Rosa*, and he's fairly punchably smug. That doesn't make me want to assassinate him – but Cardassian extremists disagree. Shakaar almost courts his own demise, insisting on parading around the station with minimal security, allowing Worf and Odo to bond over how annoying it is when people change their plans.

Star Trek has a pretty poor record when it comes to romances. They tend to be perfunctory, like Kirk's various squeezes, ludicrous like Worf and Troi, or easily forgotten whenever they're inconvenient like Crusher and Picard. The torch Odo carries for Kira is a little different. It's a tragic tale of love unrequited, seen most clearly and affectingly in the otherwise rather silly episode with Kira seemingly consumed by a giant crystal. Now, Shakaar confides in Odo that he similarly has the hots for the Major, and Odo takes his bad mood out on Quark. Neither TNG nor Voyager could ever get away with this kind of story, so it's exciting to see it attempted here, but Shakaar's bland anti-charisma manner makes him scarcely a threat to the far more appealing shapeshifter, who valiantly saves all three of them from a plunging turbolift.

While I struggled with the First Minister, I can't fault René Auberjonois and Nana Visitor, and if anything, it makes the love story play better when we see only those glimpses of it that Odo is privy to. Auberjonois in particular manages to create amazing depth from behind all of that foam latex. The whole story is written in his eyes. And then, incredibly, and rather sweetly, it's Quark who is able to put Odo back together, again (for purely financial reasons, of course).

DS9 S04E14 Return to Grace ★★★★☆

Story by Tom Benko, teleplay by Hans Beimler. Directed by Jonathan West.
TX: 5 February 1996. Featuring: Marc Alaimo, Cyia Batten, Casey Biggs.

Expertly balancing the personal and the political, about the only thing this episode does wrong is to make it all look too easy.

Kira is having to get her jabs before she goes to a Cardassian outpost with her new fancy boyfriend. In a follow-up to the excellent *Indiscretion*, she is accompanied by Dukat, who has been demoted due to following Kira's advice regarding his half-Bajoran offspring. Their verbal sparring is delightful – Dukat trying and failing to drive a wedge between the Major and her new beau – but when they arrive, Klingons have destroyed the outpost. Dukat picks a fight with a Klingon Bird of Prey and isn't fired upon – there's no honour in destroying a virtually defenceless freighter. Pretty soon, Kira and Dukat are reluctantly joining forces in hunting down and destroying the Klingons. This is typically nuanced stuff, Kira and Dukat make a great pair, and again we end with a new status quo – Dukat's daughter living on *Deep Space Nine*. It's nothing special by the very high standards of this show, but that still makes it an engrossing and worthwhile watch.

DS9 S04E15 Sons of Mogh ★★☆☆

Written by Ronald D. Moore. Directed by David Livingston.
TX: 12 February 1996. Featuring: Tony Todd, Robert Doqui, Dell Yount.

Feeble jumble of Klingon rituals and other similar nonsense, which hops from idea to idea in search of meaning and never finds it.

Not a title guaranteed to inspire enthusiasm in me, this one. Tony Todd is back as Kurn and wants Worf to murder him in some kind of ritual Klingon honour code blah de blah. This is all because Worf refused to join in with the war against the Federation, and that is not reflected on the rest of his family. Worf manages to get the blade into his bro, but he lives, and Worf is chewed out by Sisko, who thinks all this wokery has gone too far and he's no longer going to be supportive of cultural diversity that involves bloodshed. The upshot is that Kurn ends up working for Odo – a development that seems to me to be wholly lacking in interest. The writers presumably agreed and so this phase of the story bites the dust. Pick an idea and stick to it, guys. The resolution, involving mind wiping and plastic surgery, is redolent of bad pulp comics. Rather more engaging are the shady Klingon war games that Kira and O'Brien stumble over on their way back from some inspection or other. Klingons have been mining the area but not for long.

DS9 S04E16 Bar Association ★★☆☆☆

Story by Barbara J. Lee & Jenifer A. Lee, teleplay by Robert Hewitt Wolfe and Ira Steven Behr. Directed by LeVar Burton. TX: 19 February 1996. Featuring: Chase Masterson, Jeffrey Combs.

Fairly tiresome comedy episode, which inserts trade union politics into the Ferengi lifestyle but can't find anything new to say about either.

Family Business delved deeper into Ferengi society with some success and set up a new recurring villain in Liquidator Brunt. Here, Nog cos-plays as Fred Kite and becomes the Quark's Bar shop floor steward, but the satire is weak, the insights into alien races slim, and the drama almost non-existent. If you're a huge fan of the Ferengi, this is fine, but it doesn't add anything to what we know already and just feels a bit inconsequential. Equally inconsequentially, Worf is bunking up in the *Defiant*, which is… okay, I guess – the pairing of Worf and Dax certainly has its appeal. One extra half-star for the fact that Rom quits the bar and doesn't go back. Every time this series does stuff like that, I have to remind myself that this went out in 1996, when everybody 'knew' you had to design episodes to be completely self-contained and watchable in any order. And everybody was wrong.

DS9 S04E17 Accession ★★★☆☆

Written by Jane Espenson. Directed by Les Landau. TX: 26 February 1996. Featuring: Richard Libertini, Camille Saviola, Robert Symonds.

Somewhat plodding exploration of Bajoran culture and mythology, which rushes to a resolution just when it was getting interesting.

The commander of the station being adopted as a Bajoran prophet is one of the odder concepts assembled for this series. We get a quick reminder of this set-up just in time for a 200-year-old ship to come through the wormhole with a Bajoran on board who claims that *he* is the Emissary. Rather sweetly, he's a poet who learns that schoolchildren can recite his most famous works from memory. But he wants to take Bajor back 200 years and reinstall the ancient caste system, which would mean Kira becoming an artist instead of a soldier. The set-up is strong, but it's the strongest aspect – the Bajorans enthusiastically and murderously getting with the old/new programme – which has to be hastily discarded off-screen to make the ending work. We're just told that everybody believed Sisko's story without question, and spontaneously agreed to pretend that the last few days had never happened. Cool.

Elsewhere, the Battle of Britain having been holographically won once more, Bashir and O'Brien are faced with a far bigger conflict – the fit that Keiko will have once she sees the bachelor pad that her husband has made of their family home. This domestic strand really only serves to reintroduce Keiko and doesn't develop into anything resembling drama. Only **Star Trek** script from Jane Espenson, who used to write an excellent blog about screenwriting – she also worked on *Buffy*, *Battlestar Galactica* and *Torchwood* among many others. Worf has no wish to help Keiko with another birth after his experience on board the *Enterprise* in *Disaster*.

DS9 S04E18 Rules of Engagement ★★★☆☆

Story by David Weddle & Bradley Thompson, teleplay by Ronald D. Moore. Directed by LeVar Burton. TX: 8 April 1996. Featuring: Ron Canada, Deborah Strang.

Fairly routine courtroom drama with familiar tropes well deployed, and directed with class, but lacking the detail of the finest instalments.

Further isolated from the Klingon Empire, Worf is now up on charges and facing extradition. During a battle that we haven't seen, Worf commanded the *Defiant* and destroyed a Klingon transport. Far from saluting this zeal for warlike glory, Worf is accused of negligence, even though the event occurred in the heat of battle. Unable to dispute the facts, the Klingon prosecutor effectively puts his own people's battle-happy mind-set on trial.

As director, LeVar Burton includes some stylish flourishes, especially having witnesses give testimony to camera during flashbacks in a way that recalls Ray Liotta leaving the stand at the end of *Goodfellas*. The trial stuff is the usual nonsense, resembling no known judicial procedures, and the killer evidence-giving at the end barely makes a particle of sense, but Avery Brooks has fun chewing the scenery. The best material in the whole episode is the final conversation between Worf and Sisko.

Those bonkers admirals' uniforms are back. T'Lara's tailor got bored making the sleeves and added pointless black bands and extra gold braid to the cuffs. Everyone else is in their standard dress togs.

DS9 S04E19 Hard Time ★★★★☆

Story by Daniel Keys Moran and Lynn Barker, teleplay by Robert Hewitt Wolfe. Directed by Alexander Singer. TX: 15 April 1996.
Featuring: Margot Rose, F.J. Rio, Craig Wasson.

O'Brien must microwave suffer. This is real nightmare fuel material and Meaney is brilliant.

The brilliance of *The Inner Light* is that it's the reset button that isn't. Picard is returned to exactly where and when he was, but he carries (at least some of) the memory of those decades he lived as Kamin, and they contribute to who he is when he returns to his life as a starship captain. I've always thought of it as something a bit less than a real lived experience, but something a bit more than a dream. O'Brien has a similar experience here – he's been given memories of twenty years of incarceration in mere minutes – but as punishment, rather than as commemoration of a doomed society. And the emphasis is mainly on rehabilitation and recovery rather than the experience.

Unsurprisingly, he takes a while to adjust to life back on board the station, including seeing glimpses of his cellmate, about whom he is being oddly secretive. The script even finds something for Jake to do – quizzing O'Brien on which tool is which. You go, Jake. Colm Meaney is better than ever here, and this manages the excellent trick of being an episode of a science fiction adventure television series where the jeopardy is principally: will one of the characters recover from trauma? – without it ever becoming maudlin, low-stakes or boring. Whether the final revelation makes sense or not is open to debate – presumably, the Zagbars could have given O'Brien memories of him doing any appalling thing they wished – but the impact is hard to argue with.

We've seen Starfleet doctors selectively erase memories before, and so while Sisko's observation that these implanted experiences can't be removed by Bashir isn't particularly convincing, it's nice that Keiko even brings it up.

DS9 S04E20 Shattered Mirror ★★★☆☆

Written by Ira Steven Behr and Hans Beimler. Directed by James L. Conway. TX: 22 April 1996. Featuring: Andrew J. Robinson, Felecia M. Bell.

Looking Glass couldn't recapture the impact of Crossover, *and the trend of diminishing returns continues, but this is still fun in its gleefully dark way.*

Just as Jake is beginning to make sense of Nog's absence from his life, he pops home to find his dead mom sitting on the couch. She's popped over from the

Mirror Universe in what seems like it's going to become an annual event. It's a neat way of distracting us from any thoughts we might have about O'Brien's trauma last week having long-term effects. By spending most of the episode 'over there', we can keep Colm Meaney in front of the camera and not have to examine 'our' Chief too carefully or too soon.

Jennifer's visit turns out to be a ruse to lure Sisko to 'her' station. The Terrans have taken back 'Terok Nor' (as the Cardassians named *Deep Space Nine*) and have ripped off the blueprints of the *Defiant*, but can't get it to work. Once again, the *Defiant* appears to be simultaneously a super-ship that would be the envy of any force in the galaxy – and a hopelessly over-gunned, over-powered and thoroughly wonky failed prototype that is still not ready for prime time. Because Worf is in the cast now, Worf is in the Mirror Universe too. And it's the first time we've seen Garak in absolutely ages as he sucks up to his Klingon captors, in some of the episode's best scenes.

Captured by the Terrans, Intendant Kira is a tiny bit less fun than usual, and Alexander Siddig never really convinces as a hard-bitten rebel, but elsewhere it's still exciting to see the regulars adopting goatee beards and sarcastic sneers. Alas, since we know the set-up quite well now, we can't be quite so thrilled at the reinventions of those characters, and since being able to bump off the regulars is part of the point of these stories, we can't be all that shocked when Kira kills Nog either. There's a pretty nifty space battle at the end, though, where the *Defiant* manages to knock out an entire enemy fleet. Tough little ship that. Last appearance by Felecia M. Bell as Jennifer.

DS9 S04E21 The Muse ★★☆☆☆

Story by René Echevarria and Majel Barrett-Roddenberry, teleplay by René Echevarria. Directed by David Livingston. TX: 29 April 1996.
Featuring: Majel Barrett, Michael Ansara, Meg Foster.

Attack of the space MILFs and not half as much fun as that sounds.

The teaser consists of two brief moments. Jake is people-watching and coming up with loglines for short stories in the way that I don't think any short story writer has ever done. Then Lwaxana turns up and tells Odo she's pregnant. Both of these strike me as rather silly, and not in a good way. Mrs Troi has run away from her new husband whose culture believes that boys should be raised exclusively by their fathers. Eventually, Odo has to pretend that he is in love with Lwaxana and wants to marry her. None of this feels like it means anything or amounts to much, and Lwaxana obediently leaves the station once Odo's sacrifice has been made – although kudos to René Auberjonois, who never even hints that this is the worst script he's had all year. Elsewhere, a mysterious older woman spouts gibberish at Jake, promising him all sorts of 'exercises and techniques' that will make him a better writer, if he comes to her quarters tonight. She might as well be telling him there are sweets and puppies in her van.

Talk of Jake's writing career (and his career-making novel *Anslem*) brings back fond memories of *The Visitor*, but this has nothing like the level of invention and depth of feeling of that episode. Lwaxana also brings up the events of *Crossfire*. Something about this episode compels everyone to intone their dialogue at half speed and the overall effect is close to numbing in its soporific mood. Jake's 'muse' gives him amazing and innovative authorial advice like 'editing is a thing'. Eventually, the twist is that the eerie older woman with a predatory interest in Jake who isolates him from his father is actually – crumbs! – the bad guy. This is the last time we see Lwaxana and it makes rather a poor swan song for her despite (or because of) Majel Barrett's own hand in the script. That's Meg Foster as the titular muse – she was the second Christine Cagney, taking over from Loretta Swit after the pilot, and being replaced herself by Sharon Gless after the first season of *Cagney and Lacey*. Jake seemingly writes his stories with a pencil, even before his creepy friend introduces him to this newfangled 'paper'.

DS9 S04E22 For the Cause ★★★★☆

Story by Mark Gehred-O'Connell, teleplay by Ronald D. Moore. Directed by James L. Conway. TX: 6 May 1996. Featuring: Kenneth Marshall, Penny Johnson, Tracy Middendorf, Andrew J. Robinson.

Very elegant mystery-betrayal story cleverly disguised as a relationship tale, beautifully played by Johnson and Brooks.

Klingons having devastated Cardassia Prime, the Federation are having to bail out the Cardassians with industrial replicators, but there's a worry that the Maquis will try to intercept the delivery. The finger of suspicion falls upon Kasidy Yates, which creates a conflict of interest for Sisko, the pillow-sniffing softie. Disappointingly, he opts to protect his girlfriend rather than the Federation's allies (he does say Odo can search her ship if he can find a suitable excuse). Eventually, he follows her in the *Defiant*, but it turns out that this was merely a ruse to remove him from the station. This is very clever plotting, disguising a turncoat rebel story as a personal relationship drama. And the fact that it's Eddington who turns Maquis is brilliant. He's a familiar face, but we don't know a lot about him, except that he's rubbed some people up the wrong way. Gratifyingly, Sisko owns his mistake, telling Kira that everything that happens on the station is his responsibility. Meanwhile, red-blooded, all-hetero Garak is sharking after Dukat's daughter Ziyal (now played by a different actor) and they share a chaste Cardassian sauna together. Their arid flirting is absolutely horrifying, and knocks half a star off what's otherwise a typically strong episode.

DS9 S04E23 To the Death ★★★★⯪

Written by Ira Steven Behr and Robert Hewitt Wolfe. Directed by LeVar Burton. TX: 13 May 1996. Featuring: Brian Thompson, Scott Haven, Jeffrey Combs.

Once more splicing nuanced morality with Boy's Own *adventure, Federation troops are out fighting side by side with the Jem'Hadar in this utterly engrossing collision of worldviews.*

Returning in the *Defiant*, Sisko and team find that an entire pylon of the station has been destroyed, leaving multiple casualties – the work of the Jem'Hadar. It's a devastating opening, and it's smart (as well as budget-saving) to play it as a discovery by the returning crew and not have the melodrama of putting us on board the station when the attacks occur. It puts us in their shoes. On the theme of *Hippocratic Oath*, Sisko's ship ends up rescuing a bunch of Jem'Hadar grunts, but with them is the smooth-talking Weyoun, played in this and countless subsequent episodes by Jeffrey Combs (even though he's seemingly offed in the closing minutes). He's a wonderful addition to the extended cast, filling the void left by Dukat, who has been somewhat gelded over the course of recent stories.

Continuing with the **Deep Space Nine** theme of: everything is grey, it turns out that there are good and bad Jem'Hadar and this group (and the station) were set upon by renegades who are trying to build a 'gateway' that will make them 'virtually invincible' (according to Sisko). This is apparently picking up a discarded thread from **Next Gen** Season 2, but I don't think it needed to be (it reminded me more of *All Our Yesterdays*). Of far more interest is the Jem'Hadar attitude to Worf, Sisko and, in particular, Odo, whom they see as a god that has inexplicably turned against heaven. It's absolutely fascinating.

We take our sweet time getting to the Jem'Hadar Death Star, but the lengthy journey never feels like padding or busywork. The scenes with Weyoun and Odo, Worf and Sisko, and especially Dax and O'Brien, are wonderfully written and played. However, as the centre of gravity of these stories moves inexorably away from the now largely settled Cardassian–Bajoran conflict, Kira is getting less and less to do. Let's hope that she finds a place in the new landscape before too long, and we don't get many more of these 'You have the station, Major' moments. She's not Tasha Yar, for crying out loud.

Worf doesn't wear his baldric into battle.

DS9 S04E24 The Quickening ★★★☆☆

Written by Naren Shankar. Directed by René Auberjonois. TX: 20 May 1996. Featuring: Ellen Wheeler, Dylan Haggerty, Michael Sarrazin.

Standard-issue ethical dilemma, which does little to bring focus to the still frustratingly generic Julian Bashir, but there's that trademark bracing dose of **DS9** *vinegar towards the end, which helps a little.*

Quark is making public access TV commercials and spamming the station with them and his branded mugs, to the fury of especially Worf, who still isn't used to his Ferengi shenanigans. This breezy scene contrasts sharply with what follows as Bashir and Dax beam down to a plague planet. Yup, another episode, another virus, but whereas on **Voyager** this would be an excuse for a lovely camping trip with a friendly monkey (see *Resolutions*, which went out a week before this), here it looks grisly, painful, existential. The wrinkle is that those who come down with the titular (and always fatal) 'Quickening' are spirited off to a death camp, which is considerably nicer than their homeworld, but where the 'patients' are given a swift release. Despite the harder edge, this all feels a bit 'off-the-peg' to me. We've seen so many incurable plagues and brutal societies that only needed the firm hand of the Federation to set them straight, and this is more of the same.

And yes, there are occasional mentions of the Dominion and the Jem'Hadar, but this doesn't feel like it has much to do with the main season plot and the lack of specificity doesn't help tie it to our characters. That's before we get to the dreadfully shop-worn clichés like the Doctor pumping the chest of some poor guest actor, yelling 'Breathe! Breathe!' as if the thought hadn't occurred to them. I do like Dax with her hair down, though. The fourth act is a sort of Bashir Must Suffer, with some tough love from Dax, and the strength of this helps a little. The trouble is, I've become conditioned to expect bleak endings from this show just as much as I've become conditioned to expect whiplash-inducing reset buttons from **Voyager**, so it doesn't induce a sickening realisation when everybody dies, rather a feeling of 'Oh yes, that makes sense', which I don't think was the intention.

DS9 S04E25 Body Parts ★★☆☆☆

Story by Louis P. DeSantis & Robert J. Bolivar, teleplay by Hans Beimler. Directed by Avery Brooks. TX: 10 June 1996. Featuring: Andrew J. Robinson, Jeffrey Combs.

Two vaguely medical storylines running side by side, neither particularly striking, and not gaining anything by being stuffed into the same episode.

Quark is back from Ferenginar with a fatal diagnosis as a result of his annual insurance physical (and he knows it's accurate because his is the most expensive doctor on the planet, unlike that hu-man Bashir who doesn't charge anything and therefore can't be any good). Top of his list of concerns his paying off his debts before he passes on, for which reason he plans to flog off his remains, and then finds himself having to go through with the sale even after it comes to light that he isn't dying after all.

We also get our second medical ethics storyline in two episodes. A rock-climbing accident puts Keiko's pregnancy in jeopardy and – ridiculously – Bashir beams the foetus into Kira's abdomen. This is described as a 'change of address', which completely fails to account for the wholesale physical and chemical changes that occur in a woman's body during gestation. The fact that Kira is Bajoran is the least implausible part of this whole scenario, given that Klingons, Romulans, humans and Cardassians all seem capable of interbreeding. Nana Visitor was pregnant when this was filmed and that seems to be the entire reason for this narrative choice. Quite what any of this means, or why these two particular storylines have been juxtaposed, is anyone's guess.

Armin Shimerman, as usual, locates the tiny sliver of acting terrain between heartfelt sincerity and absurd overplaying with uncanny accuracy, but we've seen Quark in far more interesting scenarios than this one. Likewise, it's nice to see Jeffrey Combs back as Brunt but his impact isn't nearly as strong third time around (and I prefer him as Weyoun). Garak returns and Quark tries to hire him as a hitman (better to die than to break a contract), but the sub-*Pink Panther* shenanigans that ensue make this the Cardassian tailor's least interesting outing to date.

DS9 S04E26 Broken Link ★★★☆☆

Story by George A. Brozak, teleplay by Ira Steven Behr and Robert Hewitt Wolfe. Directed by Les Landau. TX: 17 June 1996. Featuring: Andrew J. Robinson, Salome Jens, Robert O'Reilly, Jill Jacobson.

A superb storyline for Odo, which shares screen time with various other less compelling bits and pieces in a messy episode that brings a strong season to an uncertain close.

Odo is so appalled at Garak's uncharacteristically clumsy matchmaking that he has some sort of fit and collapses in the middle of the shop. He's an irascible patient, but being laid up in sickbay does provide an opportunity for some bonding between him and a still-pregnant Major Kira. As his condition continues to worsen, Odo insists that he be returned to his people in the Gamma Quadrant.

Once they reach Dominion space in the *Defiant*, Jem'Hadar shock troops beam on board and Salome Jens attempts to separate Odo from his friends, but instead they are effectively led blindfold to the new Changeling homeworld. That Odo killed a Changeling is something they cannot forgive and that's why they forced him to return home to the Great Link for judgement. All the Odo stuff here is superb. René Auberjonois is terribly affecting, and the brief farewell scene between him and Quark is a mini-masterpiece of acting and writing. Then his punishment is to be returned to the Federation with none of his shapeshifting powers. Garak has to fit him for a uniform, he has to eat for the first time, he feels itchy and tired.

But the rest of the episode is filled out with bits and pieces that don't pay off. Relations with the Klingons continue to deteriorate, with Gowron deliberately provoking the Federation by suddenly laying claim to a system they have had no interest in for decades – the big end-of-season cliffhanger is Odo's realisation that the Klingon chancellor is a shapeshifter. Seems like a better way to keep that secret would be not to stick Odo in the Great Link in the first place. Garak also tries and fails to use the *Defiant's* weapons to destroy the Great Link and end the Dominion War before it starts – a huge story swing that is over and done with in about five minutes. And Kira continues her journey away from the centre and towards the fringes of the ongoing narrative as she's left behind, pregnant and sneezing. Compared to the apocalyptic opening, this season ends with a bit of a whimper.

When this episode is good it's sensationally good, but as a whole it's rather awkward and unsatisfying, which is a real shame as this has been a pretty incredible run of episodes overall. Shakaar is mentioned but not seen. I wonder what he thinks of Kira's sudden surrogacy! Garak fights well for a tailor.

DS9 Season 4 wrap-up

- While **Voyager** thrashes around trying to figure out what stories it can tell, and what stories it wants to tell, as we'll see towards the end of this volume, **Deep Space Nine** continues to both settle down and refuse to stand still. Episodes like *Hippocratic Oath*, *Starship Down*, *Hard Time* and *To the Death* make it clear what an asset a strong regular cast can be, combined with a really detailed and well-thought-out world.

- But there have been some big successes in the wilder swings as well, with episodes like *Rejoined*, *Our Man Bashir*, *Little Green Men* and most amazing of all, the sublime *The Visitor*. These are episodes that no other series in the franchise could even have attempted.

- Now, you can also say this about some of the less successful efforts this year, like *The Muse*, *Body Parts* and *Bar Association*. And my low tolerance for Klingon mythology has also dragged some scores down. But we still end with a very fine 3.72 average, just behind **TOS** Season 1 and approaching the dizzy heights of **TNG** Season 6.

- Character development has been strong with some amazing stuff for Odo, Quark (even if not all the comedy Ferengi episodes worked for me) and O'Brien; good material for Dax, Sisko and new arrival Worf; and Bashir and even Jake finally starting to come into focus. The only disappointment is Kira, moved to the sidelines as the focus shifts away from Cardassia vs Bajor and towards Klingons vs Federation, and ending up as a walking incubator for Keiko's baby.

- The secondary cast continues to impress as well, with familiar faces showing up in multiple episodes: Garak, Weyoun, Winn, Brunt, Dukat and more besides. There's a very deep bench here and it gets richer every year.

- What's exciting is that I get the distinct impression that the Dominion War is going to bring us even more compelling episodes and even bigger threats to the status quo. Since the end of Season 3, Worf has joined the station, Quark has been exiled, Rom has quit, Odo has been stripped of his powers and Kira is having Keiko's baby. **Voyager** has to carry the burden of launching Paramount's new network UPN. Well, let the network show hit the reset button every week. We're still in syndication and we can do what we like.

Deep Space Nine
Season 5

Starring: Avery Brooks, René Auberjonois, Michael Dorn, Terry Farrell, Cirroc Lofton, Colm Meaney, Nana Visitor, Alexander Siddig, Armin Shimerman. Featuring: Aron Eisenberg, Max Grodénchik, Rosalind Chao. Executive producers: Rick Berman, Ira Steven Behr. Creative consultant: Michael Piller. Co-producer: J.P. Farrell. Producers: Robert Hewitt Wolfe, Steve Oster, René Echevarria. Co-supervising producer: Hans Beimler. Supervising producer: Peter Lauritson. Co-executive producer: Ronald D. Moore.

DS9 S05E01 Apocalypse Rising ★★★★☆

Written by Ira Steven Behr and Robert Hewitt Wolfe. Directed by James L. Conway. TX: 30 September 1996. Featuring: Marc Alaimo, Robert O'Reilly, J.G. Hertzler, Casey Biggs.

Pulpy fun with Klingon disguises, endless subterfuge, and lives on the line. Thrilling stuff, and full of surprises, but hardly deep.

Perhaps inevitably, Starfleet elects to send none other than Benjamin Sisko to try to unmask Chancellor Gowron. Equally inevitably, but of rather more interest, is Odo's challenge of facing up to being a 'solid', which he's doing by getting drunk and melancholy in Quark's Bar. Not unreasonably, Sisko wants his security officer with him, no matter how protean he is or isn't. And since Gowron is unlikely to submit to a blood test, they have a doohickey that will reveal his true nature – but as a prototype, it's beset with design flaws. Thus, Gul Dukat is recruited to smuggle Sisko, O'Brien, Odo (disguised as Klingons) plus Worf into Klingon space, and it's tons of fun. Sisko rapidly gets the hang of his new identity, but O'Brien and Odo are both struggling, and they need to do more homework before they try to ambush Gowron at the Klingon school prize-giving. The twist that it's the Chancellor's second-in-command who's really the Changeling is not only a lovely extra wrinkle, it also retrospectively makes more sense of the Founders' actions at the end of the last episode. The inter-season gap hasn't given Kira enough time to have Keiko's baby, so she's still stuck squabbling on the sidelines, alas.

DS9 S05E02 The Ship ★★★★☆

Story by Pam Wigginton & Rick Cason, teleplay by Hans Beimler. Directed by Kim Friedman. TX: 7 October 1996. Featuring: Kaitlin Hopkins, F.J. Rio, Hilary Shepard, Ken Lesco.

Tense siege story with a beguiling mystery and very strong character work.

O'Brien and crewman Muniz (seen in a couple of previous episodes) are fishing around for rocks when a Jem'Hadar warship falls out of the sky at them, which turns out to be littered with corpses. Every time Muniz makes a good suggestion, O'Brien tells him that he maybe won't be drummed out of Starfleet, which I think is meant to be 'bonding' or 'banter' or some such. Naturally, he's the first one to be hit when more Jem'Hadar land, looking for their lost motor, which leads to the team holed up inside the crashed ship as the Jem'Hadar negotiate for the return of their property.

Kaitlin Hopkins as Vorta Kilana is very striking, claiming that this is her first mission, and making all kinds of veiled threats while continuing to maintain her coquettish demeanour. She's well matched with Sisko's bull-headed stubbornness – he's definitely the least flexible of the five captains. Equally striking is the conflict between Worf and O'Brien regarding the fate of the stricken Muniz, where the Klingon advocates letting him prepare for death and the human wants to keep him fighting. Of course, he doesn't make it (this is **Deep Space Nine**, after all), but this is no casual redshirt zapping. This hurts. It almost plays like a doomed love story, when Muniz switches from calling O'Brien 'sir' (which he doesn't like) to 'Jefe' ('boss') to 'Papa'.

What really elevates this whole story, though, is the fact that as the siege intensifies, everybody starts being dickish – even Dax! – and only Sisko can bark them back into some kind of professionalism. This breakdown of social norms isn't because of any kind of anomaly, virus or mind-parasite. It's just due to the fact that they're in dead trouble and they aren't perfect. Nor is the narrative wrapped up in a neat bow. Nobody got what they wanted, and now even more people have died. Episode 100 and we show no sign of slowing down.

DS9 S05E03 Looking for par'Mach in All the Wrong Places ★★★★☆

Written by Ronald D. Moore. Directed by Andrew J. Robinson. TX: 14 October 1996. Featuring: Mary Kay Adams, Joseph Ruskin, Phil Morris.

Divisive comedy episode, riffing on Rostand, but I bought it.

Worf is thunderstruck by the ravishing beauty of the Klingon woman Grilka, whom Quark had reason to marry in the largely successful episode *The House of Quark*. Now Quark seeks to help her again by doing some light bookkeeping. Hoping to impress the foxy Grilka, Worf picks a fight with Morn and switches his usual human prune juice for more traditional blood wine. But Worf's dishonour (yawn) prevents Grilka from expressing any interest in him as a mate. (He also seems to have forgotten about K'Ehleyr when he asserts that he has never pursued a Klingon woman romantically.) But Quark still holds a candle for Grilka and is fretting about what he's supposed to say to her during their private dinner, before ending up having to fight for her love. This sets the stage for a *Cyrano de Bergerac*-style routine where Worf is able to puppeteer Quark like something out of *Ratatouille*.

Even by the standards of **Deep Space Nine** 'comedy' episodes, this is pretty fluffy and trivial, and I understand that it's some people's favourite and some people can't stand it. I appreciated the Worf/Quark double act – each set of traditions shines a clear light on the other, making it seem both amusing and convincing – and that helps get us past the usual **Star Trek** sex and romance blind spot. Plus, Michael Dorn, Armin Shimerman, Terry Farrell and Mary Kay Adams are all doing wonderful work. It ends with Dax and Worf's sparring taking on a rather more intimate quality (to Bashir's intense disquiet). As a pairing of regular characters, it certainly makes more sense than Worf and Troi.

In the B-plot, medical ethics expert Dr Bashir is listening at keyholes (with rather less success than Quark, whose Ferengi physiognomy gives him a distinct advantage), but O'Brien claims that his domestic arrangements, which involve helping Kira out of the bath and giving her massages (all while Keiko watches) present no problems. Odo knows better, of course – it's clear that becoming a solid hasn't made him any less perceptive (or any less of a dick).

DS9 S05E04 ...Nor the Battle to the Strong ★★★★☆

Story by Brice R. Parker, teleplay by René Echevarria. Directed by Kim Friedman. TX: 21 October 1996. Featuring: Andrew Kavovit, Karen Austin, Mark Holton.

War is hell. Not a new observation, but sticking Jake into the middle of the slaughter is novel and Cirroc Lofton rises very ably to the challenge.

It's a standard move for this show to stick a mismatched pair in a runabout and have them encounter a crisis, distress call or spatial anomaly. Jake Sisko and Julian Bashir are a novel combo, though, and while Bashir is given the usual not-quite-funny-enough self-involved babbling, Jake's wry impatience rings true – Cirroc Lofton is maturing very nicely as an actor, and is beginning to develop some layers to his Generic Teen characterisation. In true **DS9** style, when they answer the distress call, the boy journalist who was eagerly looking forward to swapping the Doctor's dry academia for something with a bit more human interest, now finds himself scrubbing up, helping out, wrist deep in guts and watching people die.

None of this is especially new or insightful, but it's new to Jake and that helps give it meaning for us. Particularly giving Jake the heebie-jeebies is a young man who seemingly phasered himself in the foot to get away from the front line. Then, on a mission to get a backup generator from the Paramount backlot, Jake and Bashir come under fire and Jake finds himself in a version of *All Quiet on the Klingon Front*, clambering over corpses of Federation and Klingons alike and trying to tend to a wounded man. Because this is **Deep Space Nine**, the poor guy dies in front of him.

Back on the station, poor Odo is still forgetting to remember that he isn't a Changeling any more (rather like the Kakapo parrot of New Zealand, which has seemingly forgotten that it has forgotten how to fly and thus is prone to launching itself optimistically out of high branches when pursued by predators). While I do vaguely remember that Odo regains his shapeshifting powers at some point, I'm impressed at how long they're keeping him in this form.

DS9 S05E05 The Assignment ★★★☆

Story by David R. Long & Robert Lederman, teleplay by David Weddle & Bradley Thompson. Directed by Allan Kroeker. TX: 28 October 1996. Featuring: Rosie Malek-Yonan.

Pulpy nonsense with Keiko taken over by space ghosts. It's totally nuts and very enjoyable, but it's as thin as rice paper.

Suddenly, **Deep Space Nine** remembers that it's a **Star Trek** show and this feels like something right out of **The Original Series**, except that there weren't any family relationships on the 1960s *Enterprise*. Having Keiko's body taken over by a malevolent alien to manipulate her husband is pure pulp science fiction, which makes zero sense – O'Brien even asks why the entity didn't take *him* over instead, then they get distracted before she can answer. But the show leans into the bonkers plotting and Colm Meaney plays it with a sort of Frank Drebin earnestness, which works brilliantly against Rosalind Chao's delicious scenery-chewing. It's all a load of nonsense, so I can't give it five stars, or even four, but it's tremendously enjoyable.

DS9　S05E06　Trials and Tribble-ations　★★★★★

Story by Ira Steven Behr, Hans Beimler & Robert Hewitt Wolfe, teleplay by Ronald D. Moore & René Echevarria. Directed by Jonathan West.
TX: 4 November 1996. Featuring: Jack Blessing, James W. Jansen, Charlie Brill, Leslie Ackerman.

Ridiculous birthday fun with the whole cast in sixties costumes, faultlessly stitched into the old footage. Wonderful.

Sisko is confronted in his office by a pair of internet nitpickers who hate predestination paradoxes (and jokes). The story he tells them is one of the more absurd things ever to have happened to this particular crew but it's deliriously entertaining, even coming from someone who wasn't the world's biggest fan of *The Trouble with Tribbles*. On a pretty thin pretext, we all have to go back in time, disguise ourselves as Kirk's shipmates and sneak about putting history back the way it was, like Marty McFly in *Back to the Future Part II*. For some reason, I have scarcely any memory of most **DS9** stories except this one, and once while watching **TOS**, I recognised a scene, not because I'd seen that story before, but because it gets repurposed for this story (which includes footage not just from *Tribbles* but also from *Mirror Mirror*).

　　This is full of good jokes, warmly poking fun at the old series, while never mocking or belittling it. Plus, we get to see Kirk, Spock, McCoy, and the old *Enterprise* – inside and out. It's a brilliant coup, and very hard to do with the resources available to a TV show in 1996. Just like the original episode, it's a very smart blend of gags, engaging story and just enough stakes to not let it feel pointless, but never enough to spoil the prevailing party mood. **Voyager**'s

---

SCOTT DRISCOLL, actor, improviser, author
The intrepid crew of the *Defiant* are returning from a mission when due to some chronometric shenanigans are thrown back in time 100 years, where they are forced to interact with the crew of the USS *Enterprise* on the Deep Space station K7 during the events of *The Trouble with Tribbles*. The reason I love this episode is the pure joy it created in me with its seamless insertion of the future characters in a past episode. The love they showed the previous story and the way they resolved all the plot without descending too deep into unnecessary fan service. All the winks to us were earned and the non-explanation of the glaring physical differences between **TOS** Klingons and those in further projects still gets a big laugh from me.

celebration of thirty years of **Trek** (broadcast a bit closer to the right day) was fun, I suppose. This is glorious. The only fault I can find is – yet again, there's nothing of interest for Kira to do.

DS9 S05E07 Let He Who Is Without Sin... ★★☆☆

Written by Robert Hewitt Wolfe and Ira Steven Behr. Directed by René Auberjonois. TX: 11 November 1996. Featuring: Vanessa L. Williams, Monte Markham, Chase Masterson, Frank Kopyc.

Puritan Worf is enmeshed in the anti-pleasure rhetoric of a local crank in a story that has gained more relevance in the passing years, but which still doesn't entirely work.

Morn is bringing an ensign flowers, the old softie. And there's love in the air. Worf and Dax are taking shore leave on Risa, accompanied – whether they want it or not – by Bashir and Leeta, and Quark too. Former Miss America Vanessa Williams appears as Arandis, who made sure that Curzon Dax died happy. While scowling at his bathing shorts, Worf receives a visit from a Make The Federation Great Again nutjob who wants the whole planet shut down. And so, Worf swaps his shiny trunks for a tinfoil hat and falls down a puritanical conspiracy theory rabbit hole. Alas, Monte Markham lacks the loopy charisma that this kind of part really needs – he comes across as an earnest local government type rather than a firebrand orator.

This divides Worf and Dax, and he tells her a sad – in fact murderous – story about his childhood, growing up with human children. I think it's supposed to give us an insight into their relationship, but the context makes the whole thing feel like a 1970s sitcom with ultra-masculine jealous dad getting all worked up by what he sees as his out-of-control wife. Having got this story off his chest, Worf does an obedient about-face and even manages not to turn round and murder Markham when he gets slapped. Bashir's subplot, in which he ritually breaks up with Leeta, is mired in unspoken puritanism of its own, as the mere idea of an open relationship is seen as utterly absurd, if not profoundly immoral – seen that is by the writers as well as many of the characters. Indoor hoverball is just wrong.

DS9 S05E08 Things Past ★★★★☆

Written by Michael Taylor. Directed by LeVar Burton. TX: 18 November 1996. Featuring: Marc Alaimo, Victor Bevine, Andrew J. Robinson, Kurtwood Smith.

Weird spooky return to the days of the Cardassian occupation, which feels a little like The Twilight Zone, *but not in a bad way.*

Is this actually a time-travel franchise? This is our fourth time-travel story in five episodes – and we have *First Contact* rapidly heading our way. Odo, Dax, Sisko and – hurrah! – Garak are found slumped unconscious in a runabout on their way back to the station. They quickly find themselves mentally transported back to the time of the Cardassian occupation. This is a very odd form of time travel. They have travelled only in their minds, the other inhabitants of Terok Nor see them as Bajorans, and they are wearing Bajoran clothes. When dream Garak gets punched in the face, his body lying in Bashir's sickbay starts bleeding. And worse is to come – Odo recognises that the identities they're living as are three people who were (falsely) executed for the attempted assassination of Gul Dukat.

There's a delicious spooky atmosphere to this one, with Odo seeing familiar figures in the crowd, hallucinating bloody hands and so on, Garak seeing things from a whole new perspective, and Dax becoming Dukat's new 'friend'. The ghost story aesthetic adds a nice extra dimension to this unusual tale, which expertly blends science fiction mystery with **DS9**'s trademark politicking and double-dealing, as well as delving into Odo's complicated relationship with the Founders, the Bajorans and the truth. Because Odo knew what was happening all (or at least most of) the time, and because this is essentially a rerun of past indiscretions, it's worthwhile for what it tells us about Odo, but it doesn't push the story on in any meaningful way, and what it tells us about Odo is a minor variation on much we knew already. It's well handled, though, René Auberjonois is as good as ever, and it's nice to see that somebody has remembered that Nana Visitor is still on the payroll. Kurtwood Smith (Boddicker in *RoboCop*) appears as Thrax, the Cardassian (or is he?).

DS9 S05E09 The Ascent ★★★★☆

Written by Ira Steven Behr and Robert Hewitt Wolfe.
Directed by Allan Kroeker. TX: 25 November 1996.

Two character studies in two different genres makes for a slightly weird mix, but it can't be denied that both know what they're trying to do and both pull it off.

Jake is moving in with a returning Nog on the other side of the station, while Odo is simultaneously escorting Quark to face a Federation grand jury, giving rise to a signature **DS9** two-people-in-a-runabout sequence involving Quark's predilection for card games and Odo's dubious taste in literature. They are nearly at their destination when a (very small) bomb cripples their ship, including knocking out the replicator, which leaves them stranded on a remote planet with minimal food rations and only one survival suit. There's some lovely location work as the mismatched pair haul their salvaged transmitter up the side of a mountain (although it's striking how every habitable planet in the galaxy looks like southern California).

This is very serviceable Legolas-and-Gimli-style stuff, if a bit contrived, with the quarrelsome pair gradually establishing common ground as they struggle to survive, and Auberjonois and Shimerman are at the peak of their powers. It's quite bleak when they come to blows and tumble down the slopes, breaking Odo's leg in the process. And while intellectually I know they aren't going to kill off two hugely popular characters in the middle of the fifth series, I can't see a way out of their predicament, which is thrilling.

Back on the station, Jake discovers that his roommate is a new Nog, up at 04:30 to hit the gym, cleaning their living quarters (just on the odd and even-numbered days), showing no interest in Dom-jot or holosuites. He also tidies up Jake's spelling and grammar. Even Rom barely recognises him. So, while the (ex) Changeling and the Ferengi bartender are re-enacting *The Lord of the Rings*, the human and the Ferengi cadet are re-enacting *The Odd Couple*. It's a weird blend but both halves of the story are strong even if they're playing by very different rules.

DS9 S05E10 Rapture ★★★☆☆

Story by L.J. Strom, teleplay by Hans Beimler. Directed by Jonathan West. TX: 30 December 1996. Featuring: Penny Johnson, Ernest Perry Jr, Louise Fletcher.

Sisko has a turn and comes over all Space Jesus and refuses to let Bashir turn off the funny lights in his head. Not my favourite topic, but nice to see Louise Fletcher again.

With no explanation, everyone's in new togs. Well, I say new – they're the same as the ones that the *Enterprise* crew (including Worf) were all wearing in *First Contact*, with grey quilted shoulders, the division colours relegated to the now more detailed undershirt, and a striking band on the cuff – perhaps my favourite part. It's another step on the journey away from the tsunami of Technicolor that is **The Original Series**, but the added texture is very helpful, or would be if we had HD restorations of this footage (they look great in the movies). Stranded in the Delta Quadrant, Janeway's crew doesn't get wind of Starfleet's new fashion choices. The change is never mentioned in dialogue and the visiting admiral is still a riot in red. It takes Sisko a few goes to get his combadge in the right place.

In the main plot, rather like Richard Dreyfus in *Close Encounters*, Sisko starts seeing mysterious shapes in his food and this sends him off on a vision quest in Quark's holosuites and then a mission to find Bajoran Atlantis, which he does in five minutes flat. At the same time, Bajor is being considered for admittance to the Federation, and Kasidy Yates is returning from jail, so a great many of my least favourite things are coalescing in one story. On the other hand, we get a return visit from Kai Winn for the first time in ages. Her nuanced villainy is always fascinating, and it's fun that she ends up as Sisko's spiritual guide.

I've been getting more and more invested in Sisko, and more and more used to Avery Brooks's performance style – or he's been getting better and better. But all the talk of prophecy, visions and messiahs generally leaves me cold, and it seems obvious from the jump that the Captain will be cured of his doomsaying before the episode's end.

DS9 S05E11 The Darkness and the Light ★★☆☆☆

Story by Bryan Fuller, teleplay by Ronald D. Moore. Directed by Mike Vejar. TX: 6 January 1997. Featuring: Randy Oglesby, William Lucking, Diane Salinger, Jennifer Savidge.

Kira rehashes existing debates about the morality of resistance fighters, but there's little depth to this Grand Guignol raving and ranting.

Like the opening of a spy film, members of Kira's old resistance cell are being bumped off in a variety of novel ways. Alas, Kira's too pregnant to investigate in person, so she sends Dax and Worf, who only come back with a corpse. The remaining survivors save her the trouble and they sneak onto the station, before being offed in turn. Eventually, Kira is taken and tied to the railway tracks while her tormentor strokes his waxed moustache. Compared to nuanced villains like Kai Winn and Gul Dukat, Silaran Prin, with his disfigured features and his penny-dreadful posturing, is pretty one-note and boring, so while it's nice to finally have an episode built around Nana Visitor again, the slow build-up gives way to a lot of hysterical clichés at the end. First credited **Star Trek** work for Bryan Fuller, who will go on to co-create **Star Trek: Discovery**.

DS9 S05E12 The Begotten ★★★☆☆

Written by René Echevarria. Directed by Jesús Salvador Treviño.
TX: 27 January 1997. Featuring: Duncan Regehr, Peggy Roeder,
James Sloyan.

Odo becomes a father and Keiko becomes a mother in this domestic episode, which tends to put squabbling where there's usually deep conflict, but has some stronger moments towards the end.

Quark sells Odo a baby Changeling in a bottle and he ends up playing wet nurse. This is the same week that Kira is finally having Keiko's baby, so everyone is getting used to new arrivals. Also, Shakaar exists and is dropping by to hold his girlfriend's hand – and so is Dr Mora, the Bajoran who reared Odo. Odo tells him to back off, but he insists on staying to 'observe' (which actually means 'interfere').

René Auberjonois is terrific here, as he always is. Odo is a perfect example of the difference between personality and backstory. Being a Changeling is one element of the character, but the writing and performance layer in far more besides. The actual storyline is a bit talky and plotless, though. The tug-of-love stuff between O'Brien and Shakaar is all very silly and feels like synthetic conflict. In fact, you could say the same about the presence of Mora. Odo celebrating his success with a very suspicious Quark is a much stronger scene. Quark has never seen Odo like this and neither have we. Of course, because this is **Deep Space Nine**, Odo can't stay happy and so while Keiko cradles her baby, Odo's 'child' doesn't make it. However, it manages to merge with Odo as it dies, returning his shape-shifting abilities, which seems like a low-key way to discard what seemed like a very big story thread that has not ended up going anywhere very interesting. The final scene between Odo and Kira is lovely, though, with no hint of the adolescent longing that Odo was once burdened with. Now they're just two old friends, sharing a little sadness together.

Solid Odo is a hypochondriac with bad posture.

DS9 S05E13 For the Uniform ★★★★☆

Written by Peter Allan Fields. Directed by Victor Lobl. TX: 3 February 1997.
Featuring: Kenneth Marshall, Eric Pierpoint.

Expert blend of adventure and character as a very determined Sisko pursues Maquis leader Eddington through the Badlands in a barely functional Defiant.

Sisko is searching for turncoat officer Michael Eddington, last seen hightailing it out of *Deep Space Nine* in the similarly titled *For the Cause* – and finds him very rapidly. Their conversation spells out the debate with clarity and drama. Who's to blame: the Federation for giving away planets to Cardassia in the name of peace, or the Maquis for keeping the futile hope alive that those displaced will get to go home?

The Chief has a new kind of holographic Zoom call, which he's keen to play with. Since it just requires the other actor to stand on the set, rather than being inserted into a viewscreen, it's probably a cheaper effect for the production team (although it's only seen in one other episode). Eddington cripples the *Defiant* and tells Sisko not to make this personal. He also leaves them alive because the Maquis aren't killers. He's another nuanced villain and I can tell Kenneth Marshall loves delivering these speeches that Peter Allan Fields has written for him.

Starfleet brings in another captain to take over the hunt for him. Sisko takes this as well as you might expect. Worse is to come, as Mr 'I am not a killer' detonates a nerve agent targeted at Cardassians over one of the planets the Federation gave them. The *Defiant* has been barely patched together but it's the closest ship to Eddington so ~~Ahab Javert~~ Sisko takes it out and gets on his trail. Eddington forces Sisko to choose between pursuing him and rescuing a stricken transport evacuating Cardassians from the next planet he poisons.

Since Eddington sees himself the hero of his own romantic melodrama, Sisko obediently adopts the role of villain, poisoning a Maquis-occupied planet for all humanoid life before Eddington can threaten the next Cardassian colony. It's not a bluff and it forces Eddington into a noble surrender. This is a truly fascinating dissection of the traditional roles of hero and villain as well as an examination of the political forces at work in this universe and the passions and motivations of these characters in particular. Only the crippling of the *Defiant* fails to pay off in any meaningful way – once they've got it off the station, it's the same tough little ship it's always been, just with Nog doing his Lieutenant Tawny Madison bit.

Eddington doesn't even need to give orders to a computer to beam out. He just pushes a button on a little doohickey and away he goes.

DS9 S05E14 In Purgatory's Shadow ★★★★★

Written by Robert Hewitt Wolfe and Ira Steven Behr. Directed by Gabrielle Beaumont. TX: 10 February 1997. Featuring: Marc Alaimo, Melanie Smith, J.G. Hertzler, Paul Dooley, James Horan.

Thrilling curtain-raiser, full of delicious twists, which melds personal relationship stories with existential threat in the way that only this show can.

The station picks up coded Cardassian signals emanating from the Gamma Quadrant, and so Sisko sends for Garak, who blithely tells them that it's nothing to get excited about before swiftly exiting the station in a runabout. The message is actually a distress call from Garak's old mentor Enabran Tain and when Bashir finds out what he's up to, he dobs him in, and so it's Worf that Sisko despatches to look after the duplicitous tailor. This occasions a mild domestic between Worf and Dax in which Dax refuses to wish him a good death in battle, and Worf frets that she might lose the Klingon operas she's borrowing.

Worf and Garak are a new combo for the regulation mismatched pair on a runabout signature **Deep Space Nine** scene, while Dukat attempts to control his daughter's friendship circle by picking a fight with Kira. This kind of scene can easily come off as soapy, but we have so much history with these characters, and the actors are so strong, that it plays very well.

Maybe not surprisingly, it looks as if Garak's incursion into the Gamma Quadrant has poked the hornet's nest. The inhabitants of the runabout are captured by the Jem'Hadar, where Worf discovers General Martok (who was unmasked as a Changeling in the season opener) and Garak discovers Tain, who is dying. More surprisingly, they find Dr Bashir! The old uniform is a handy way of dating his abduction (some time before *Rapture*). This is a fabulous twist, impossible to see coming and it emphasises the insidious nature of the Dominion threat. (Apparently, due to episodes being filmed out of order, Alexander Siddig almost never had to 'play' imposter Bashir, he just played Bashir, and then read this script and discovered what had been happening.)

Garak, who blithely espoused the importance of lying to Worf, now pleads with Tain to be truthful and acknowledge that they are father and son. His father's dying wish is for Garak to escape and avenge his death. It's an amazing scene and Paul Dooley makes the most of his exit. Sisko determines that collapsing the wormhole is his only option, and O'Brien and Dax get to work, aware that if they succeed then Garak and Worf will be trapped on the other side of the galaxy. The attempt fails, no doubt thanks to sabotage on the part of Changeling Bashir. Dominion ships pour through – to be continued…

Michael Westmore must have been letting the trainees have a go. Caucasian skin shows through around the eyes on both Andrew Robinson and Marc Alaimo. Melanie Smith takes over as Ziyal, Dukat's half-Romulan daughter.

DS9 S05E15 By Inferno's Light ★ ★ ★ ★ ★

Written by Ira Steven Behr and Robert Hewitt Wolfe. Directed by Les Landau. TX: 17 February 1997. Featuring: Marc Alaimo, Melanie Smith, J.G. Hertzler, Paul Dooley, James Horan, Robert O'Reilly.

More thrilling edge-of-the-seat adventure full of great character beats and wonderful plot turns. The Dominion make devilishly insidious foes.

The last episode ended with everything going to hell. Amazingly, the teaser ups the ante even more with the revelation that the Cardassians are joining forces with the Dominion. It was only a couple of weeks ago that Sisko was tracking down ex-Federation officers and protecting Cardassian colonists. Now Dukat wastes no time in smugly telling Major Kira that they're no longer on the same side. His urgent insistence that Ziyal join him on his homeworld makes much more sense now, and his parting shot is to prevent Garak from being released along with the other Cardassian prisoners. Bashir stuffs him in a claustrophobic wall void to fix a communications array, which causes him some anxiety, and eventually sends him nuts.

On the station, the attempt to collapse the wormhole has only made it more robust. *Faux*-Bashir suggests a new round of blood screening to try to find the saboteur. Gowron and Sisko are able to secure a new partnership between the Klingon Empire and the Federation without anyone else in the chain of command needing to sign it off. But Changeling Bashir is still up to no good.

Dukat, meanwhile, has his sights set on the station and offers Sisko a deal since he owes the Captain his life (several times over). Sisko naturally refuses and we end up with Klingons and Romulans joining forces with the Federation to take on the combined might of the Cardassians and the Dominion. With Worf being ritually pummelled for the edification of the Jem'Hadar troops, and Garak's subterfuge on the brink of discovery, it looks bleak for the Gamma Quadrant contingent, until suddenly, the interrogators are vaporised by a surprise ~~Mandalorian~~ Breen agent.

Changeling Bashir now takes a runabout into the Bajoran sun – using it as a bomb to destroy the entire system, fleet and station. But not the Dominion fleet, which was never really there. This is an amazing crescendo – and we've half a season still to go.

DS9 S05E16 Doctor Bashir, I Presume? ★★★☆☆

Story by Jimmy Diggs, teleplay by Ronald D. Moore. Directed by David Livingston. TX: 24 February 1997. Featuring: Brian George, Chase Masterson, Fadwa El Guindi, J. Patrick McCormack, Robert Picardo.

Amusing if superficial episode, which makes a refreshing change but doesn't reinvent the formula.

So, we have our new status quo for the back half of Season 5. Bashir has been returned to the station. Dukat is heading up the Cardassian government and has formed an alliance with the Dominion. General Martok is in charge of a bunch of friendly Klingons who are helping out with station security. Kira is done being brood mare for the O'Briens. Dax and Worf are a couple. Nog is strutting about the station in Starfleet togs. You can forgive the show for giving us a breather while we wait for the actual Dominion war fleet to turn up.

We open with Nog trying and failing to chat up Leeta. We smash into the titles with the appearance of **Voyager**'s Robert Picardo as Lewis Zimmerman in more of that inter-franchise corporate synergy, uniting the two active strands of the **Star Trek** Televisual Universe. Like a 1990s riff on ChatGPT, everyone is worried that light-based medics might replace real flesh-and-blood doctors, and Zimmerman is offering to use Bashir as the model for a new long-term Emergency Medical Hologram. There is no EMH on the station because the Cardassian infrastructure is not compatible with Starfleet technology. Thus, Zimmerman has come to the station to develop his new Starfleet technology. Why he has not asked Bashir to join him at a Starfleet facility is never made clear. Picardo is as good as ever, but Zimmerman and Rom's adolescent leering over Leeta date this episode rather uncomfortably.

This all builds to the revelation that Bashir is the product of Khan-style genetic engineering. It's interesting as far as it goes, but it's a line in his biog, not a character note that an actor can play (especially as it's information that Bashir already knew). (I'm going to give the show the benefit of the doubt and assume that this plot line isn't motivated by the stereotype of pushy Indian parents who want their kids to be top of the class.) But while this doesn't deepen his character in any meaningful way, Alexander Siddig is so much more comfortable now than he was back in Season 1, he is now well able to make the young doctor a believable character, if not a terribly rich and complex one. He's best when paired with ripe performances like those of Picardo and best of all, Brian George and Fadwa El Guindi as his mum and dad, and he pulls off the big scenes with aplomb. But this is pretty much all sitcom stuff (complete with comedy mistaken identity), with no ambitions to be anything more, except a demonstration of 1990s visual effects, all of which are pretty seamless.

DS9 S05E17 A Simple Investigation ★★☆☆☆

Written by René Echevarria. Directed by John T. Kretchmer.
TX: 31 March 1997. Featuring: Dey Young, John Durbin, Nicholas Worth.

Fairly dire Philip Marlowe rip-off, which doesn't shine much light on either the pulp fiction that inspired it, or our familiar characters.

We're back in the mode of someone-turns-up-on-the-station-and-they've-brought-a-plot-with-them. Odo is embroiled in the pulpy story of bionic femme fatale Arissa, whose contact is vaporised before he can pass on the MacGuffin he brought her. Odo's just grateful not to be playing holosuite games with Dr Bashir, but he's embroiled in a pastiche narrative with just as many clichés and tropes, it's just Raymond Chandler instead of Ian Fleming, and the banter here is pretty dreadful. Rather than elevating the world of the series, as in *Our Man Bashir*, here the over-familiar elements end up as a chain around the characters' necks, condemning them to spend the whole episode mouthing second-hand phrases and obeying the rules of the genre instead of being true to themselves. The sight of Odo, reduced to a blushing schoolboy in Arissa's presence, is quite ridiculous. And then he seeks out Dr Bashir for advice. Dr Bashir! The relationship ends badly, of course, thanks to a *Total Recall*-style twist that serves only as a reset button. Having this story take place while Odo was a humanoid might have made more sense, but honestly, this one was doomed almost from the start. The Changeling's very human-looking chest is rather distracting. Had Michael Westmore run out of latex?

DS9 S05E18 Business as Usual ★★☆☆☆

Written by Bradley Thompson and David Weddle. Directed by Siddig El Fadil. TX: 7 April 1997. Featuring: Lawrence Tierney, Steven Berkoff, Josh Pais.

Weapons is a growth industry. But Quark unexpectedly finds that a conscience can be an expensive thing.

Quark is broke and so has no choice but to go into business with his death-dealing cousin who wants him to charm customers as well as turn around his financial fortunes. The third partner in their tripod of evil is the always-entertaining Steven Berkoff, whose theatrical style fits very well into this world of rubber faces and apocalyptic storylines. They team up to demo holographic weapons, which means that technically they aren't bringing any forbidden items onto the station and thus Odo can't touch them.

Lo, he and his associates do start making money, but it belatedly dawns on Quark that being a weapons dealer means that he will be providing people with weapons and some of those people won't be very nice. Gaila does the 'cuckoo clock' speech from *The Third Man*, but Josh Pais is no Orson Welles and David Bell smothers the scene with pounding music, which robs it of the lightness of touch that makes the original so chillingly effective. Thus, what starts as a passably amusing Quark-as-Arthur-Daley story loses its way amid a mire of melodramatic clichés, including a dream sequence populated by corpses who ask 'Why did you kill me?' following which, Quark awakes and asks nobody, 'What have I done?'

In a B-plot, O'Brien must suffer... his whining baby, which he ends up palming off onto Worf, ho ho ho. Alexander Siddig directs because everybody gets a turn now, reverting to Siddig El Fadil for this credit. Unlike many other **Star Trek** actors, he didn't go on to much of a directing career. People still can't decide whether it's 'Quark' or 'Quork', and it seems very late in the day to be unsure of how to say a regular character's name. Imagine if half the cast had been referring to 'Captain Quirk' or 'Mr Spork' for three years.

DS9 S05E19 Ties of Blood and Water ★★★★☆

Story by Edmund Newton & Robbin L. Slocum, teleplay by Robert Hewitt Wolfe. Directed by Avery Brooks. TX: 14 April 1997. Featuring: Lawrence Pressman, Marc Alaimo, Thomas Kopache, William Lucking, Jeffrey Combs.

Enthrallingly intricate meshing of the political and the personal, finally centring Kira again (it's been too long).

'Cardassian politics are very complex,' muses Worf, having had the bonkers events of *Second Skin* recapped for him. That was a very strong episode, however, and I'm excited to see what this series, above all, can do in revisiting it. It would be unusual indeed for it to bring back an old character just in order to tell the same story again. And Worf's right – seeing Kira so pally with a Cardassian does seem wrong. And that's fascinating.

Pretty soon, Gul Dukat (yes, still Gul) wants him back, and I enjoyed Sisko telling the Cardassian government where they and their Dominion paymasters could shove it, almost as much as Sisko himself. But Ghemor is dying (inevitably) and there's nothing Dr Bashir can do. Now he wants to download years of Cardassian secrets to Kira, but she doesn't know if she wants to participate in this act of planetary betrayal, not least because it feels like she's denying her own (late) father by accepting this paternal surrogate in this way. It's a fascinating dilemma and it's great to see Kira in the spotlight for the first time in ages. And when Dukat swaggers onto the station to collect his bounty, he's accompanied by none other than Jeffrey Combs as Weyoun – whom we saw die, but I remembered that his part in the story was far from over. Wouldn't you know it, the Vorta are a clone race. This establishes him as part of the DS9 secondary cast and he's a wonderful addition. Shakaar is namechecked but does not appear.

DS9 S05E20 Ferengi Love Songs ★★☆☆☆

Written by Ira Steven Behr and Hans Beimler. Directed by René Auberjonois. TX: 21 April 1997. Featuring: Chase Masterson, Jeffrey Combs, Cecily Adams, Hamilton Camp, Wallace Shawn.

Sitcom level stuff only without the discipline of having to make a studio audience laugh twice a minute.

Quark's Bar is infested with voles, leading him to somewhat hysterically claim that he hates his life. Rom only makes matters worse when he reveals that he's getting married to Leeta. Returning to Ferenginar to see mom brings even worse news – Moogie is shacked up with Liquidator Brunt. Cecily Adams is fine, but I miss Andrea Martin, who was a force of nature. I'm also weirdly perturbed by the low arched doors with thick yellow frames, which I don't remember noticing before. They look like something out of Dr Seuss. The versatile Jeffrey Combs shows up for his second episode running, but playing a different recurring character, and Wallace Shawn is back as Grand Negus Zek, hiding in Moogie's wardrobe in the hope of concealing their romantic secret from Quark. Back on the station, Rom and Leeta enact a variation on the same theme. It's all pretty trivial and unamusing. The only reason this is watchable at all is that Armin Shimerman is so accomplished. Moogie is right – leave your action figures in their original packaging.

DS9 S05E21 Soldiers of the Empire ★★★★☆

Written by Ronald D. Moore. Directed by LeVar Burton. TX: 28 April 1997. Featuring: J.G. Hertzler, David Graf, Rick Worthy, Sandra Nelson, Scott Leva.

Tremendous showcase for Terry Farrell, matching wits and fists with her Klingon shipmates.

Martok is being patched up by Bashir who is (winkingly) more worried about the state of his carpet than the risks to the Klingon's life. J.G. Hertzler is a real asset to the show, providing a fascinating link between Federation officer Worf and the wider Klingon Empire. Now, he and Worf are despatched to retrieve a missing Klingon vessel, meaning that Worf is no longer subject to Starfleet regulations – and the other members of the regular cast have to pick up the slack, except for Dax, who is coming along for the ride. It's the sagacious yet playful Trill on board the Bird of Prey that kicks this one up a notch. Like *A Matter of Honor* with Riker participating in the officer exchange programme, we learn much more about them through this juxtaposition. In a signature **Deep Space Nine** move, the episode is concerned far more with the journey than the destination, with the demoralised crew confused by Martok's unwillingness to pick fights, and Dax more than holding her own. Cunningly, Worf challenges Martok in order to lose, and thus re-energised, Martok gets his mojo back and leads his rackety old ship to a famous victory. Confusingly, Klingons speak mainly English, with smatterings of Klingon dialogue, implying that they are not talking Klingon to each other. Why not?

DS9 S05E22 Children of Time ★★★★☆

Story by Gary Holland and Ethan H. Calk, teleplay by René Echevarria. Directed by Allan Kroeker. TX: 5 May 1997. Featuring: Gary Frank, Jennifer S. Parsons, Davida Williams, Doren Fein.

Amazing counter-factual tale, which shows our people their futures and leaves them profoundly altered.

The pitch sounds more like a **Voyager** episode than anything else. Unwisely stopping off to check out a mysterious planet, the *Defiant* is cheerily greeted by a bunch of humans who claim to be our crew's descendants, a situation that arises when the hardy little ship is flung back in time 200 years, er, in two days' time. In **TNG**, this would definitely be a trick, but here it appears to be genuine, and the game plan involves preserving this timeline as well as getting our people home. Shockingly, it's this that turns out to be the deception. Sisko has to choose between going home, which means erasing this timeline with its 8,000 people – or letting time repeat itself and condemning everyone on board to painful years of isolation and rebuilding (except Kira, whose injuries prove fatal).

Speaking of Kira, Shakaar, who hasn't appeared since forever, is written-out off-screen. This is another symptom of a season of the show displaying an unease and uncertainty about decisions made in past episodes that was rarely if ever seen in Seasons 3 and 4. Odo here completes his journey back to his previous incarnation: isolated, shapeshifting, mooning over Kira. But while that's a concern, it's not something that hurts this particular episode, because while 'our' Odo is poured into a jar, a 200-years-older Odo confesses his love for Kira, and that's what makes this a **DS9** episode. It's an incredible scene, building expertly on almost five years of shared history, and Nana Visitor and René Auberjonois play it beautifully.

It's just a shame that a crew of nearly fifty people is rendered just as six members of the regular cast. Surely, the others should have at least been consulted? That's a bit of fridge-logic, but it just barely knocks half a star off what's a superb hour of television on the whole.

DS9 S05E23 Blaze of Glory ★★★★☆

Written by Robert Hewitt Wolfe and Ira Steven Behr. Directed by Kim Friedman. TX: 12 May 1997. Featuring: Kenneth Marshall, J.G. Hertzler, Gretchen German.

Nog disciplines some Klingons, and Eddington likewise faces off with Sisko one last time. A small-ish story built on what initially sounds like a huge premise.

According to Cadet Security Officer Nog, the Klingon security forces are obnoxious, disobedient and frequently intoxicated. Sisko's advice to pick a fight with one of them doesn't strike me as particularly sound, and Nog and Jake's B-plot is hardly ever interesting. In the rather more compelling A-plot, Martok's forces have picked up a Maquis message intended for Michael Eddington, which asserts that missiles are heading for Cardassia – missiles that might be cloaked. Maquis missiles killing millions of Cardassians means Cardassia demanding that the Dominion exact equally bloody revenge on their behalf, which means that the missiles – if they exist – have to be stopped.

Michael Eddington and Benjamin Sisko make a fine pair, and **Deep Space Nine** loves nothing more than sticking a pair of characters in a shuttle/runabout/the *Defiant* and having them put the galaxy to rights. As invincible forces meeting impenetrable objects go, these two manage an enviable level of tension and wit and detail. It's very good stuff and Kenneth Marshall makes the most of his final appearance. Sisko tries to force Eddington's hand by leading the ship towards a Jem'Hadar fleet and Eddington's solution seems to involve putting Sisko in as much jeopardy as possible. It's pretty much standard-issue shaky camera, technobabble dialogue and lots of pixels – but both actors play it with commitment. However, this intimate mano-a-mano stuff feels almost trivial compared to the apocalyptic threat we were promised in the teaser. And indeed, it turns out that the missiles never existed, which is clever but still feels like a let-down. In keeping with the theme of this season – tying off loose ends – that seems to be it for the Maquis, introduced way back in **TNG** Season 7.

DS9 S05E24 Empok Nor ★★★★☆

Story by Bryan Fuller, teleplay by Hans Beimler. Directed by Mike Vejar.
TX: 19 May 1997. Featuring: Tom Hodges, Andy Milder, Marjean Holden,
Jeffrey King.

*Satisfyingly nasty haunted house adventures with O'Brien, Garak, Nog and a team
of redshirts.*

A gizmo on the station has failed and it 'can't be replicated', for reasons it's
probably best not to enquire about. Thus, O'Brien, Garak, Nog and a bunch
of fungible engineers are despatched to a derelict station of the same design,
which is bound to be booby-trapped. Naturally, because this is **Deep Space
Nine,** we can't be expected to cut to the station – we have to hang out with the
team during the journey while Garak plays meaningful board games with Nog
and O'Brien, one of redshirts gives away his desire for trinkets, and everyone
gets suitably tense.

When they arrive, two Cardassian operatives are defrosted, one of whom
blows up the runabout, stranding our heroes, which is a nice way to raise the
stakes. There follows a very tense game of cat-and-mouse, recalling movies like
Alien or *The Thing.* The trouble is, in those movies audiences are constantly
trying to guess who will live and who will die. Here, we know the four guys
we've never seen before are killable and nobody else is. That could easily
undermine a lot of the suspense, but there's another wrinkle, as Garak himself
becomes affected by the drug designed to inflame the murderous instincts
of the Cardassians left behind and goes on the rampage himself. Everything
else is very well handled, with Robinson and Meaney on wonderful form. In
particular, Garak's needling of O'Brien regarding his war record is some of the
episode's best material, and it's these deeper themes that elevate a four-star
adventure story to near five-star status. I also greatly appreciate that we don't
keep cutting back to *DS9* for some tedious B-plot.

DS9 S05E25 In the Cards ★★☆☆☆

Story by Truly Barr Clark & Scott J. Neal, teleplay by Ronald D. Moore.
Directed by Michael Dorn. TX: 9 June 1997. Featuring: Jeffrey Combs,
Brian Markinson, Chase Masterson, Louise Fletcher.

*Weird mix of low-stakes baseball card shenanigans with Jake and Nog and a prelude
to war with Sisko and Kai Winn. It doesn't entirely work.*

The threat from the Dominion is increasing. Federation ships are going
missing. Thefts on the station are spiking. And now, Kai Winn wants a chat.

No wonder Sisko has the glums. Luckily, Quark is preparing to auction off a Willie Mays baseball card (among other more exotic items) and Jake proposes to buy it to raise his dad's spirits, with all that post-scarcity money he doesn't have. Unluckily for them, they are outbid by a trader who believes he has found a cure for death, the details of which are ridiculous even by **Star Trek** standards. They embark on a (disappointingly stem bolt-free) game of secret favours and swapsies across the station in order to secure their prize, which is rarely funny enough to distract me from how irrelevant and over-familiar it all is.

Meanwhile, Winn and Weyoun are meeting on the station, which is certainly a more eye-catching prospect, but it too fails to catch fire, even when the two narrative threads collide. Having two teens seemingly make a fool of your chief villain is a weird way to ramp up the stakes before things take a turn for the apocalyptic, and if you're going to attempt something so seemingly counter-productive, I think you need to do more than dust off an old plot line and give it another spin. The ending is rather sweet, though.

Nobody told Cirroc Lofton how to say 'neodymium', which is unfortunate. Dr Giger's name is the source of a truly dreadful *Wizard of Oz* pun.

NATHAN BOTTOMLEY, host of several podcasts, including the *Doctor Who*-**themed** *Flight through Entirety* **and** *Untitled Star Trek Project*
The Dominion War will be starting in a week, but Jake and Nog have found themselves embroiled in a classic sitcom plot – performing a series of tasks in order to get hold of a Willie Mays baseball card that Jake believes will make his gloomy father happy. However, the man who has the baseball card is Dr Giger, the inventor of a machine that not only entertains your cells, but can also change the rules of the episode's narrative. Suddenly, we're in magic realism mode, as each of the boys' tasks incidentally brings moments of happiness, not just to Sisko, but to O'Brien, Bashir, Kira, Worf and even Weyoun. For just one episode, the grim march of an oncoming war is alleviated by a story of kindness, coincidence and tiny moments of joy.

DS9 S05E26 Call to Arms ★★★★☆

Written by Ira Steven Behr and Robert Hewitt Wolfe. Directed by Allan Kroeker. TX: 16 June 1997. Featuring: Jeffrey Combs, Marc Alaimo, J.G. Hertzler, Chase Masterson, Melanie Smith.

Doom–laden episode with great character beats for most of the regulars and supporting cast, but it feels like more prelude and I'm still waiting for the beat to drop.

'I wish they'd just attack and get it over with,' grumbles O'Brien, and I know how he feels. Meanwhile, the Dominion is signing up more and more worlds to the kind of non-aggression pact that Bajor might have signed if not for Sisko's intervention. There are so many Dominion ships coming through that Sisko plans to mine the wormhole to put a stop to them. They're losing the peace, so the risk of starting a war sounds like one worth taking. Weyoun, who is now seemingly the only Vorta on hand, tells Sisko he can remove the mines or surrender the station. Sisko estimates they have barely a day until a real attack begins, and Starfleet seems to have other things to worry about (destroying Cardassian shipyards, it later transpires).

Elsewhere, things are coming to a head with Kira and Odo. After the weird narrative cul-de-sac of Odo becoming a solid, and Kira's relationship with Shakaar fizzling out off-screen, we pick up where we left off to a certain degree. But, with a degree of maturity, Odo suggests that they mentally shelve their complicated feelings until the current crisis is past. It's a bleakly funny scene, resting on the depth of characterisation built up over five years.

Sisko protects Bajor by now insisting that they sign the non-aggression pact. He evacuates civilians from the station (including Dukat's daughter) and performs Rom and Leeta's wedding ceremony. It all feels like something pretty bad is going to go down. And before long, a combined Weyoun/Dukat armada comes calling. Battle stations. As usual with DS9, it's about the journey as much as it is the destination. We have no long runabout voyage to go on, but while we wait for the fighting to start, there are plenty of scores to settle, alliances to shore up and running jokes to revisit.

Luckily, there's some budget left at the end of the season because the space battles look pretty snazzy. The station shields prove surprisingly durable, and Worf is able to pick off various Jem'Hadar and Cardassian ships while the *Defiant* struggles to complete the minefield (which oddly can't be activated without every single mine in place).

Although victory appears to be within his grasp, Sisko orders the Federation evacuation of the station. This separates Worf and Dax, who depart having agreed to get married. Even Garak leaves on the *Defiant*, which means that Kira, Quark and Odo are the only members of the regular cast left behind and they fry the station's systems. Oh, but oops, war reporter Jake has stayed behind too.

The sight of Cardassian and Jem'Hadar troops swarming through the station is an apocalyptic one to be sure. Pretty soon, the Starfleet armada returns, but the rematch is going to have to wait till next season. As forty-five minutes of TV, this feels like it simmers but never boils – it's a long drum roll that never resolves. However, by the time the titles roll, almost every piece has been swept off the chessboard, meaning that – initially at least – Season 6 is going to feel like an entirely different show.

DS9 Season 5 wrap-up

- It's clear to see why this show is such a fan favourite. It's by far the most complex, nuanced, powerfully acted and moving series of the Berman 'big three' – but it's also the most demanding, requiring careful viewing and a good memory.
- That's partly why the goofy episodes are so important. If every episode was misery porn and O'Brien-must-suffer, then we'd stop tuning back in because it wouldn't be a good time. So outings like *Looking for par'Mach*, *Ferengi Love Songs* and *Trials and Tribble-ations* are a real tonic – even if not all of them worked for me.
- However, in the context of the arc of the series, this run of stories betrays a certain lack of confidence. Like winter in *Game of Thrones*, or Christmas in the Narnia books, the Dominion War is always coming and never arrives, so seemingly apocalyptic episodes like *By Inferno's Light* fizzle out. Worse, some of the big swings taken at the end of Season 4 are rolled back without comment. Odo spends a few episodes as a solid and then just isn't anymore – but wouldn't *A Simple Investigation* have made much more sense if he wasn't a Changeling?
- Kira and Odo's relationship finds a weird way to come full circle too. Kira's relationship with Shakaar is quietly ditched off-screen, and the two outsiders do finally confess their true feelings for each other (with a bit of timey-wimey help) but then they conclude they don't have the headspace to get into this now, because there's a war on. Is there? Isn't there?
- The final episode, in which they give up the station, feels huge, but even though this is a series about consequences – standing in stark contrast to the adventures of the good ship *Reset Button* over on UPN – I know just as well as Dukat (even without that totemic baseball) that Sisko will be back before long. I just hope 'before long' doesn't mean Season 6 episode 3.
- The numbers betray my ill ease, but the average season score is still a very impressive 3.67, down a little from the excellent 3.72 of Season 4 (itself beaten only by **TOS** Season 1 and the magnificent **TNG** Season 6) and there were any number of great episodes this time, including the incredible *In Purgatory's Shadow* two-parter, the terrific *The Ship*, the excellent *For the Uniform* and of course, *Trials and Tribble-ations*.
- Nothing got less than a 2, but I didn't enjoy *Let Who is Without Sin*, *Ferengi Love Songs* or *In the Cards* and I really thought I'd get more out of the season finale.

The S-Word

If there's one thing that makes **Deep Space Nine** stand out from the shows surrounding it, both within and without the **Star Trek** universe, it's the word that Rick Berman preferred not to hear from his writing staff: serialisation. **TNG** had broadly followed the **TOS** model of adventure-of-the-week. On the sixties show, it was barely possible to predict how many of the 'regulars' you'd see in any given episode, let alone expect shocking developments like Uhura having her memory wiped to be picked up on the following week. Even when new cast member Chekov joins, he's just there. He doesn't get a joining story and nor does Yeoman Rand get written out; she just doesn't appear again.

That was ideal for syndication. Local stations could show **Star Trek** episodes in whatever order they chose, confident that any viewer could readily understand what was going on. This kind of 'light touch' continuity also meant that creators of shows could get away from poor decisions made early in the run, and just ret-con how the *Quantum Leap* time-travel chamber worked, or how many people were on board *Red Dwarf*, confident that nobody was expecting a developing story that unfolded seamlessly week to week.

Soap operas played by different rules, but were cheaply shot on videotape, and essentially never rerun, and so there wasn't much that glossy primetime dramas could learn from their daytime little siblings. The only exception to this rule was *Peyton Place*, commissioned by ABC in the mid-1960s, specifically to try to duplicate the success of *Coronation Street* in the UK. It worked, and *Peyton Place* was soon airing three half-hour episodes a week and topping the ratings. But few tried to repeat the experiment until 1978, when CBS commissioned a five-part miniseries called *Dallas* about feuding oil barons in Texas. Before the year was out, a whole season of twenty-four episodes had been ordered, continuing the story, and pulling in massive audiences. ABC hit back with *Dynasty* a few years later, and suddenly it seemed as if there was an audience for ongoing storylines in prime time after all.

This was helped by the rise in popularity of home VCRs. The first home video tape machine with a built-in timer and dual tuner (so you could watch one show while recording another, or have a show automatically recorded while you were away) was released in 1975 – but it cost around $2,000, which put it out of reach of most consumers (well over $10,000 in today's money). Once VHS hit the market, the price of both recorders and blank cassettes started to fall and by 1987, the home video market was worth $5 billion. Suddenly, it didn't matter if you weren't going to be home when your favourite show was on – you could tape it and watch it later. That meant that programme-makers could demand a bit more dedication from their audience.

Steven Bochco had been writing for television since the early 1970s (his credits include *Columbo*, *Ironside*, *McMillan & Wife* and many more). In 1981, he created *Hill Street Blues* for NBC. What looked at first like another police procedural was as concerned with the private lives of the characters as with the criminals they caught and the crimes they committed. Its sprawling ensemble cast meant that it wasn't always possible to wrap up storylines in one-hour chunks and so bits of narrative would spill over into subsequent episodes. Bochco repeated the trick with hospital show *St Elsewhere* and legal drama *LA Law*. And other shows began to get in on the act. Previously, case-of-the-week shows like *Cagney and Lacey* began rewarding loyal viewers with ongoing storylines that spanned multiple episodes or even whole seasons. Sitcoms like *Cheers, Roseanne* and *Friends* began to experiment with longer stories too, even ending seasons on a cliffhanger.

This was the environment that **TNG** was born into in 1987, but the famously risk-averse Rick Berman was already out on a limb, rebooting a show that everyone 'knew' relied on the chemistry of its original cast, transmitting in first-run syndication, costing a ridiculous amount per episode, and putting science fiction drama on television at a time when nobody thought that was possible. The last thing he was thinking about was making life harder for the local TV stations who were paying for the damn thing. So, little bits of serialisation crop up in some episodes, like the bizarre thread which culminates in Season 1's *Conspiracy*, the increasing threat of the Borg, or the return of characters like Q, or Lore or Leah Brahms (but then even Kirk met Harry Mudd twice). As story material accretes around the characters, threads like the Maquis and the Bajoran/Cardassian conflict become more attainable, but if you *really* need to have watched a previous episode, it's clearly signposted because the on-screen title includes the explicit words 'Part II'.

So, that was the plan for **Deep Space Nine**. Create an ensemble cast. Tell adventure-of-the-week stories against this backdrop. Ensure that local stations can rerun the episodes in any order once the show goes off the air. But the very conception of the series pulled away from that approach. Yes, Picard was periodically summoned back to Federation HQ for a talking-to from his superiors, but fundamentally, the *Enterprise* always flew off at the end of the story to find a new adventure somewhere else. Sticking the cast on a space station means that all of the choices your characters have made this week will still be there next week. The end of the episode won't always be the end of the story. Before long, the writers in general and Ira Behr in particular were begging for the chance to do longer story arcs. Paramount told Berman no way and Berman told Behr no way.

And yet – here we are at the beginning of Season 6, about to start a multi-episode arc in which basically nothing makes sense unless you've watched most of the previous 120 or so episodes. How did we get here? Was **Deep Space Nine** such a ratings behemoth that, like *Dallas* and *Dynasty* before it, it could do what it liked? Well, actually, no. **Next Generation** had been remarkably consistent in its ratings, averaging between 10 and 12 million viewers an episode every year for seven years (which would generally put it just outside the top thirty shows for the year). **Deep Space Nine** started very strongly with its pilot episode pulling in nearly 19 million, slightly better than the finale of **TNG** a couple of years later. But it never hit those heights again, and its own finale in 1999 was watched by just over 5 million viewers.

The thing is, Paramount didn't really care what was happening to **Deep Space Nine**. **Voyager** was the flagship of their proposed fifth network, UPN, and that needed to be a ratings smash. **Voyager** held its own in the ratings, but that didn't mean that it was setting any records. **Voyager**'s third year averaged 6.87 million viewers, while **Deep Space Nine**'s contemporaneous fifth year averaged 5.75 million. But just as **Deep Space Nine** was going all-in on serialisation, Berman, Jeri Taylor, Paramount, and anyone else who cared, was busy revitalising Janeway's show, with added Borg. Ira Behr and his writers could do what they wanted. It's not like anyone was watching, anyway.

By this stage, it was accepted that serialisation was just part of how we tell stories on TV now, and Steven Bochco, the man who started the trend, sealed the deal with *Murder One* in 1995, which explicitly told you that you were watching one story in twenty-three chapters. And shows like *Lost*, *The West Wing* and *24* continued this evolution. Today, streaming services mean that we can watch episodes whenever we like, and only miss one or get them in the wrong order by accident, so programme-makers are free to be as serialised as they want. If anything, with shows like **Strange New Worlds**, there's even a slight tilt back towards adventure-of-the-week.

For what happened to **Voyager**, UPN and the Borg, see the later sections of this book, and the first section of *Volume III*.

Deep Space Nine
Season 6

Starring: Avery Brooks, René Auberjonois, Michael Dorn, Terry Farrell, Cirroc Lofton, Colm Meaney, Nana Visitor, Alexander Siddig, Armin Shimerman. Featuring: Aron Eisenberg, Max Grodénchik, Marc Alaimo, Andrew J. Robinson, Jeffrey Combs, J.G. Hertzler. Executive producers: Rick Berman, Ira Steven Behr. Creative consultant: Michael Piller. Co-producer: J.P. Farrell. Co-supervising producers: Steve Oster, René Echevarria. Supervising producers: Hans Beimler, Peter Lauritson. Co-executive producer: Ronald D. Moore. Story editors: Bradley Thompson & David Weddle.

DS9 S06E01 A Time to Stand ★★★★☆

Written by Ira Steven Behr & Hans Beimler. Directed by Allan Kroeker. TX: 29 September 1997. Featuring: Brock Peters, Casey Biggs, Barry Jenner.

Very satisfactory curtain-raiser continuing the war at an unhurried pace, which means great character moments sometimes at the cost of tension.

The war has started, and Dominion forces have the station. Bashir gives us barely a 30 per cent chance of prevailing, which is no comfort to Garak. Even the captain's log is completed by Dukat. Worf and Dax, who bid a tearful farewell in the season finale, are reunited before the opening credits this time round and begin bickering about the details of their wedding. On the station, an eerie peace has descended. As Quark notes, things could be a lot worse.

Just as it once played Kira being stripped of her role on the station as a tragedy, now Sisko losing not just the station but also his role as captain of the *Defiant* is accompanied by gloomy chords and is deemed a strong enough plot twist to take us into the commercials. He should be worried about Jake – who has reinvented himself as Sisko Jr, Federation News Hound – and who is only just now learning the value of keeping important contacts onside.

Finally, we get something with a bit of forward momentum. Sisko has been given a salvaged Jem'Hadar ship and the regular cast is sent on a covert mission to destroy the Alpha Quadrant's main supply of Ketracel White – the drug which the Founders keep their soldiers hooked on to ensure their obedience. Another two weeks go by as they learn to pilot their new craft. While I admire the patience of this series, and revel in the character beats (like the terrific Kira/Dukat scene in the third act) I can't help thinking that this is a very relaxed and almost genteel war.

Kira's the heart and soul of this episode. With shorter hair than usual, and a pinched, grim expression, she looks defeated and yet still determined to fight back. Weyoun's bland propaganda doesn't give this ex-freedom fighter a target she can aim at, and she feels helpless. The Ketracel White mission is a bit more by-the-numbers but it's exciting enough with the unfamiliar ship adding a few extra wrinkles, and it gives us a great cliffhanger to go out on. It's also a good episode for Bashir, now embracing his custom-built heritage, which makes much more sense of his character generally and does give Siddig something new to play.

DS9 S06E02 Rocks and Shoals ★★★★☆

Written by Ronald D. Moore. Directed by Mike Vejar. TX: 6 October 1997. Featuring: Phil Morris, Christopher Shea, Paul Eckstein.

The war continues on a more personal footing in an exemplary episode, full of wonderful moments.

Continuing where the previous episode left off, our crew is limping along in their crippled Jem'Hadar ship. This is starting to feel like a modern fully serialised show – there's no 'Part II' on-screen, but clearly you need to know in detail what happened last week (and during the previous five years) to make any sense of this. It's also very dramatic, with Dax on the receiving end of a pretty shocking injury before the titles.

They end up stranded on a barren world where an injured Vorta and a gang of Jem'Hadar are also working hard to survive. Garak and Nog are captured, and Garak is forced to admit that there is a doctor in their party. Jem'Hadar troops have orders to reconnoitre but not engage – they're too trigger-happy, though, due to lack of White. The details of the Dominion – Founders, Vorta, Jem'Hadar – are all fascinating, Sisko's ability to spin the foot soldiers is compelling and Avery Brooks has never been better, slightly underplaying but with soft intensity. There's great location work here too.

On the station, a particularly nasty protest takes place in front of Odo, Kira and – horribly – Jake, whose boy reporter persona still isn't quite working. For Kira, clocking on for her shift the next day, surrounded by Cardassians and Jem'Hadar, is like a nightmare. An impossibly brutal act of self-harm changed nothing. The sense of helplessness is overpowering. Truly, we are approaching the moment of darkest before the dawn.

DS9 S06E03 Sons and Daughters ★★★☆☆

Written by Bradley Thompson & David Weddle. Directed by Jesús Salvador Treviño. TX: 13 October 1997. Featuring: Marc Worden, Melanie Smith, Casey Biggs.

A pause in the action, which isn't unwelcome, but nor is it particularly exciting.

Our characters have made it to a starbase with some help from General Martok and are being debriefed by Starfleet top brass. Worf joins Martok's ship and he discovers that his own son is among the troops. Brian Bonsall having retired from acting, the part is now taken by Marc Worden, the fourth actor after Jon Paul Steuer, who played him in his original **TNG** appearance (*Reunion*), and James Sloyan, who was the adult Alexander in the very odd *Firstborn*. Heavy make-up does make it easier to hide this kind of recasting (see also Ziyal, Moogie, that Ferengi who fell through a wormhole and so on) but it saps the hoped-for sense of history between these two. Speaking of Ziyal, she's struggling to find her place too, given that she's living among Bajorans when her father is waging a war against their most exulted living religious leader. She paints some pictures and then gets to wear the dress that her dad bought for Kira, who's somewhat gone off the sadistic Cardassian dictator and butcher, much to his surprise.

Viewed as part of a daily binge-watch, it's nice to catch up with familiar characters and look at how the unfolding war is affecting each of them. But watched week to week, I can't help but think that it might have been a bit frustrating to have so little movement in the main season plot with seven days to wait for this episode and another seven to wait before the next one. Plus, much of this is more bafflegab about Klingons, their honour codes, and their houses, which is apparently terribly meaningful and moving to some people, but leaves me completely cold.

War is much more fun when you're winning, according to Martok.

DS9 S06E04 Behind the Lines ★★★★☆

Written by René Echevarria. Directed by LeVar Burton. TX: 20 October 1997. Featuring: Casey Biggs, Barry Jenner, Salome Jens.

Odo learns about his people. Sisko gets a desk job. Dukat practises smiling. Little actually happens, but it's fascinating to watch it all unfold.

Our people are stationed on a Starbase, running sorties with the *Defiant*, and making some inroads, but always finding the enemy one step ahead. Now Sisko's team is charged with taking out their intelligence-gathering array. And that's not the only thing worrying the Dominion. Without a supply of White, they can't keep the Jem'Hadar in line. And on the station, Kira has made sure that they get wind of the Cardassian plan to bump them off before they go berserk and turn on their masters. The fun here is less in Kira's slightly clunky narration of events in the teaser, it's in Act One, with Weyoun encouraging Dukat to keep smiling as they figure out what to do next. Dukat isn't a talented smiler.

Sisko figures out how to nobble the array, but Admiral Ross mysteriously kicks him upstairs, as obviously the best use of his most able tactician during a brutal war is behind a desk and not on the bridge. Of more interest is the fencing between the Founders, the Cardassians and Odo – strung between worlds, neither collaborator nor rebel, neither Changeling nor solid, neither leader nor lackey. Salome Jens's quiet authority continues to play very strongly. In fact, that's the tone of this whole episode. Talky, low-key and quietly effective – even Dax's mission against the array takes place off-screen – I can't imagine this episode being anybody's favourite, as it's largely concerned with setting the table for future storylines and tying off a few loose ends, but it's discreetly compulsive viewing nevertheless because the character work is so good, and the acting is so strong (Nana Visitor and René Auberjonois are amazing here).

We get our first admiral's uniform with grey quilted shoulders on Barry Jenner. It actually looks as if he's part of the same fleet as Sisko, which might be a first for this franchise, even if his silly gold belt buckle looks like a leftover from *The Motion Picture*.

DS9 S06E05 Favor the Bold ★★★★☆

Written by Ira Steven Behr & Hans Beimler. Directed by Winrich Kolbe. TX: 27 October 1997. Featuring: Melanie Smith, Casey Biggs, Chase Masterson, Barry Jenner, Salome Jens.

Once again, not much really happens, but it's still compelling while it's on.

The *Defiant* is seemingly dead in space, but it's a ruse to lure Dominion ships to them (and the *Rotarran*). Dax and Worf's love language is tactics and battle plans. But it's clear that the Federation is on the back foot and that morale is slipping. Sisko's new plan is to retake *Deep Space Nine*. I can't decide whether I'm impressed we made it this long before bringing this up or whether four episodes out of a seven-year run is pretty footling. But this is still **Deep Space**

Nine, where it's always about the journey at least as much as the destination. So, this is an episode about plans being put in place, tensions simmering, and positions being entrenched. The biggest development isn't the two colossal attack fleets facing each other, it's the blow-up between Odo and Kira, which once again is an incredible display of writing and acting.

Thankfully, we're spared The Female Changeling (hereafter TFC) asking Odo 'What is this thing that the solids call love?' and we join them when he's got through showing her. Garak prefers asking the questions and wonders if Bashir has a tinfoil hat handy. Weyoun has weak eyes but good ears.

DS9 S06E06 Sacrifice of Angels ★★★★★

Written by Ira Steven Behr & Hans Beimler. Directed by Allan Kroeker. TX: 3 November 1997. Featuring: Melanie Smith, Casey Biggs, Chase Masterson, Salome Jens.

Landmark episode, which builds to an amazing crescendo as loyalties are tested and high prices are paid. Amazing work by all concerned.

This isn't identified on-screen as 'Part II' but it does begin with 'Last time on **Deep Space Nine**'. Is it part two? Or part six of the arc that began with *A Time to Stand*? Or part 130 of the story begun in *Emissary*? Bashir and O'Brien trade off gloomy stanzas as they approach the enemy fleet, and then we get all the CGI that Dan Curry can muster as we go into the opening titles.

Let's talk about Rom and Nog. Armin Shimerman has been doing wonderful work week after week, but since the show started, his brother and nephew have been little more than comedy sidekicks for him or Jake to bounce off. With Rom's devotion to the Federation/Bajoran cause and Nog's earnest enthusiasm for Starfleet, each has grown considerably over the course of recent episodes. Wisely, the actors haven't drastically altered their approach to reflect this very different characterisation on the page – rather, they've subtly modulated, giving the careful impression that this potential was there all along. It's a wonderful lesson in how to handle secondary characters in a long-running series (see also Kai Winn, Gul Dukat, Garak and so on, but everyone goes on about them).

Sisko's strategy seems sound, but on the station, it looks like Dukat is one step ahead. And while Kira and friends are laying new plans to prevent the Cardassians from removing the minefield and allowing reinforcements to come pouring through – they are all held for questioning. It's always exciting when the bad guys are smart. It's too easy to resolve plot problems by just having the bad guys do something dumb (just as it's too easy to create plot problems by just having the good guys do something dumb). This feels like a real clash of intellectual titans. And the shifting status patterns between Cardassians, Vorta, Founders and Jem'Hadar continue to fascinate.

With a bit of help from Worf, the *Defiant* punches through the enemy lines and meanwhile, it's Quark and Ziyal of all people who team up to break Kira, Rom, Jake and Leeta out of jail. When the Ferengi bartender has to slay two Jem'Hadar, he stares at the corpses, unable to process what he's just been forced to do. It's a tiny moment, which doesn't slow down the action, but it's a wonderful detail, giving us a glimpse of a powerful internal conflict brewing in – again – another character conceived simply as comic relief. But amazingly, all of their efforts are in vain as the minefield is successfully detonated, leaving only the *Defiant* between the Dominion fleet and *Deep Space Nine*. But the *Defiant* has Bajoran gods on its side. Gods out of a machine? Not really; this was set up 160 episodes ago. And the final scenes between Dukat, Damar and Ziyal approach grand opera for their tragic power. Not bad for a syndicated adventure series about people with rubber faces wearing silly clothes.

Dukat can't understand why there are no statues of him on Bajor, after everything he did for them.

DS9 S06E07 You are Cordially Invited ★★☆☆☆

Written by Ronald D. Moore. Directed by David Livingston.
TX: 10 November 1997. Featuring: Marc Worden, Shannon Cochran, Chase Masterson.

With a key victory won and the station theirs again, everyone has a chance to let their hair down and party. Not really what I'm looking for from this show.

Sisko's opening narration awkwardly tries to square the circle of everything's-okay-again-now and let's-not-forget-we're-still-at-war. Marc Worden returns as Alexander, present for his dad's hasty wedding to Jadzia. 'It's sort of like a best man,' says the Trill, translating Klingon customs into human concepts for the benefit of a Klingon. She gets her comeuppance soon enough when Martok's wife Sirella spots her using replicated candles and threatens to block Dax's entry to the House of Martok. As usual, Ron Moore can't think of anything more enthralling than making up absurd Klingon rituals, and I can't think of anything more tedious. Dax vs Sirella is a little more interesting, but not much. So, while it's nice to have the gang back together, this is inessential to say the least. Odo and Kira's thread is the most interesting and their 'big talk' happens off-screen, which is audacious but not entirely satisfactory. Hungover Dax is funny, though, and Terry Farrell is always watchable. Quark gets a few good laugh-lines too.

DS9 S06E08 Resurrection ★★☆☆☆

Written by Michael Taylor. Directed by LeVar Burton. TX: 17 November 1997.
Featuring: John Towey, Philip Anglim.

*Continuing the downward trend of Mirror Universe stories on **DS9**, this ignores all the great character and plot development of recent episodes in favour of bringing back Bareil, who was only ever stiff and dull in our universe.*

Kira and Odo having resolved their five years of deeply complicated emotional entanglements off-screen last episode (seriously, what the hell?), Kira is considering (and rejecting) various different options for a date to bring over to Mr and Mrs Worf's. This cheerful domesticity is interrupted when some guy beams onto the station and everyone freaks out. Despite watching these episodes at the rate of one a day, I had to pause and Google him. It's the Mirror Universe version of Kira's earlier squeeze Vedek Bareil, who fell victim to Julian Bashir's tender ministrations in *Life Support*, back in Season 3.

It's only after he's been disarmed and locked up that anyone speaks his name. He's stunned to discover that his counter-part is a) dead and b) used to be a religious leader. Cue a lot of mumbling in robes and trudging through dimly lit caves. His presence does solve Kira's social dilemma, however, and everyone seems super-impressed when he's a dick to Worf, especially Kira, who jumps into bed with him – a development that urgently requires Odo's presence if we're going to make emotional sense of it, but he's nowhere to be seen. Later, the Intendant turns up, and so this nonsense turns out to be merely a ruse to cover the theft of a Bajoran Flashback Box. Even Nana Visitor can't seem to bring much to Goatee Kira this time round. Maybe that's why Mirror Bareil switches sides at the end, obediently phasering his actual girlfriend and resolving the plot.

DS9 S06E09 Statistical Probabilities ★★★★☆

Story by Pam Pietroforte, teleplay by René Echevarria. Directed by Anson Williams. TX: 24 November 1997. Featuring: Tim Ransom, Jeannetta Arnette, Hilary Shepard, Michael Keenan, Casey Biggs, Faith Salie.

Series-best stuff for Alexander Siddig in this gloomy version of One Flew Over the Deep Space Station.

Bashir's backstory regarding his genetic superiority, which seemed to energise the actor without really transforming the way the character was written or played, is now made into a story in its own right, as we get the chance to

Promo shot of Avery Brooks as
Benjamin Sisko.

Promo shot of Nana Visitor as
Kira Nerys.

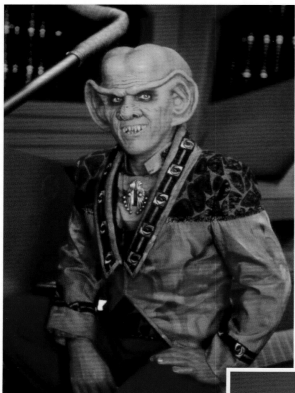

Promo shot of Armin Shimerman as Quark.

Promo shot of Terry Farrell as Jadzia Dax.

Promo shot of Cirroc Lofton as Jake Sisko.

Promo shot of Nicole de Boer as Ezri Dax.

The **Deep Space Nine** regular cast.

Publicity still from *Trials and Tribble-ations* featuring Colm Meaney and Alexander Siddig.

Terry Farrell behind the scenes on *Trials and Tribble-ations*.

Andrew Robinson (Garak) at Startopia Convention 2017 in Mannheim, Germany, 2017.

Kirk vs Soran from *Star Trek: Generations*.

Picard and Data in stellar cartography from *Star Trek: Generations*.

Publicity still from *Star Trek: Generations* featuring Malcolm McDowell and Gwynyth Walsh.

Walter Koenig, William Shatner and James Doohan.

William Shatner and Patrick Stewart saddle up for *Star Trek: Generations*.

Whoopi Goldberg in *Star Trek: Generations*.

Publicity still from *Star Trek: First Contact*.

Robert Picardo in *Star Trek: First Contact*.

Alfre Woodard and James Cromwell in *Star Trek: First Contact*.

Publicity still from *Star Trek: First Contact*.

Patrick Stewart and Alice Krige in *Star Trek: First Contact*.

Jonathan Frakes shooting *Star Trek: First Contact*.

Publicity still of Kate Mulgrew as Kathryn Janeway.

Promo shot of Robert Duncan McNeill as Tom Paris.

Promo shot of Tim Russ as Tuvok.

Promo shot of Roxann Dawson as B'Elanna Torres.

Promo shot of Robert
Picardo as The Doctor.

Promo shot of Jennifer Lien as Kes.

Promo shot of Garrett Wang as Harry Kim.

Voyager Season 1 cast.

Publicity still of Kate Mulgrew and Ethan Phillips.

USS *Voyager*.

examine how the Federation manages citizens with behavioural problems. Riffing on movies like *Rain Man*, *The Dream Team* or *12 Monkeys*, which had proven popular in the previous decade or so, this pits Doc Julian against and eventually alongside Tim Ransom as Jack, who seemingly draws on Hoffman, Keaton and Brad Pitt to create this manic character.

Alexander Siddig began his **DS9** journey working a shade too hard with scripts that did little more than portray him as an overly cheerful sex pest. While other characters like Odo, Kira and Dax flourished, Bashir languished – and although Siddig relaxed, his character never really got the depth that even secondary characters like Nog and Dukat were getting. But watching him discuss the collection of unhappy people he'd just met, and stepping through the minefield of his similarity to them and yet utter difference from them, I was struck by the delicacy and clarity of his performance. He really is a very fine actor, and the franchise was lucky to have him.

Meanwhile, the Cardassians have remembered that they declared war on the Federation, and Damar starts making speeches live on YouTube about seeking peace talks. The patients see through the deception – this is the old story of the idiot savant – and Bashir sees giving them access to holotapes of the conference as a therapeutic tool. And maybe it will give the Federation an edge in the negotiations.

Taking a page from Asimov's *Foundation* series, Bashir reckons that his team of mad geniuses can tell the future – confoundingly, their predictions getting *more accurate* the further into the future their analysis goes. And while we're paying tribute to the science fiction giants of the twentieth century, Bashir puts on a celebratory rendition of 'The Blue Danube' when their report is accepted by Sisko. But their celebrations turn sour when their predictions show that the only sensible course of action for the Federation is to surrender to the Dominion now and save countless lives.

This is all good, serviceable Trolley Problem stuff, with a dash of Racism Is Bad M'kay thrown in, but undermined slightly by the overplaying of the Four Who See All, who too often come off as *Batman* villains rather than troubled souls seeking peace. And it's not the most enlightened depiction of mental health issues you're likely to see either.

DS9 S06E10 The Magnificent Ferengi ★★☆☆☆

Written by Ira Steven Behr & Hans Beimler. Directed by Chip Chalmers. TX: 1 January 1998. Featuring: Cecily Adams, Josh Pais, Christopher Shea, Hamilton Camp, Chase Masterson, Iggy Pop.

Quark seems to value public adoration almost as much as latinum in this rather insipid movie-inspired romp.

Quark is holding court and telling tall tales about fake floods and supplies of syrup when Bashir and O'Brien turn up having performed some actual (off-screen) derring-do. Apparently, earning profit is not considered heroic outside of Ferenginar, and thus Quark and Rom are off on a Nagus-sponsored rescue mission, with Moogie as the damsel in distress. But first, they need to assemble a team, and it needs to be all-Ferengi, which means return appearances for Josh Pais and Jeffrey Combs (as Brunt rather than Weyoun) as well as Cecily Adams as Moogie. But it's all fairly silly stuff, which fails to comment in any interesting ways on the works of either John Sturges or Akira Kurosawa – in fact, it ends up more *Weekend at Bernie's* than *Seven Samurai* – and it doesn't add much to the Ferengi corpus either. The one big laugh this elicited from me was the look on Sisko's face as Quark and Rom pop up through a hatch in the wall of his office, but the rest is all pretty grim. Bizarrely, Iggy Pop turns up as the Vorta negotiating the prisoner exchange.

DS9 S06E11 Waltz ★★★★✬

Written by Ronald D. Moore. Directed by René Auberjonois.
TX: 8 January 1998. Featuring: Casey Biggs.

Yet another riff on The Odd Couple in Space *with Sisko and Dukat but this is still richly fertile ground and there are other twists besides.*

Sisko comes to see Gul Dukat in prison. Everything on this show has consequences that reverberate through the characters long after the events. It looked like Dukat's arc was concluded as he experienced what he describes as his 'momentary instability' while cradling his dead daughter, but here we are following up, and the teaser devotes almost five full minutes to a simple dialogue scene between Marc Alaimo and Avery Brooks, both of whom are tremendous. But this is still a science fiction adventure series, so the prison ship they're on is duly attacked and destroyed and Kira sends out a search party.

This isn't the first time that this series has paired two traditional enemies and forced them to work together to survive (it isn't even the first time that this series has done it with Dukat) but it's a good ploy and this is a particularly fascinating pairing, richly marinated in over 100 prior episodes' worth of history, and so it works very well, even after an apparition of Weyoun satirises the very idea of this story concept. Pretend Weyoun is joined by Phantom Damar and Hallucinatory Kira as the time-constrained search continues.

These imaginary friends distract Dukat long enough for Sisko to get the distress beacon working (which Dukat had secretly disabled). On **Voyager**, we might have been left to believe in the reality of Dukat's companions a little longer, which might have made for a neat plot twist, but playing it honestly means we can clearly dissect the psychological state of this dictator-brought-low. And in any case, we have another bait-and-switch later when O'Brien and Dax pull off a *Silence of the Lambs*-style piece of misdirection, making us think it's Dukat and Sisko they've locked onto, when it's just two other random survivors.

And if anything, what happens on board the *Defiant* is almost more interesting than what happens on the barren planet. Worf insists on calling off the search, and has to order Bashir off the bridge when the Doctor suggests that Kira's message was too garbled to understand. It's a delicious moment of tension and uncertainty (and Worf still disobeys the order).

DS9 S06E12 Who Mourns for Morn? ★★☆☆☆

Written by Mark Gehred-O'Connell. Directed by Victor Lobl.
TX: 4 February 1998. Featuring: Gregory Itzin, Brad Greenquist, Bridget Ann White, Cyril O'Reilly.

Minder in Space, not for the first time. Insubstantial and only fitfully amusing.

As I understand it, Morn was a spare costume that was knocking around which helped fill out Quark's Bar and made it feel a bit busier. Because the costume wasn't articulated, and because the performer inside was paid as a supporting artist not as an actor, the thing couldn't talk, which gave rise to a very funny running gag about how he never shuts up. Now his death is the source of (some) genuine pathos. So far, so **Deep Space Nine**.

But by and large, this is a comedy Quark episode and those are a bit hit-and-miss as far as I'm concerned. For every hilarious *Little Green Men*, there's a tiresome *Ferengi Love Songs* waiting. Here, despite having a perfectly serviceable wife, Morn's will bequeaths everything to Quark instead, and so this is more towards the tiresome end, with Quark trying to track down Morn's riches, and various knobbly gangsters shaking him down. Nothing we haven't seen before, although while René Auberjonois is largely wasted, Armin Shimerman never lets his energy flag.

For those who care, we finally nail down what 'gold-pressed latinum' is in this episode. Quark's bargain basement hologram is insubstantial, compared to most holograms in this franchise, which can be touched as well as seen. That's Morn actor Mark Allen Shepherd whom Quark invites to sit in Morn's chair.

DS9 S06E13 Far Beyond the Stars ★★★★★

Story by Marc Scott Zicree, teleplay by Ira Steven Behr & Hans Beimler. Directed by Avery Brooks. TX: 11 February 1998. Featuring: Brock Peters, Penny Johnson.

*One of the biggest swings this or any **Trek** series has ever attempted, and it's a thing of beauty, burning with heartfelt rage. I'd give it six stars if I could.*

Ben's pa has come to stay, since the war still seems to be enjoying an intermission. It's not only his first time on the station, it's his first time off-world. Despite the cessation of on-screen hostilities, Sisko feels as if it's someone else's turn to make the tough decisions, and this leads him to try to talk Kasidy out of continuing her delivery runs. Suddenly, and impossibly, he's in the middle of a mid-twentieth-century New York street. Is this timewimey shenanigans or some kind of hallucination?

Well, in fact, it's little more than an excuse to see all our regular cast out of make-up, and/or acting out of character (it's almost more disconcerting to hear Michael Dorn talking in a normal cadence than it is to see him without rubber forehead ridges). It's also a love letter to the pulp science fiction writers of the 1950s who gave birth to the concepts that Gene Roddenberry built upon. And it's a passionate exploration of the civil rights movement – old ground to be sure, but given an extra sting when put into this context. Suddenly, what was subtext becomes furiously angry text and it's shocking to see these issues dealt with so frankly and straightforwardly. **Star Trek** is so completely post-racial, it's easy to forget that America's racist past still casts a very long shadow, to the extent that in the mid-1990s, **Deep Space Nine** was pretty much unique among American television shows for having a Black lead. (Alexander Siddig seems to count as white, maybe because he's British.)

So, this is wonderful fun in the same way that *Trials and Tribble-ations* was; it's about **Star Trek** itself, in the way that *First Contact* was; and it has something to say about humanity which even if it isn't all that new, is said with tremendous clarity and feeling. The flimsy plot fig leaf of the real Sisko lying in sickbay with a broken brain needn't detain us unduly – I almost wish they hadn't bothered. This is why you take time out from your arc plot. I loved it, and my only complaint is that Andrew Robinson wasn't included. Avery Brooks directs, which is pretty impressive given how much is going on here, and how much of it involves Sisko/Benny.

DS9 S06E14 One Little Ship ★★★☆☆

Written by David Weddle & Bradley Thompson. Directed by Allan Kroeker.
TX: 18 February 1998. Featuring: Scott Thompson Baker, Fritz Sperberg,
Leland Crooke.

*Honey, I Shrunk the Spaceship. Filler episode composed mainly of familiar tropes,
although the Jem'Hadar continue to fascinate.*

Again, the war can be trusted to fight itself, while the *Defiant* goes off on
a research expedition, and we take a run at that doughty science fiction
standby the-crew-is-shrunk-and-sees-things-from-a-new-perspective. The
guinea pigs are Dax, O'Brien and Bashir, who are willing to go through this
uncontrollable process based on the fact that a single unmanned probe didn't
come to any harm. But it's those left behind on the *Defiant* who hit trouble
first when a Jem'Hadar raiding party holds them at gunpoint. There's a nifty
wrinkle here – a new breed of Alpha Quadrant Jem'Hadar who regard the
Gamma Quadrant versions as old timers. And I don't think I've said enough
about make-up man Michael Westmore's design for the Jem'Hadar, which is
one of his very best. They are compelling foes and their tactical fencing with
Sisko is highly entertaining.

On board the teeny tiny runabout, things are more familiar, and not in a
good way. It takes ages to get to the 'money shot' of little human figures running
around the *Defiant*, O'Brien and Bashir cracking gags fails to convince me that
their reduction in size is a genuine problem, and the phenomenon is treated with
the usual lack of plausibility seen in every prior example of this trope going back
at least as far as the 1957 film *The Incredible Shrinking Man* as well as at least
one prior **Star Trek** episode. The visual effects are pretty nifty, though, and this
is fairly good fun if you can get past the silliness. Kira certainly seems to think
the premise is risible, judging by her near-hysterics in the teaser.

DS9 S06E15 Honor Among Thieves ★☆☆☆☆

Story by Philip Kim, teleplay by René Echevarria. Directed by Allan
Eastman. TX: 25 February 1998. Featuring: Michael Harney, Carlos
Carrasco, John Chandler, Leland Crooke, Joseph Culp, Nick Tate.

Limp and predictable reprise of Donnie Brasco *(or* **TNG***'s* Gambit*) with O'Brien
undercover, but not in a way that stretches the actor or illuminates the character.*

O'Brien is lurking in a dive bar eavesdropping on a bunch of ne'er-do-wells
who are exchanging listless banter. They are part of the Orion Syndicate and

O'Brien's job is to find out who is giving them information about Starfleet Intelligence. It seems to me that going undercover in Starfleet Intelligence would be better a more appropriate plan if the aim is to find the mole in Starfleet Intelligence, but I am not a wooden plank who lurks in the shadows and exchanges flat exposition with affable Irish fix-it men, so what do I know?

This parade of gangster movie clichés (the bad guy even has a white cat) never feels like this show, and not in the transcendent way that *Far Beyond the Stars* didn't. It just feels like a less good, less interesting show. Colm Meaney is dependable, but this never lets him reveal any new sides to O'Brien, and the guest cast are interchangeably bland. It does make the Chief's life easier that these gangsters are the kind who give makeovers, appreciate constructive criticism, talk wistfully about doing something else with their lives, and offer up the very information he's after without even being prompted.

Meanwhile, in the absence of the Chief, the station almost falls to bits. His idea of succession planning seems to be giving tips to Nog.

DS9 S06E16 Change of Heart ★★★☆☆

Written by Ronald D. Moore. Directed by David Livingston.
TX: 4 March 1998. Featuring: Todd Waring.

Slackly plotted episode where Dax and Worf potter about on a planet until one of them gets shot, and Bashir learns to play Tongo. Quite sweet if mainly uneventful.

Dax and Worf are busy getting busy when Kira despatches them to the Badlands to collect this week's MacGuffin. They are a very cute couple, and as we spend the usual requisite travel time hanging out with them, their amiable bickering and Michael Dorn's deadpanning is fairly amusing, even if this all feels a bit like padding. When they get to the jungle planet where the rendezvous is due to take place (full of unusually exotic fauna), they work together very well, which is refreshing, if not super-interesting.

The story begins, very late in the day, when they cross paths with a squadron of Jem'Hadar, and Dax receives a wound in her side, the bleeding from which can't be stopped for... reasons. Dax's gallows humour quips are devoid of wit and there's little in this situation that we haven't seen before, although I do appreciate the specificity that comes from it being this couple in particular, and Farrell and Dorn continue to completely inhabit these roles, with Farrell really selling Dax's weakened state as the blood loss continues. I can't help wondering whether this would not have been more interesting if the big strong Klingon was the one having to be left behind with pain meds and the young woman (or so she appears) had to decide between completing the mission and coming back to rescue him. Maybe it's better the way it is, and maybe that's a testament to the strength of these characters. This way round it also foreshadows things to come (to the extent that Farrell thought this would have been a better exit for Dax, and I don't disagree, although I wouldn't have wanted to lose her half a season early). When they return, Sisko has the brilliant insight that he should probably stop sending married couples off on missions together. Ya think?

In a rather silly B-plot, Quark is winning at Tongo and O'Brien of all people wants to take him on, so he recruits Bashir to assist, in a sequence that helps itself to all of the usual clichés of the rookie-beats-experts-at-their-own-game trope, and then just stops. Irishman O'Brien hopes to win Scotch whisky from Worf for some reason. Bashir reads and understands every rule of Tongo with one glance at O'Brien's PADD, which is ridiculous even for a meta-human, but still pretty funny.

DS9 S06E17 Wrongs Darker Than Death or Night ★★★☆☆

Written by Ira Steven Behr & Hans Beimler. Directed by Jonathan West. TX: 1 April 1998. Featuring: Leslie Hope, David Bowe, Wayne Grace.

Time travel with Kira's mum in Dukat's bed, which has some strong moments but doesn't amount to a whole lot.

Exotic alien duo Worf and Dax, who once were part of a fascinating alien culture, have now been reduced to a sitcom couple who squabble about social engagements. Similarly, Gul Dukat, who was once a superbly nuanced political operative, is now being rendered as a one-dimensional ranting villainous lunatic, torturing Kira just for kicks. Is it possible that we're past the DS9 peak?

Kira reacts to Dukat's taunting by generally being a dick to everyone she works with, and even Odo can't get through to her. Only the Bajoran flashback boxes can give her peace of mind – and lo! she gets to wander through her own infant past during the occupation, venturing wisdom such as 'Why are we fighting each other? We should band together and fight the common enemy.' (To which the answer is presumably 'Yes – the Bajoran People's Front!') Kira and her mum are both selected to be 'comfort women' to Gul Dukat, which does seem to match the tale he told adult Kira.

As ludicrous as this all is, once Dukat assembles his harem on board 'Terak Nor', the story does generate a certain amount of grim power. There is something weirdly, horribly invasive about the Cardassian healing Kira Meru's scar without her permission and Leslie Hope (Mrs Jack Bauer from *24*) plays the moment with real feeling.

We don't cut away from this timeline until the end, so this is all about Kira, her mum and Dukat. It's great to see Nana Visitor with some decent material again, but the whole structure of this episode makes it feel like a doodle in the margins, rather than a major piece of the bigger story.

DS9 S06E18 Inquisition ★★★★☆

Written by Bradley Thompson & David Weddle. Directed by Michael Dorn. TX: 8 April 1998. Featuring: William Sadler, Samantha Mudd, Benjamin Brown.

Bashir is accused of having committed plot holes in past episodes in a dystopian story that makes decent and sometimes compelling viewing.

Bashir is off to a sunny resort to deliver a paper at a medical conference, much to O'Brien and Odo's sneering dismay. But he doesn't get to go, because Death from AC-12 (I mean, William Sadler as Sloan from Internal Affairs) turns up and accuses the entire senior staff of being Dominion spies. This sort of paranoid, anti-corruption, who-can-you-really-trust storyline is not new to **Star Trek** – it's not even new to **Deep Space Nine** – but the mood of this series being generally bleak, and its habit of painting in shades of grey, means that it works best here, compared to sunny **TNG** or sometimes goofy **TOS**. Sloan's MO of going back over old episodes and picking holes even recalls Remmick's behaviour in *Coming of Age*, back in **TNG** Season 1. And true to form, the **DS9** version is grimmer than any of the earlier goes at this storyline. Bashir's genetic enhancement makes him the target of an investigator consumed by hatred due to a personal tragedy. The presumption of guilt not just from him but from his security guards is chilling, and Alexander Siddig rises ably to the challenges the script sets him. Back on **TNG**, Remmick was all 'Not only are you not guilty, I want to be just like you when I grow up.' Here, Bashir is beamed out by Weyoun because – it seems – everything that Sloan said was true. He was turned while in captivity and then brainwashed back into being a loyal Starfleet officer until he was needed.

The trouble is, once you start playing these games, the story trains the audience to disbelieve everything. So, it's fortunate that the script doesn't try to sustain the fake rescue team for very long, as I suspected the truth almost immediately. The revelation that virtually the whole episode had been a fantasy was harder to spot. Michael Dorn as director brings a nicely tense and claustrophobic atmosphere to proceedings, so even if this isn't revolutionary, it's a nice introduction to Section 31 and a fine examination of the eternal moral quandary – who watches the watchers?

There's barely anything here for Dax, which is a shame, given that I know what's coming at the season's end. She and Worf are excluded from the final conference.

DS9 S06E19 In the Pale Moonlight ★★★★★

Story by Peter Allan Fields, teleplay by Michael Taylor. Directed by Victor Lobl. TX: 15 April 1998. Featuring: Stephen McHattie, Howard Shangraw, Casey Biggs.

A landmark episode, a turning point in the war, a profound exercise in moral ambiguity, and deserving of its glittering reputation.

Here it is. This is the big one. When the conversation turns to best-ever **Star Trek** episodes, the same few names keep coming up. From **TOS**, it's *The City on the Edge of Forever, Amok Time, Arena, Balance of Terror, The Devil in the Dark.* From **TNG**, it's *The Best of Both Worlds, Yesterday's Enterprise, Darmok, Chain of Command, The Inner Light.* And from **DS9**, it's *The Visitor, Duet, Trials and Tribble-ations, Far Beyond the Stars* – and this one. And for some people, this is the best episode the franchise has ever produced.

It begins with a seemingly shell-shocked Sisko having to confess what sound like appalling crimes to his log. One of his wartime duties has become posting weekly casualty lists every Friday. There's always a familiar name for somebody. Bringing the neutral Romulans into the war seems like the only way out – but as Dax points out, why would they get involved when they can just sit back and watch their rivals annihilate each other? The two officers role-play the negotiations and it kind of backs Sisko into a corner. Where can he find the evidence that it would take to get the Romulans to alter their position? Answer – he probably can't, but maybe Garak can. Or one of Garak's old friends? While he makes some calls, the Dominion takes Betazed. Everyone Garak contacts is murdered within hours of the contact. So, the human and the Cardassian decide that if they can't find the evidence they need then they should deepfake some.

The master forger that Garak introduces to the station turns out to be violent and a drunk, which means Sisko has to pony up a substantial bribe to prevent Quark pressing charges and creating a record of this guy's presence on the station. (Quark thinks much more highly of Sisko after this, which is very neat.) Any doubts about the wisdom of his course are swept aside next time he posts the weekly casualty list. And to complete the deception, Sisko has to provide quantities of bio-memetic gel, a substance that the Federation closely controls.

It's the centring of Sisko that really makes this work. Unlike Picard or Janeway, the lead of this series has tended to be a fixed point around whom other characters orbit, and upon whom responsibilities are heaped, as opposed to a complex character with his own foibles and arc. Here we dig deep into his convictions, moral compass and willingness or not to compromise. It's a compelling portrait and a wonderful performance by Avery Brooks. The Romulan commander thought he'd be taller. He also uncovers Sisko's deception, proclaiming the evidence to be a fake. Days later, the same Romulan's ship is destroyed and the Dominion are seen to be to blame. This was Garak's true plan, and it might just work. Grimly, horrifyingly, Sisko thinks he can live with it. Can't he? Computer. Erase recording. Wow.

***

UNA McCORMACK, *New York Times* **bestselling science fiction author**
AKA 'The One With the Faaaaaake!', this is the episode that lit a bonfire beneath **Star Trek**. Constructed as a series of monologues to camera, in which Sisko reflects upon the events that have brought the Romulans into the Dominion War, *In the Pale Moonlight* charts the corruption of a Starfleet officer by everyone's favourite Cardassian, Elim Garak. Fast-paced and well-structured, the story shows how far even a perfect Federation citizen might go if desperate enough. The supporting cast are outstanding, but it's the central, crackling performances by Avery Brooks and Andrew Robinson as Sisko and Garak – driven despite mutual distaste into an acid alliance – that make this episode burn so very bright.

DS9 S06E20 His Way ★★☆☆☆

Written by Ira Steven Behr & Hans Beimler. Directed by Allan Kroeker.
TX: 22 April 1998. Featuring: James Darren, Debi A. Monahan, Cyndi Pas.

Come back Joe Piscopo, all is forgiven.

One of the more remarkable things about **Deep Space Nine**, as compared to its nineties stablemates, is that it manages to be simultaneously the most subtle, complex and dark of all the shows, and the goofiest. This instalment introduces us to holographic lounge singer Vic Fontaine, who is approximately 25 per cent Frank Sinatra, 25 per cent Tony Bennett and 50 per cent cheese. And Odo, of all people, is mysteriously taken with him and decides to ask him for lessons in seduction. James Darren has fun with the part but it's a weird narrative cul-de-sac for the series to pursue, especially this late in the overall arc, and especially *especially* after the huge turning point we witnessed last week.

The Odo/Kira relationship, which was once so potent, and which was then summarily dismissed during an off-camera conversation, probably can't be resuscitated at this point, and it feels a bit desperate and a bit 'oh god, how many more episodes before the end of the season?' for the writers to attempt to disinter it. Worf prefers Klingon opera, and I think I do too. Nana Visitor as 'Lola Crystal' crooning the old standard 'Fever' is quite a treat but overall this has none of the loopy energy of bonkers holosuite episodes like *Our Man Bashir* and little of the detailed character work of the best Odo/Kira stuff from Seasons 3 and 4. Changeling Odo from the twenty-fourth century includes references in his dialogue like 'Nanook of the North' and 'Romeo'. This is always going to be an issue in shows like this, but it stands out particularly when characters go wandering around in recreations of early 1960s Las Vegas.

DS9 S06E21 The Reckoning ★★★✯☆

Story by Harry M. Werksman & Gabrielle Stanton, teleplay by David Weddle & Bradley Thompson. Directed by Jesús Salvador Treviño. TX: 29 April 1998. Featuring: James Greene, Louise Fletcher.

*Slightly inelegant collision of two big **DS9** themes – Bajoran mysticism and the Dominion War. It's a bit of a pudding but some of the parts are excellent.*

The Dominion have control of Betazed and now have eyes on Vulcan, but the Romulans have forced them back from Benzar. Despite the fact that – as Dax tartly points out – there is a war on, Kira, Jake and 'The Emissary' are going digging through old Bajoran pottery instead of defending the Alpha Quadrant. Finding a slab seemingly addressed to him, Sisko takes it back to the station for analysis. This attracts the attention of Kai Winn, who wants to see his manager.

When translated, the inscription on the tablet seems to spell doom for *Deep Space Nine* and it's fun to see this news pinging off some of the other regulars, all of whom have different reactions to the very idea of religious prophecy. Meanwhile, to add verisimilitude to these prognostications, the wormhole seems to have a bad case of gas. Confoundingly unable to cope with the pressure, Sisko ends up smashing the thing and releasing colourful vapour-spirit-whatsits, of which no trace can subsequently be found. This is not uninteresting, and the verbal fencing between Bajor's twin religious leaders is engrossing, but it feels a bit like a series of scenes hunting for a story.

When that story finally turns up, it turns out to be one of those damned pah-wraiths from the extremely silly episode *The Assignment*. Now instead of Keiko O'Brien, the evil force takes over Kira – and Sisko's first thought is to evacuate the station, rather than prevent the war of the gods taking place. He sees this as payback for the prophets' help with the Dominion fleet. But it's Kira in the blue corner and, darn it, Jake in the red corner, and they stand firing pixels at each other from their tummies, in what's meant to be a dramatic twist, but which just ends up looking ridiculous.

Despite Terry Farrell, Avery Brooks and Louise Fletcher's best efforts, it's hard to take this seriously, and it never really feels as if the station is under threat. It's one of those stories in which things happen because it feels like drama, rather than unfolding naturally or because people are genuinely pursuing their goals. And I simply don't buy Kai Winn's actions at the end, prioritising Jake's life over the will of gods she professes such unwavering belief in. The cast is so good, though, and they manage to put all of this over with class, as uneven as it is. It's also our first sight of Kira and Odo as a real couple, and they're very sweet.

DS9 S06E22 Valiant ★★★☆☆

Written by Ronald D. Moore. Directed by Mike Vejar. TX: 6 May 1998. Featuring: Paul Popowich, Courtney Peldon, David Drew Gallagher, Ashley Brianne McDonogh, Scott Hamm.

One of those Jake-centred episodes that we get once every couple of years or so. In this case, it's a sort of Bugsy Malone in Space *with teens play-acting as grown-ups on their secret lost battleship.*

Quark lusting after Dax rather puts me in mind of the early years of this show in which the dynamic between the Trill and Bashir resembled something out of *On the Buses* or *Carry On Trekking*. Meanwhile, Jake is hoping to get an exclusive with the Grand Nagus and has lied to Nog in order to get it. Victims of a surprise Jem'Hadar attack, they're rescued by the second *Defiant*-class ship in Starfleet – the USS *Valiant*, with a crew of Red Squad cadets. Nog is made chief engineer on this ship of children and Jake goes moon-eyed over a moon-dwelling officer – and he's raked over the coals by the equally pint-sized senior staff for distracting her when she's on duty.

What's happening on this ship and with these officers is all fairly standard issue – we have to turn off the safeties to fix the warp core, we're all super-dedicated to the mission, the captain is working too hard and popping pills. It's supposed to be given a bit of extra spin because the crew are all inexperienced cadets given field promotions. Trouble is, they're being played by inexperienced actors, and so the whole thing feels a little more 'school play' than is ideal. But as they gear up for their suicide mission, the tension builds quite nicely and it's cool to see the Federation and the war from another perspective. Ultimately, though, the loss of the *Valiant* is too inevitable to be shocking and the improbable survival of Jake and Nog prevents it from having much in the way of tragic power.

DS9 S06E23 Profit and Lace ★☆☆☆☆

Written by Ira Steven Behr & Hans Beimler. Directed by Siddig El Fadil. TX: 13 May 1998. Featuring: Henry Gibson, Cecily Adams, Chase Masterson, Wallace Shawn.

That Ferengi version of Tootsie *I didn't know I wanted. And I really didn't want it.*

The title is a giveaway. This is going to be a comedy Quark episode, probably involving Brunt, Moogie and – if his schedule permits – Wallace Shawn. There are worse ways to spend an hour, but this is also a pond that I think might have been overfished. We start with a libidinous Quark sleazing over his waitstaff, in another scene that feels like it's dated very badly. And you ain't seen nothing yet in that regard…

Luckily, Vizzini's diary could accommodate this filming, so we do get the Grand Nagus – as a surprising women's libber allowing women on Ferenginar to wear clothes. This has led to a financial meltdown and now it's up to Quark and chums to retake the planet. I can't tell you how little I am invested in this storyline, and when Quark is forced to dress up as a female to take his mother's place, it's all I can do to keep watching. Even Henry Gibson can't save this one. Poor Alexander Siddig had to direct in what I can only assume was the result of a very foolish wager on his behalf.

DS9 S06E24 Time's Orphan ★★★☆☆

Story by Joe Menosky, teleplay by David Weddle & Bradley Thompson. Directed by Allan Kroeker. TX: 20 May 1998. Featuring: Rosalind Chao, Hana Hatae, Michelle Krusiec.

Latest in a long line of family/relationship/time-travel stories and it feels a little bit rote and repetitive, although Colm Meaney and guest star Michelle Krusiec do fine work.

Hey, everyone, Keiko exists – and so does Molly, who's looking forward to going on a space picnic. The title of this one, plus the opening shots, kind of gives the premise away: some subset of Miles, Keiko, Molly and Kirayoshi will fall into a time hole and a moral dilemma will ensue. This kind of thing can work – see *Children of Time* for a wonderful example – but especially against the background of the Dominion War, it feels off the peg. And the script wastes no time in dropping Molly (of course) into a puddle of nineties computer graphics goo even before the opening titles.

Sending a strong signal that this is going to be a the-gang-works-together-to-solve-a-science-problem story rather than an O'Brien-must-suffer episode, the parents of the missing child are all business, with only the Chief's frustrated cry of 'bollocks' betraying any emotion at all. Even Keiko takes hours to show any worry or concern. When the now teenage and feral Molly is plucked back out of the temporal ooze, it is a strong moment, but despite what everyone says as they tend to her medical needs, I can't help feeling that a reset button is in Girl Tarzan's future.

It's greatly to the credit of this show that we take our time rehabilitating her (when we aren't cutting away to Worf playing *Mr Mom* with Yoshi) but the price we pay for that is that, again, Molly's parents seem perfectly content with losing their child as long as they can imagine that she might be happy where she is. No wonder that the episode quickly finds a way to have its tragic sacrifice and eat its status quo too.

DS9 S06E25 The Sound of Her Voice ★★★★☆

Story by Pam Pietroforte, teleplay by Ronald D. Moore. Directed by Winrich Kolbe. TX: 10 June 1998. Featuring: Debra Wilson, Penny Johnson.

A doomed rescue mission shines a strong light on some of our regulars. Quark and Odo's B-story is barely C-grade, though.

With all the time spent recently on Pah-wraith possession, Ferengi cross-dressing, school plays, and toppling through time holes, you might have been forgiven for forgetting that the Alpha Quadrant is riven by war and that *Deep Space Nine* is a station of major strategic importance. The *Defiant* picks up a distress call from a stranded Starfleet officer, but they're six days away. This is the **DS9** MO of conversations-on-the-journey taken to its logical conclusion, as the whole episode is just Sisko and crew trying to reach poor doomed Lisa Cusack in time (when Quark and Odo aren't indulging in would-be amusing 'hijinks', of course).

Weirdly, I have clear memories of a chilling episode of Steven Moffat's *Press Gang*, based on a similar premise. Spike is buried in a building collapse, but although he can't move, he is able to talk to a girl similarly buried. She sounds close, so he's optimistic then when he's saved, she will be okay too. But horribly, it turns out that her voice was making its way to him through a long pipe and she is quite out of reach of the rescue team. 'It's a pity you're late, guys. You missed one hell of a nice girl,' he tells the paramedics, having heard her expire. (Season two, episode two, 'The Rest of My Life', first aired 22 March 1990.)

Lisa's chipper demeanour again signals that she's not long for this world, but her other purpose is to bounce off our regulars and give each of them a chance to explore their own attitudes to life, love, the war and duty. It's not pulse-pounding excitement but it's absorbing character stuff of the kind that only this show can do. When they arrive at the planet, the latest in a long line of exotic radiations makes beaming impossible, so a shuttlepod is called for. The crash site is impressively rendered but at first, there's no sign of cheerful Lisa. Until there is – a long-dead skeleton. They're three years late and the exotic radiation messed with time – a detail which oddly didn't come to light during any of their lengthy chats. They bury her on the station, apparently without contacting any of her family. An odd episode, tonally very uncertain, but with strong material especially for Bashir, so often under-served on this show.

We're heading to the end of the season, so Jake and Kasidy show up, although there's no sign of the other key supporting cast members: Garak, Martok, Weyoun, Dukat, Winn, Nog or Rom.

DS9 S06E26 Tears of the Prophets ★★★☆☆

Written by Ira Steven Behr & Hans Beimler. Directed by Allan Kroeker. TX: 17 June 1998. Featuring: David Birney, Casey Biggs, Barry Jenner, James Darren.

'That's different. The Founders are gods.'

A Bajoran festival of thanks has taken place despite the war and Odo is getting a tongue-lashing from Kira because he arrested a Vedek, like a ninny. Sisko is getting a commendation (the 'Christopher Pike Medal of Honor'). It all feels positively valedictory, but the war is far from over, and Sisko has been chosen to lead an offensive (finally), and mount an attack on the Dominion shipyards and munitions factories.

Definitely making this feel like a party is the list of names in the opening credits. Even Vic Fontaine is in this one. And Dax keeps talking happily about the future, although I've been aware of what's coming for some time (without knowing the details). But at the top of the episode it's Sisko that Dukat has in his sights and the Wormhole Aliens aka the Prophets. And those same Prophets sound like they are warning the Captain not to leave *Deep Space Nine*, on the eve of the planned attack.

That might have been good advice as Dukat manages to summon a Pah-wraith from an old Bajoran gewgaw and when Dax prays to the Prophets on the station, Dukat appears and cuts her down with a blast of orange pixels. It's virtually a Tasha Yar end to a great character. It adds to the apocalyptic nature of the episode, but it doesn't have any meaning or poetry to it. I'll talk more about Terry Farrell's exit in my season round-up. More notable for this episode is the fact that Dukat's actions have sealed the wormhole.

Some nifty space battles ensue with the Klingon attack wing crippled by Jem'Hadar suicide runs, while the Cardassians race to get their fancy new defence grid up and running. It doesn't survive for long either. The Federation/Klingon/Romulan victory is thus short-lived and sour. The Dominion is crippled, cut off from home and on the run. But Bajor is cut off from the Prophets (as is Sisko) and Jadzia Dax is dead.

There's something vaguely synthetic about this episode. It feels bolted together, rather than emerging organically from the story threads that were already present. The attack on Cardassia, the easily destroyed weapons platform, the sudden return of Dukat, the seeming end of the wormhole, and the death of Dax all feel jarring and ill-fitting. Maybe that reflects the fact that deaths (especially in war) do come unexpectedly, but that fact alone doesn't make this a television masterpiece. There's lots of good stuff here, but it's a shame that more care wasn't taken over the fit and finish.

DS9 Season 6 wrap-up

- We end another season with a loss. Last year ended with losing the station. This year we lose the wormhole and Jadzia. She does at least get a goodbye with Worf, which is suitably heartbreaking. And Sisko leaves, taking his baseball.
- Mid-run cast changes we've come to expect. Season 3 of **TNG** saw the return of Dr Crusher, and Wesley was phased out during Season 5. **Deep Space Nine** added Worf to its regular cast in Season 4, and **Voyager** also swapped Kes for Seven in its fourth year. But a change in the final season is unhelpful, removing a cast member with years of history and introducing a new one who will barely have time to establish themselves.
- And it does seem as if letting Terry Farrell leave was a goof. Not as big a goof as the similar situation which J. Michael Straczynski found himself in with the final year of *Babylon 5*, as here there was actually time to write her out,

whereas Claudia Christian just wasn't there at the start of the final season, despite the enormity of what she'd gone through in the previous episode.

- Why did she leave? Farrell was keen to accept the offer to star opposite Ted Danson on *Becker* and was convinced that a deal could be struck that would allow her to appear on both shows – probably by not appearing on every episode of **Deep Space Nine**'s final season. **Deep Space Nine**'s producers seemingly were incensed that anyone on their show would want to appear on anyone else's show ever and insisted that Farrell was either in or she was out – her standard six-year contract having come to an end.

- Turning to other matters, Season 6 was surprisingly bumpy. After a stellar run of episodes at the end of last year and the start of this one, during which I thought this was a show that could do no wrong, it suddenly turned into a very inconsistent viewing experience. Almost as soon as the gang was back on the station, it seemed as if a duff episode was every bit as likely as a classic for the ages. *The Magnificent Ferengi* aired next to *Waltz*. *In the Pale Moonlight* was followed by *His Way*. And the less said about *Profit and Lace* the better. Maybe Robert Hewitt Wolfe, who left at the end of Season 5, was the secret sauce that really made the show sing.

- However, this was still the year that gave us *Rocks and Shoals*, *Inquisition* and the amazing *Far Beyond the Stars*, and any show that can give us that and *In the Pale Moonlight* in the same season must be doing something right.

Deep Space Nine
Season 7

Starring: Avery Brooks, René Auberjonois, Nicole de Boer, Michael Dorn, Cirroc Lofton, Colm Meaney, Nana Visitor, Alexander Siddig, Armin Shimerman. Featuring: Casey Biggs, Jeffrey Combs, James Darren, Aron Eisenberg, Max Grodénchik, J.G. Hertzler, Barry Jenner, Salome Jens, Andrew J. Robinson. Executive producers: Rick Berman, Ira Steven Behr. Creative consultant: Michael Piller. Co-producers: J.P. Farrell, Terri Potts. Co-supervising producers: Steve Oster, René Echevarria. Supervising producers: Hans Beimler, Peter Lauritson. Co-executive producer: Ronald D. Moore. Executive story editors: David Thompson & Bradley Weddle.

DS9 S07E01 Image in the Sand ★★★★☆

Written by Ira Steven Behr & Hans Beimler. Directed by Les Landau.
TX: 30 September 1998. Featuring: Brock Peters, Megan Cole, Deborah Lacey.

Melancholy episode, which resets the status quo, while barely hinting at future directions for the final season.

In some ways, it's convenient that it was Terry Farrell who quit. Probably only Odo and Worf were genuinely irreplaceable. Losing Sisko would have been tough, but Kira could have stepped up to run the station; we could have got a new doctor; Rom could have taken over the bar; O'Brien and Kira we could have worked around. Obviously, **Deep Space Nine** works without Worf, but his connection back to 1987 is difficult to replace. And having a Changeling on the station was clearly needed for the final stages of the Dominion War to have personal as well as Galactic stakes.

But the nifty thing about Dax is that, just as Curzon gave way to Jadzia, so Jadzia can give way to Ezri, and we can have a whole new angle on this interesting bit of science fiction biology. It's just a shame that it curtails the Worf/Jadzia relationship so decisively. Nicole de Boer doesn't appear until the episode's end (which seems tactful) so we'll discuss her next time.

In the inter-season gap, various things have changed. Major Kira is now Colonel Kira, and she has a new all-business hairdo. She's in charge of the station in Sisko's continuing absence (and she calls Admiral Ross 'Bill' now). The invasion of Cardassia has ground to a halt (according to Worf, who is drowning his sorrows in Vic Fontaine songs). Sisko is back on Earth, seeing visions of a woman's face peeking out of some sand dunes, and she turns out to be a figure from his dad's past.

It's a slow burn, this episode, rather reminiscent of TNG's excellent *Family*, all people talking miserably in rooms, rather than the epic space battles we were treated to at the end of the last season. It's almost a relief when a creepy guy in a red hood slices Sisko's belly open. But the rich characters make a check-in episode like this worthwhile, even if it doesn't start us off with a bang.

DS9 S07E02 Shadows and Symbols ★★★★☆

Written by Ira Steven Behr & Hans Beimler. Directed by Allan Kroeker.
TX: 7 October 1998. Featuring: Brock Peters, Megan Cole, Deborah Lacey.

Who are you and what have you done with Jadzia?

There's no 'Part II' caption, but this continues nearly seamlessly from where *Image in the Sand* left off, and here's where we meet Ezri for the first time, learn her backstory, and start deciding whether we like her or not. Well, she's no Terry Farrell, but the producers have clearly decided to take the character in a very different direction. If Jadzia was an old head on young shoulders, Ezri is a blur of personalities, still coming to terms with fundamental facts about her biology, with none of the support that was offered to her predecessors. She turns to Sisko for guidance, and you can see immediately how much it helps him to have someone to help in turn, so, they're off to seek the Wizard. I'm less impressed when she starts barfing on the runabout. It would be a shame to replace one of the most capable, experienced members of the team with a little girl character who's nervous about everything and space in particular.

Quark volunteers to join Worf's mission to get Jadzia into Sto'Vo'Kor. I confess I don't entirely understand how this works – how does Worf risking his life guarantee someone else's place in the afterlife? And – as mentioned by other characters – is Klingon Valhalla really going to be Jadzia's idea of a good time? Of more interest to me is Kira negotiating to get those Romulan weapons off Bajor's moon, even if it means setting up a blockade.

Dax is right, Sisko is getting stranger. And in a quite brilliant flourish, his story is partly told through the eyes of his 1950s alter ego Benny Russell. This is very fine stuff, expertly melding mysticism, character drama, science fiction adventure and meta fiction in a very complex way – and the crosscutting between this and Kira's brinkmanship adds tension to both strands. Only the Klingon story thread is a let-down, and even that has a strong ending. However, it can't be denied that the chief function of this episode is to undo much of the exciting developments from the end of last year, which gives me a queasy feeling. Are we going to start yo-yo-ing back and forth instead of forging on to new situations? Meanwhile: 'Worf, we have to talk.' Er, yes.

DS9 S07E03 Afterimage ★★★☆☆

Written by René Echevarria. Directed by Les Landau. TX: 14 October 1998.

Low-key relationship-y episode centred on Ezri Dax, cementing her position on the station and resetting some character dynamics.

Weird times for Ensign Ezri Dax, who walks around the station, and even examines the Bajoran wormhole doom box where Jadzia met her end, and has clear memories of all these places despite never having been there before. As Kira says, it's a lot to get used to. She also claims she isn't staying on the station. We'll see about that. When Worf appears over her shoulder at Quark's, the Ferengi comments drily, 'I bet the two of you have a lot to talk about,' which is pretty soggy scriptwriting, as that's almost exactly what Ezri said right to his face last episode. The Klingon's initial fury at seeing Ezri is a powerful evocation of grief but risks making the proud Klingon seem petulant and immature.

Garak is being kept far too busy by Starfleet Intelligence to make silly costumes for O'Brien and Bashir. He's also more tetchy than usual and eventually he suffers from a claustrophobic attack and – lo! – Ezri Dax is a counsellor-in-training and Sisko thinks she might be just what Garak needs. I still struggle to connect Nicole de Boer's lisping lost-little-girl performance to the assured swagger that Terry Farrell brought to Jadzia. She's appealing enough as a performer, but definitely a downgrade in terms of capability and, I fear, story possibilities. Her attempt to counsel Garak out of his claustrophobia by sharing stories about her space-sickness at first only ends up with Garak feeling claustrophobic and her feeling space-sick.

Of all people, it's Julian Bashir who forms the strongest bond with the newly promoted Lieutenant Ezri Dax, who – somewhat inevitably – does end up as station counsellor. And that's the job of this episode, which it does smoothly but rather unsurprisingly.

DS9 S07E04 Take Me Out to the Holosuite ★★★☆☆

Written by Ronald D. Moore. Directed by Chip Chalmers.
TX: 21 October 1998. Featuring: Gregory Wagrowski, Chase Masterson,
Penny Johnson.

Great vehicle for Avery Brooks and Sisko even if the premise is both thin and somewhat ridiculous.

Sisko greets the visiting Vulcan coldly. After waving their medals at each other, the rivals decide to settle their differences via a Holographic baseball game. I don't share Ron Moore's enthusiasm for this most American of sports, but I do like Sisko cutting corners, treating rules as guidelines and acting from the gut (just as much as I like seeing Picard following the book, finding loopholes instead of ignoring inconvenient statutes and articulating detailed reasons for his actions). It possibly hasn't occurred to the grinning station commander as he beams at his senior staff that there isn't one American human among them, but the Irishman, Anglo-Indian, Bajoran, Klingon, Trill and Ferengi agree to give it a try and begin studying up. It's complex stuff, full of confusing and unfamiliar terminology. Thank goodness they aren't playing cricket.

It's nice seeing Ezri included as part of the crew without issue. Sure, it's quick, but there are only so many episodes left, and we spent much of the last two (and almost all of the last one) dealing with the fact that she was here and Jadzia wasn't. If she's going to be an outsider for much longer, it's going to get repetitive. But the antics of watching the mismatched crew struggle to achieve any kind of competence, together with rum-tee-tum music from David Bell to tell us how amusing it all is, does test my patience over this kind of length. I know sports movies and I know how they go. This one is fine, and it's nice to see our characters as a gang of friends, but it's not really what I'm here for.

After one brief establishing shot, Sisko elects to have the computer delete the holographic (and expensive) spectators for most of the rest of the match.

DS9 S07E05 Chrysalis ★★☆☆☆

Written by René Echevarria. Directed by Jonathan West. TX: 28 October 1998.
Featuring: Tim Ransom, Faith C. Salie, Hilary Shepard Turner,
Michael Keenan.

Harpo speaks! Or lovesick Bashir re-enacts Awakenings *in this by-the-numbers soapy medical melodrama.*

In something of a regressive move, once socially awkward Dr Julian Bashir, who found it hard to make friends, who developed into a much more confident, likeable self-aware character, begins this show acting awkwardly in social situations and finding it hard to make friends. The bad-tempered admiral who summons him to sickbay at 3:00 am turns out to be one of the four McMurphys who told Starfleet to surrender to the Dominion last year. Now they want Bashir's help to treat silent Sarina, who is nearly catatonic. Sisko, for whom rules are very often little more than vague suggestions, gives him a slightly hypocritical tongue-lashing about how many rules his friends have broken.

Bashir's impossible-seeming medical breakthrough is accomplished without much fuss, and the delight that the other three mutants take in being reunited with their lost comrade is suitably heart-warming (although the barbershop segment does go on a bit – Miles, I sympathise). But we spend altogether too long with Sarina just enjoying her new life and nothing else very interesting happening – good or bad. And then, the twist is that Bashir and Sarina fall for each other, which means splitting up the gang of odd-balls so they can live together unethically ever after. Even on this All Consequences All The Time show, I find it hard to believe that Bashir and Sarina will be standing side by side come the end of the Dominion War after another twenty or so episodes. So, I still think the dead hand of the reset button will visit itself upon this story very shortly (regardless of the good doctor's assertion that he isn't going to give up on her, ever).

And, lo, it swiftly comes to pass, leaving me unmoved, a little bored, and feeling that the potential of these four returning characters has been somewhat squandered. I'm just pleased that Sarina got to leave the station still able to communicate, once free of Bashir's overwhelming charisma.

DS9 S07E06 Treachery, Faith, and the Great River ★★★★☆

Story by Philip Kim, teleplay by David Weddle & Bradley Thompson. Directed by Steve Posey. TX: 4 November 1998.

Tense cold-war-esque drama, enmeshed in the details of this intricate world. Oh, and Nog is trying to buy a whoosit from some guy.

Turns out that there are some advantages to having a Changeling as a boyfriend. The scene of Odo rubbing Kira's back makes me think things about their sex life that I can't unthink. Yikes. He's next summoned to meet a high-ranking Cardassian who turns out to be a defecting Weyoun. Naturally, I don't trust this story for a second, and equally naturally neither does Weyoun. Love may have softened him (if you see what I mean) but it hasn't stopped him from being cautious.

You'll remember that the Vorta are a clone race, thus here the versatile Jeffrey Combs plays two Weyouns (six and seven – five died in a transporter accident). And now, Damar and Seven are faced with a terrible decision. Allow Six to defect and tell the Federation everything he knows, or destroy the runabout with him and Odo on it and murder what to the Vorta is a god.

Salome Jens returns as TFC and Seven has to start hastily covering his tracks. But TFC is also suffering from a debilitating and fatal pox, which manifests itself as dry cracks across her face and hands. This malady is affecting the whole of the Great Link – every Changeling except Odo. Six's vision is for Odo to assume the leadership of the Dominion when he becomes the last surviving Changeling. This is marvellous stuff: complex, specific, engaging and detailed, and played by two magnificent actors.

In a tedious Nog/O'Brien subplot, the Ferengi teaches the Chief the subtle art of queue-jumping and dealmaking. I can't tell you how much I didn't want this stupid B-plot to be part of this otherwise excellent episode, although the metaphor of the Great River is neat enough.

DS9 S07E07 Once More Unto the Breach ★★★☆☆

Written by Ronald D. Moore. Directed by Allan Kroeker.
TX: 11 November 1998. Featuring: John Colicos, Neil C. Vipond,
Nancy Youngblut, Blake Lindsley.

More Klingon posturing, which even the excellent John Colicos can't make me care too much about.

Oddly, the presence of a real war on their doorstep has not dimmed O'Brien and Bashir's enthusiasm for re-enacting famous battles – although Worf seems to think that Davy Crockett is a legendary figure who may not have existed. And this is a Worf episode, alongside a returning John Colicos as fellow Klingon Kor, who frets that there's no place in this violent universe for a tired old warrior. Hoping to die with honour, he wants a posting on the front line. Oddly, General Martok has no interest in sending a bewildered old captain out on one of his ships to pilot it to its destruction, and so he tells Worf to get lost.

This is a combination of two things I tend not to like. Lots of Klingon honour rituals, and lots of telling stories about places we've never been to and people we've never met. Regardless of the General's wishes, Worf finds a ship for the old man, who is catching up with Dax, in whom he brings out some of the old Jadzia swagger. Quite why this has to be Martok's ship isn't at all clear – to me or to Martok's fussy aide-de-camp.

In the heat of the battle, Kor rapidly gets confused, imagining that he is fighting the Federation, and Worf comes to regret putting him in that position. Even Martok feels sorry for him. Naturally, he comes good in the end, and he has the opportunity to blow himself up for a purpose, instead of because he's forgotten which button is which. This whole episode felt like it was running on rails, despite the best efforts of the cast – guest, recurring and regular.

Kira tries out her therapy style on Dax. I like it. I think it would work for me.

DS9 S07E08 The Siege of AR-558 ★★★★☆

Written by Ira Steven Behr & Hans Beimler. Directed by Winrich Kolbe. TX: 18 November 1998. Featuring: Raymond Cruz, Annette Helde, Patrick Kilpatrick, Bill Mumy.

Danger Will Robinson! Actually, the CVs of the guest stars is the least interesting thing about this tense and atmospheric episode, with Quark's point of view an unexpected highlight.

God help me, I'm even getting to enjoy Vic Fontaine's appearances. That doesn't extend to Rom's mangling of old standards, and for a moment there, when Vic was talking about hiring a comic, I feared Joe Piscopo was going to make a return appearance. Speaking of Ferengi, Quark is on board the *Defiant*, having been sent on a fact-finding mission to the front lines by Grand Nagus Zek.

Sisko beams down at the head of the away team with supplies for some pretty desperate and demoralised Federation troops, defending a captured Dominion communications array. Even by the usual gloomy standards of this show, the tales of the remaining soldiers are remarkably grim, but never melodramatic. Of particular note is Bill Mumy as engineer Kellin. A veteran of both *Lost in Space* and *Babylon 5*, he jumped at the chance to do a part with no prosthetic make-up, having suffered for years as Minbari ambassador Lennier.

I don't really buy Quark's reason for being there, but his take on humans is always fascinating, and Nog has his own perspective as a Starfleet officer. Sisko takes charge of what remains of the battalion, but they're quickly outwitted by the Jem'Hadar, who use holograms to pinpoint the enemy position without risking their own lives. Behr and Beimler's typically tough script piles on the suspense and sacrifice, but keeps the focus where it should be: on the attitudes, choices, fears and beliefs of the characters, not on meaningless action and *Boy's Own* heroics. And yes, sure, this is something of a collection of doughty war-is-hell clichés but they're clichés because they work, and they feel fresh when reflected through these very specific and familiar characters.

The exception is New Formula Dax, who still isn't clicking. Every time she's on-screen, she simply repeats the same lines about not being Jadzia (or Curzon or Tobin). Let's find out who Ezri is – and soon because there aren't all that many episodes left. Her momentary qualm about using the enemy's weapons against them is something, but I need more.

DS9 S07E09 Covenant ★★★☆☆

Written by René Echevarria. Directed by John Kretchmer.
TX: 25 November 1998. Featuring: Jason Leland Adams,
Maureen Flannigan, Norman Parker.

Dukat reimagined as cult leader re-enacts Jonestown on Empok Nor with Kira in attendance. Bonkers, but compelling while it's on.

Life on board *DS9* seems rather relaxed considering the conflict raging nearby. So relaxed that an old friend of Kira's has come to call, but the tchotchke he's brought her as a gift turns out to be a transponder, which takes her to Empok Nor, at the behest of the Pah-wraith sect led by none other than Gul Dukat, whose descent into demented one-note villainy continues unabated, although Marc Alaimo's class still shines through. Kira's old teacher attempts to prove that their death cult is benign, which is arguably more interesting than tying her to the railway tracks, but makes the early going a little light on drama, except for some insults hurled at the Cardassian.

Maddeningly, when she manages to finagle a gun and point it at Dukat, his disciples form a Bajoran shield in front of him – Dukat odiously whispering, 'Now do you see how much they love me,' as she lies defeated on the floor. In rather a soapy turn, when a Bajoran acolyte gives birth, the infant looks Cardassian, which Dukat explains away as a Pah-wraith miracle. Apparently, there's no ultrasound in the twenty-fourth century.

More miracles follow as Dukat stages an airlock malfunction and the mother almost asphyxiates – but Kira gets to her just in time. It's a curious treatment of religion. Most stories along these lines present the charismatic cult leader as making up stories to tell his followers in order to build his personal power, often at the expense of those same followers. So it is here, but the difference is that we know the Pah-wraiths are real, and so we know that at least some of what Dukat claims is true. Moreover, there are a lot of moving parts here and it strains credulity slightly that Dukat, who must have suspected that the child was his, would wait until the birth was about to occur before summoning Kira to watch what happened next. Anyway, Dukat starts doling out the Cardassian Kool-aid, but he does at least arrange for Kira to go home first. And her method to unmask his villainy is satisfyingly clever.

DS9 S07E10 It's Only a Paper Moon ★★★★☆

Story by David Alan Mack & John J. Ordover, teleplay by Ronald D. Moore. Directed by Anson Williams. TX: 30 December 1998. Featuring: Chase Masterson.

Remember when I thought Nog enlisting in Starfleet was just a gag? Look at him now.

I should have known better. This series isn't just unwilling to hit the reset button, it's practically addicted to consequences. So, Nog losing a leg and needing a prosthetic wasn't just a gimmick to raise the stakes in a thrilling action sequence. It's a real and painful reality for a fully rounded character who is struggling to adjust not just to his new medical circumstances but how friends, colleagues, shipmates, professionals and holographic entertainers treat him. Callous doctors tell him that the pain is just in his head – but of course, all pain is just in the head.

And speaking of things that were once just a gimmick, Vic Fontaine has a suite in the virtual hotel he entertains at – which presumably means that this holosuite is now given over to running this program full-time. Nog moves in with him and they sit watching Jack Palance as *Shane* on a 1960s TV.

Just as this story in another medium might have involved Nog digging a ditch or bussing tables in a restaurant to learn the value of a hard day's graft, here Nog is put to work doing Vic's books using a pencil and a ledger. But Ezri, not unreasonably, is concerned that hiding out in a pretend world might not be in Nog's continuing best interests. My only concern with this heartfelt and charming episode is that – once again – I could have sworn that there was a war on, and too many episodes with no science fiction adventures, real jeopardy or proper high stakes will make me itchy. This is a series-best performance from Aron Eisenberg too.

DS9 S07E11 Prodigal Daughter ★☆☆☆☆

Written by David Weddle & Bradley Thompson. Directed by Victor Lobl. TX: 6 January 1999. Featuring: Clayton Landey, John Paragon, Kevin Rahm, Mikael Salazar, Leigh Taylor-Young.

Irrelevant side quest which asks me to get deeply invested in thinly drawn and unlikeable characters I've never met before. I decline.

I wasn't a huge fan of *Honor Among Thieves*, so I've no particular interest in Chief O'Brien tying up any loose ends left from it. Nor am I fascinated by supplies of Gagh ordered by Jadzia and now being Ezri's problem to dispose of (Worf is absent, one assumes dealing with the Son'a and the Ba'ku in the Briar Patch). Having Ezri meet up with her family, who keep talking about the person she used to be, and who don't want to be psychoanalysed by her, doesn't help bring her into focus – given that her problem as a character is that she keeps talking about who she used to be and is a fairly useless counsellor. The rest of the episode largely rehashes the earlier Orion Syndicate story, so it was all I could do to keep watching this one.

DS9 S07E12 The Emperor's New Cloak ★☆☆☆☆

Written by Ira Steven Behr & Hans Beimler. Directed by LeVar Burton.
TX: 3 February 1999. Featuring: Wallace Shawn, Chase Masterson.

Ponderous comedy episode, which squanders its few promising ideas and contradicts previous stories.

Grand Nagus Zek is trapped in the Mirror Universe and it falls to Rom and Quark to mount a rescue (when Quark isn't praying for some misfortune to befall Bashir before he can take his relationship with Ezri to the next level). Weirdly, it's an un-joined Ezri Tigan who is despatched to bring Quark this news. What's the price for the Nagus's freedom? Cloaking technology, which the Alliance seems to have forgotten it once possessed. Both Ferengi shenanigans and the Mirror Universe seem to me like overfished ponds at this stage, and I've no particular interest in seeing what happens if they get mashed together. It's nice for Nicole de Boer that she gets to wear the Lilac Eyeshadow of Ultimate Evil at least once during her year on the show, but the rest of this is repetitive, sophomoric and dull. The cloaking device is invisible. Lol.

DS9 S07E13 Field of Fire ★★★☆☆

Written by Robert Hewitt Wolfe. Directed by Tony Dow.
TX: 10 February 1999. Featuring: Art Chudabala, Leigh McCloskey,
Marty Rackham.

Plodding whodunnit requiring Ezri to manifest a previous host and try to think like a killer, but Joran is no Hannibal Lecter.

Starfleet's latest hotshot flying ace is the toast of Quark's, and flirting with Dax. 'I wish they could have been here to see this,' he announces, holding a photo of his old Academy buddies, while the neon sign flickers into life above his head reading 'I am about to die'. And lo, he is found shot to death in his quarters next morning. Odo is swiftly on the case, armed with his knowledge of Raymond Chandler novels, but Dax feels responsible, as the last person to see him alive. Her guilt-ridden dreams, in which the dead pilot blames her for his death, and she looks down and sees literal blood on her hands, are all pretty clichéd stuff, alas, shot in familiar this-is-a-dream ways. We learned in *Equilibrium* that a previous Dax was a murderer and Ezri now decides that it's only by imaging talking to him that she will understand how a killer thinks. I'm still struggling to get to know Nicole de Boer's take on Dax, and pairing her with this very standard-issue TV bad guy doesn't do much to bring the character into focus. The killer's transporter-rifle is pretty cool, if a bit over-engineered. And Worf is back.

DS9 S07E14 Chimera ★★★★☆

Written by René Echevarria. Directed by Steve Posey. TX: 17 February 1999. Featuring: Garman Hertzler.

Moving exploration of shapeshifters in a world of solids, with the best Kira/Odo material we've had in ages.

Returning to the station in a runabout, Odo and O'Brien encounter another Changeling – one of the hundred sent out to gather information. While not one of the Founders, the new arrival has a rather sour attitude towards humanoids, and his conversations with Odo are fascinating. But it's the way his feelings about solids and shapeshifters reflects off Kira and Odo that is the heart of this show. Nana Visitor and René Auberjonois both do superb work and the climax, in which Odo seemingly leaves with the new arrival, is stunning. Weirdly, the new Changeling is played by General Martok actor J.G. Hertzler, under a pseudonym.

DS9 S07E15 Badda-Bing Badda-Bang ★★★★☆

Written by Ira Steven Behr & Hans Beimler. Directed by Mike Vejar. TX: 24 February 1999. Featuring: Marc Lawrence, Mike Starr, Robert Miano, Bobby Reilly.

Ocean's 11 *reimagined in the twenty-fourth century by way of a synthetic 1961. Blitheringly stupid both in conception and on its own terms. I enjoyed myself enormously.*

I've observed already that **DS9** staked out its ground as dealing with complex characters in richly detailed, highly realistic situations, whereas over on **Voyager** you could expect something wilder, sillier and much broader. But **DS9** also has its fair share of Ferengi-falling-over episodes and, of course, Vic Fontaine. The difference is that when **Voyager** goes for those ludicrous big swings, it plays them with a straight face. But **DS9** plays its comedy episodes winking at the audience.

This time we're on the holosuite and that means something's going wrong with it, natch. And these problems can't be solved by unplugging it and plugging it back in again, natch natch. Instead, our flesh-and-blood characters have to play along with the story and do their debugging that way. In this case, mobsters have taken over Vic Fontaine's casino and made it unnecessarily vulgar, which forces O'Brien and Bashir into immediate action.

Given that this intrusion was a part of the way the program was designed, what follows is essentially a televised escape room and so it should be very hard to get seriously invested. Once more, hologram characters can't be backed up (even though in this same episode, O'Brien and Bashir talk about moving Vic into their Alamo program where he'd presumably be safe from anything that happened in Vegas) so they work their way through the puzzle designed by 'Felix' with their usual easy camaraderie.

That this works at all is a huge testament to the strength of the cast, how careful the script is to keep us from asking too many tricky questions, and how much fun this all is. We don't even bother with that old standby 'the safety protocols are off'. It's assumed that needing to restore Vic's is high-stakes enough. Elsewhere, Sisko makes some excellent points about the dangers of fantasy depictions of the past, but his scene with Kasidy feels like a remnant of an earlier draft, written in a very different style from the freewheeling

ROB LLOYD, actor, improviser and comedian

DS9 is known for its groundbreaking multiple season narrative arcs, powerful character explorations and dark, grim, sometimes bleak storylines. So... what's my go-to episode of my favourite of the **Star Trek** franchise? *Badda-Bing Badda-Bang*. This exciting, playful tribute to good-old heist movies is nestled comfortably in the middle of **DS9**'s final season and is a welcome palette cleanser from all the war, space battles, death and intergalactic politics. Head Writer Ira Steven Behr along with Hans Beimler have a blast throwing every homage and expected plot point into this lighter-than-air episode. There is simply nothing more thrilling or downright cool than seeing the entire **DS9** crew in full 1950s threads proudly strutting down the promenade in slow motion. Utterly joyous.

nonsense of the remaining forty-one minutes. Once again, a regular crops up playing a different role under a barely disguised name ('Bobby Reilly' is Robert O'Reilly, aka Gowron).

DS9 S07E16 Inter Arma Enim Silent Leges ★★★★☆

Written by Ronald D. Moore. Directed by David Livingston.
TX: 3 March 1999. Featuring: Adrienne Barbeau, John Fleck, William Sadler.

Gorgeous layering of deceptions, which recalls The Prisoner *(or possibly Kafka's* The Trial*) in its baffling complexity, but which entertains throughout.*

Section 31 has an assignment for Dr Bashir, and their theatrical flair extends to William Sadler's Sloan sitting with steepled fingers in his bedroom for what might have been hours until he stirs and turns on the lights. Aligning themselves with Garak's cynical outlook, they want the Doctor to use an upcoming conference as an opportunity to assess the Romulans, likely to be among the fittest of the victors when the Dominion War concludes. Sisko wants Bashir to go along with the plan, but for the purposes of finding out more about Section 31, which is a delightful set of wheels-within-wheels.

Once the conference is underway, Bashir's best guess is that Sloan wants him to provide a diagnosis as cover for the assassination of a sabre-rattling Romulan, but it's Starfleet's Admiral Ross who ends up in sickbay – and Bashir who ends up drugged and tortured by the Romulans, along with Sloan, whom the Romulans believe made up this rubbish about there being a 'Section 31', and who is seemingly killed trying to escape. Alexander Siddig has never been better (until his hysterics at the end) and although it's hard to take all of this double-dealing entirely seriously, I thoroughly enjoyed each successive rug-pull and revelation.

Adrienne Barbeau adds to the roster of impressive guest stars essaying ice-cold Romulans. Those white *Insurrection* dress uniforms show up again, looking just as sleek.

DS9 S07E17 Penumbra ★★★☆☆

Written by René Echevarria. Directed by Steve Posey. TX: 7 April 1999.
Featuring: Penny Johnson, Deborah Lacey, Michelle Horn.

Potpourri instalment, which shuffles up various bits of plot and tries to call that an episode.

Worf's ship is reported destroyed by a Dominion patrol. Fearing the worst, and hearing Jadzia's voice in her head, Dax breaks into Worf's quarters and tortures herself with memories before taking a runabout and finding him herself. No one else on the station seemed ready to say goodbye to him, so I wasn't convinced he was gone. This is really just an excuse to stick Dax and Worf in a runabout together – a signature **Deep Space Nine** move. Before long, Ezri and Worf are abandoned on a jungle planet, much as Jadzia and Worf were in the middle of Season 6.

Over with Weyoun and TFC, there is still no cure for the sickness infecting The Great Link, and Damar's trust in his allies is wavering, while Sisko is discovering that he can either be the Emissary of the Prophets, or marry Kasidy in front of a handful of close friends, but not both. We end with Worf and Dax prisoner, Dukat disguised as a Bajoran and Sisko discovering that his dead mom doesn't approve of his girlfriend. This is a handful of unrelated bits and pieces, which is no doubt setting the table for some good stuff to come, but which isn't all that satisfactory as an episode of television in itself.

DS9 S07E18 'Til Death Do Us Part ★★★★☆

Written by Bradley Thompson & David Weddle. Directed by Winrich Kolbe. TX: 14 April 1999. Featuring: Louise Fletcher, Penny Johnson, Deborah Lacey, James Otis.

Sisko's hasty nuptials are rather sweet but this is more set-up, with no pay-offs to speak of, and it still feels aimless, instead of a propulsive acceleration into the endgame.

The ultra-mysterious prophets having been reduced to Sisko's quarrelsome stepparents, it might come as a relief to only have to deal with Kai Winn's supercilious treachery. 'The prophets have never spoken to me directly,' she laments, which the Pah-wraiths take as their cue to make her their instrument. Also picking up where we left them are Dukat and Damar, Weyoun and Dax, and Worf. Although I think Worf carrying on with Ezri is rather ridiculous, Nicole de Boer flickers into life as she lists off her cellmates' failed attempts at escape, criticises the prison catering and speculates about Breen grooming needs underneath their VR headsets.

Everyone moves one further square towards the endgame, but again this is a bit unsatisfactory as an episode. Why have Dax and Worf been shunted into their own side plot? Why are Odo, O'Brien, Bashir and Quark very nearly MIA? Even Kira only gets a handful of bland lines. And am I supposed to be as interested in Sisko's wedding plans as I am about the future of the Alpha Quadrant? Because I'm super-not. Half a star up on last week's for a strong ending, finally colliding two of these disparate plot lines.

DS9 S07E19 Strange Bedfellows ★★☆☆☆

Written by Ronald D. Moore. Directed by René Auberjonois.
TX: 21 April 1999. Featuring: Louise Fletcher, Penny Johnson, James Otis.

We stumble a bit closer to the finale, at last, but the price we pay is that the plot twists start to strain credulity.

TFC grows ever more decrepit. It's a nice touch that her scabies affects her 'clothing' as well as her 'skin' (because it's all just shape-shifting, after all). On meeting the Breen, she's able to 'pull herself together', which is a curious feature of this ever-more mysterious pox. On board the Breen ship, Worf and Dax briefly get the upper hand and manage to off Weyoun (but as Damar points out, they should have killed him instead; he can't be replaced as easily). It also finally dawns on Kai Winn that the prophets who have brought her her guide are Pah-wraiths. Was that meant to be a surprise to us all? I just assumed that's what they were from the beginning. Sadly, it doesn't change anything. Dukat continues to manipulate her with distressing ease. It might raise the stakes (a bit) but it fatally undermines a once complex and fascinating character.

Speaking of which, Dax and Worf endlessly re-litigating their relationship doesn't do much to keep my attention. If I have to hear one more time that Ezri is not Jadzia, I'll put my foot through the TV. And then, wildly improbably, Damar turns around, guns down his own guards and sets them free. The Cardassian leader feels like a helpless puppet, enslaved by the needs of the plot. Sure, Weyoun is being a dick to him, but this is just stupid. And we still have half the main titles cast given nothing to do.

DS9 S07E20 The Changing Face of Evil ★★★★☆

Written by Ira Steven Behr & Hans Beimler. Directed by Mike Vejar.
TX: 28 April 1999. Featuring: Louise Fletcher, Penny Johnson, James Otis, John Vickery.

We're building momentum towards the endgame now, but there's still a feeling of pieces being hammered into place, rather than storylines emerging organically. And it's still tertiary characters doing a lot of the heavy lifting.

Following two episodes in which nobody seemed the least bit concerned that Dax and Worf were missing, believed dead, O'Brien and Bashir greet them happily with tales of how nobody talked about anything else while they were gone. But the bigger news is that the Oculus Quest aliens have attacked Earth, and the race is on to discover their Kryptonite. Luckily, Damar is there, sowing seeds of dissent, *Yojimbo*-style. Dukat and Kai Winn remain in their holding pattern. They want access to a Bajoran Book of the Dead, but the pages are blank, so nothing happens. Her assistant unmasks Dukat, but Winn is too far gone, so she doesn't alter course, and nothing happens. The pages of the book get filled in but – oops – no time for any consequences now, it's the end of the episode.

The *Defiant* takes on the Breen and – in the first sign that we're actually moving to the climax – is summarily destroyed, leaving Sisko and his crew in escape pods. But when Damar acts against the Founders, things really feel like they're starting to ramp up – even though most of our main characters are stuck standing around and watching events unfold. I can barely even remember what Jake looks like, and Odo, Kira and Quark get maybe three lines each, while all O'Brien and Bashir do is idly discuss the Battle of the Alamo. Even Sisko is just commenting from the sidelines. The only reason we see any more of Worf and Dax is that – in possibly the least convincing love affair in the franchise (and that's a highly contested prize) – Ezri has decided that Julian Bashir is The One – the same Julian Bashir whose clumsy advances Jadzia spent two toe-curling seasons rebuffing. Nobody touches Sisko's peppers.

DS9 S07E21 When It Rains... ★★★✭☆

Story by René Echevarria and Spike Steingasser, teleplay by René Echevarria. Directed by Michael Dorn. TX: 5 May 1999.
Featuring: Louise Fletcher, Robert O'Reilly, John Vickery.

The pattern of continuing to push half a dozen plot lines slowly uphill continues, as do the pacing problems, but we are gathering momentum, slowly.

Thanks to the Founders' novel military strategy of leaving alive as many witnesses as possible (especially those who feature in the show's opening credits), the Federation now has plenty of intelligence regarding Breen weaponry, and O'Brien has found a possible weakness – at least where Klingon ships are concerned. One of my frustrations with this climactic arc has been how little our main characters are involved, and the pivotal Cardassian rebellion against the Founders is a great example – it's all about the relationship between Damar and Weyoun. These are fascinating characters, but they aren't the ones I'm most invested in.

Having Kira (and Odo and Garak) despatched to go and teach Damar about guerrilla warfare then is a big improvement, putting a main titles character in the thick of the action, and Sisko is fully aware of the irony. Kira even puts on a Starfleet uniform for the first time. But Kira's tutoring is incredibly basic – not quite on the *Blackadder* level of explaining to Baldrick how many beans make five, but close. Yes, Damar, mounting a resistance against the Cardassian–Dominion alliance will mean attacking Cardassians, since they are members of the Cardassian–Dominian alliance, which is what you are resisting.

While not poring over a sample of Odo's 'goo', Bashir is busy misunderstanding Ezri's attitude towards him, which I guess counts as a plot line for a main titles character, but O'Brien and Quark are largely stuck as Someone For Bashir To Talk To, and Sisko just pops up to issue orders once in a while. Gowron is also here for the endgame, and even finds ten seconds to completely forgive Worf for everything and welcome him back into the Klingon fold. Who knew it would be so easy? Maybe least successfully, Dukat and Winn have yet another scene in which they do nothing but explain the status quo to each other, until finally Dukat has the good grace to let the Book of the Dead blind him, which feels like their plot line is finally staggering forward, even if it isn't exactly clear yet what this means or how it will affect the other plot strands.

DS9 S07E22 Tacking Into the Wind ★★★☆☆

Written by Ronald D. Moore. Directed by Mike Vejar. TX: 12 May 1999. Featuring: John Vickery.

The End, part 6, inching towards the finale with good material for Kira and bits and pieces for Worf, but otherwise continuing to cede the floor to secondary and tertiary characters.

The Kira Nerys School of Terrorist Resistance is in session, but she's having to keep some of her pupils back after class. Despite their obstinate foolishness, the Cardassians are winning some small battles – even if that means doing Starfleet's dirty work for them. But Odo has the pox too (in fact, he's patient zero) and now Garak knows this as well – as does Kira, who didn't need to be told. We check in with Bashir and O'Brien simply to reiterate what we were told last time (no recap at the beginning of the episode, and maybe this is why). In other words, all the characters who had a storyline at the end of the last episode remain in their holding patterns and all the characters who didn't still don't. Finally, Sisko brings Worf off the subs bench in an attempt to put the suicidally reckless Gowron back in his box, but at first, it seems his role is just to give a stricken general a pep talk. He ends up taking a bit more of an active role, but quickly hands the conch of agency back to Martok.

Of more interest is Kira's conflict with Gul Rusot, who believes that her reason for volunteering her services is to kill Cardassians, and whom Garak suggests Kira murder while she still breathes. But the deepest emotional story belongs to Damar, whose family have been wiped out by the Dominion. It's a strong moment between him and Garak and Kira, even if, again, it comes at the expense of decent material for the supposed stars of the show. Jake is entirely absent, as he has been for most of this climactic arc, so is Quark, and Dax makes only a token appearance. The mission to nick the Breen weapon is tense and well handled and gives the episode a strong ending, but it feels a bit as if this final epic arc could have lost a couple of instalments quite easily. Also MIA are Winn and Dukat, which is strange.

DS9 S07E23 Extreme Measures ★★★★☆

Written by David Weddle & Bradley Thompson. Directed by Steve Posey. TX: 19 May 1999. Featuring: William Sadler.

Fine surrealistic exploration of Section 31's darkest secrets, with Siddig and Meaney on top form.

Kira and what's left of Odo are back on the station, and their seeming goodbyes are rather touching. René Auberjonois and Nana Visitor are superb – never grandstanding, but totally believable, despite all the latex. This might be the most successful love story in the whole of the franchise. O'Brien and Bashir now break ranks and reveal to Sisko their plan to lure Section 31 to the station. And lo! there's William Sadler doing his steepled-fingers-while-you-sleep routine. While there was good stuff in the last episode, it was dragged down by the bad. Here we have long-gestating storylines finally coalescing, and we're putting our major characters at the centre of the action – both things we've been getting only very occasionally since *Penumbra*.

And because this is **Deep Space Nine**, solving his problem also means Bashir stepping over some ethical lines – using illegal Romulan mind-mashing gizmos to root around in Sloan's consciousness to find the information he needs to save Odo. It's rare indeed to see heroes of mainstream American television shows as the ones using torture to get what they want (Jack Bauer comes to mind). If anything, I could have done with a bit more handwringing from Siddig, who switches a bit too easily from 'isn't the irony horrific' to 'oh goodie, a hard problem for me to get my teeth into'.

The hard problem involves O'Brien and Bashir walking through a dreamscape of Sloan's memories (relocated to the station in a budget-saving move) and watching him give an account of himself to his imagined loved-ones and then setting guards on them. There being no shuttlecraft for them to talk on, so they confess deep feelings while slumped injured against a wall.

We've seen versions of this scene before, of course, but this has seven years of history behind it, and the extraordinary high stakes of the situation bolster it considerably.

While I appreciate the storytelling efficiency, having the miracle cure for the Changeling Pox reverse every symptom inside three seconds of the drug being administered is completely ridiculous, and very unwise for an episode that was playing games with plausible realities. And while I appreciate the novelty of an episode that actually told a complete story this late in Season 7, the price we pay is that we learn nothing new about Weyoun, Damar, Dukat, Kai Winn, TFC, Martok, the Breen and everything else that was until recently being parcelled out over multiple episodes, and once again there's literally nothing for Jake and Quark and next to nothing for Sisko, Kira, Dax and Worf.

Okay then – two episodes to go.

DS9 S07E24 The Dogs of War ★★★☆☆

Story by Peter Allan Fields, teleplay by René Echevarria & Ronald D. Moore. Directed by Avery Brooks. TX: 26 May 1999. Featuring: Penny Johnson, Chase Masterson, Juliana McCarthy, Wallace Shawn, Cecily Adams.

*Everything that **DS9** can do put in a blender and served up in an apparently random order. Some great scenes don't make up for some inconsequential and some deeply stupid ones.*

Following last week's refreshing devotion to a single strong plot line, this penultimate instalment hops from strand to strand with an almost ADHD-like frenzy. Bashir and Dax finally cement their relationship, with barely any shows left. The *Defiant Mark II*, aka the USS *Sao Paulo*, docks at the station, and Sisko is given the big chair. Damar is adding further Cardassian troops to his anti-Dominion cause, but the Jem'Hadar is one step ahead and he, Garak and Kira end up trapped. Hilariously, Garak arranges to have them hidden by his old housekeeper. Odo finally learns the truth about his illness and he's understandably peeved to think that his Federation friends are the ones who plotted the genocide of his people. Also – there are Ferengi on the station, remember, including (*sigh*) the Grand Nagus, who has chosen his replacement.

Some of these work better than others, some feel like the seven-year story is coming to an end, some of them feel like arbitrary busywork. Still no sign of Dukat and Winn, which is completely baffling, especially given that *everyone* is in this one, including two different Jeffrey Combs characters (who don't meet each other). It plays rather like the last five seasons on shuffle, with scenes in wildly differing tones coming one after the other.

'Seskal' probably wasn't the best choice of name for the doomed Cardassian as when Kira hisses that word and urges him to beam them up, it sounds like she's saying 'Sisko'.

DS9 S07E25-26 What You Leave Behind ★★★★☆

Written by Ira Steven Behr & Hans Beimler. Directed by Allan Kroeker. TX: 2 June 1999. Featuring: Louise Fletcher, Rosalind Chao, Penny Johnson, Deborah Lacey, Julianna McCarthy, Hana Hatae.

*The journey here has been bumpy and fragmented, but **DS9** saves some of the best for last with a rousing finale that surprises and satisfies, despite some of the same pacing issues.*

Here it is then – the culmination of the biggest, most complex story the **Star Trek** franchise has ever attempted. A very different problem to the one faced by *All Good Things*, five years ago. That needed to end a story designed never to end. This needs to definitively end a story that has been spread over 175 episodes. Commitment to serialisation has wavered over the last seven years, but every instalment since *Penumbra* has been part of this climactic arc, and it's all been building to this.

Sad to say, judged by the standards of modern serialised TV, it's been a bit of a mess. Early episodes tended to flit from scenario to scenario, barely inching the disparate plot lines along, and this lent a disjointed and sluggish air to proceedings. Some developments were thrilling and moving – Kira's role in the Cardassian rebellion, Odo's near-fate at the hands of Section 31, the Breen's part in the ongoing war. Some continue to seem irrelevant – Winn's acquisition of the Pah-wraith Book of the Dead, Ezri and Bashir failing to get it on, who gets to be number one Klingon. And although **Deep Space Nine** is blessed with a tremendous bench of secondary and tertiary characters, it's bizarre to see so little material for the series regulars: Quark has been very badly served, O'Brien just follows Bashir around, Dax has had little to do except to coach other people, Jake has been completely MIA, and even Sisko has been routinely sidelined, despite his unique position in both Federation and Bajoran societies.

But with ninety minutes to play with, and a war to win, hopefully everyone will be on their game. Last episode's big revelation was Kasidy's pregnancy, but we open on Bashir and Dax (who have enjoyed a big night, it seems). Their pact to both come home alive is rather sweet. Not for the first time, the *Defiant* takes its place in a huge Federation-led armada, taking the fight to the retreating Dominion. Not for the first time, there's plenty of time for meaningful conversations along the way (deadpan Worf is the best Worf).

While we're waiting, there's a great deal of satisfaction to be gained from the ongoing fracturing of the Dominion/Breen/Cardassian alliance, which we see both from their claustrophobic bunker and on the ground as Damar, Garak, Kira and Mrs Hudson plot to stay alive and ideally escape alive. And Kai Winn and Dukat finally emerge from their plot chrysalis and helpfully recap what they were up to half-a-dozen episodes ago before getting around to doing what they first discussed back in *Penumbra* – releasing the Pah-wraiths.

When the action starts, it's quite spectacular with both the CGI exterior shots and the shaky-camera, exploding console interiors looking very dramatic and convincing. Dominion suicide runs don't seem to me to be playing fair, but it ramps the stakes up wonderfully, especially as Kira and her Cardassian allies are being captured at the same time – and TFC won't waste time with elaborate scenarios that give them time to escape; she wants them executed immediately. Weyoun's decision to raze a Cardassian city to punish the rebels rebounds, and first Cardassian soldiers save Kira, and then Cardassian ships turn on the Dominion. It's a fast victory, but nevertheless a convincing one, built on threads established patiently – if not always engagingly – over many previous episodes.

Also visually impressive are the Bajoran Fire Caves, the flames of which seemingly restore Dukat's sight (so the point of him being blinded was… nothing?) as well as stripping Winn of her hypocrisy (and much of her clothing). Garak and Kira's assault on the Dominion stronghold is more par for the course, but Andrew Robinson makes the most of the mini-arc he's given, gleefully roaring 'for Cardassia!' along with the other rebels before eliminating the last Weyoun clone.

In an act of pure spite, TFC refuses to give the order to surrender, caring more for taking Federation lives than sparing Jem'Hadar. Odo tries to talk her round and they're able to link despite her pox. As Bajorans side with Cardassians, it's Odo the outsider who finally brings peace – and who returns to the Gamma Quadrant in her place. The pain of his and Kira's separation is testament to the detailed work put in by both actors, as well as some tremendous writing over the years, creating by far the most convincing love story in the franchise. (Bashir and O'Brien are in second place.)

And just as no journey from A to B ever happens during a commercial break on this show, we end the war with thirty minutes of episode left. Much of this is tying up loose character ends: Garak philosophising about what Cardassia was and will be, Worf becoming an ambassador, Kira and Odo saying goodbye, Bashir and O'Brien saying goodbye, Vic Fontaine singing goodbye. But the big loose end is those damned Pah-wraiths who have apparently kept Winn dementedly monologuing on that cliff edge for hours, if not days. Inexplicably, Sisko decides to join her at that exact moment – no time seemingly passes while he leaves the holosuite, charters a runabout, gets clearance to leave the station, sets course for Bajor, navigates into their orbit and beams himself down, where he finds a resurrected and reconstituted Dukat, still in moustache-twirling pantomime villain mode. Winn obediently switches sides at the last moment and Space Jesus is, if not resurrected, then certainly given what feels like a less than permanent exit. Even Jake barely seems to register that his dad is missing, presumed dead, and Kasidy's pregnancy is never even mentioned.

So, this isn't flawless, and the Dukat/Winn subplot is the worst aspect, but there are weird ebbs and flows of momentum throughout, partly due to the fact that the preceding episodes did so little to build up a head of steam. And yet, the whole is so much more than the sum of its sometimes carelessly assembled parts, and if the trippy psychobabble in the last act makes very little sense, it does at least centre the star of the show once more, something which we've had very little of lately.

Last episodes play by different rules. There's no reset button, no plot armour and no guarantees of happy endings. If writers Beimler and Behr don't take advantage of all of those opportunities, it's hard to criticise them for it, when so much of what we do get is so engrossing, fulfilling and heartfelt. And Quark's final line is pretty much perfect.

Last appearance of quite a lot of folks. Only Kira and Quark turn up (briefly) on **Lower Decks** and although Alexander Siddig was seen on **Picard**, he wasn't playing the actual Bashir. Janeway and Seven are all over the animated spin-offs, and Kate Mulgrew even filmed a scene for *Star Trek: Nemesis*, but this series ends as it began – the obscure syndicated spin-off, albeit now in the shadow of the big network show instead of a similarly syndicated older brother. So this is it for the family Sisko, Worf (on television), Dax, Bashir and O'Brien, as well as Dukat, Garak, Ross, Damar, Kasidy, Weyoun, Keiko, Nog, Martok, TFC, Winn and Vic Fontaine. Rom and assorted Ferengi we said goodbye to last time.

DS9 wrap-up

- There's no question that **DS9** sits very oddly in the **Trek** canon, and there's no way that it could possibly have birthed a franchise on its own, or even that it would have carried the flame the way that **TNG** did, if **TNG** hadn't come first.
- As noted elsewhere, it tends to be overlooked as it always shared the airwaves with shows that had higher profiles, but **DS9** exists in the shadows and in the grey areas. No other show of this era could have pulled off queasy, morally compromised episodes like *For the Uniform*, *In the Pale Moonlight*, *The Siege of AR-558* or *The Ship*, to say nothing of the magnificent *Far*

Beyond the Stars. All of this pays off the promise that we saw way back in Season 1 with the extraordinary *Duet*.

- Of course, this show also gave us dross like *Profit and Lace* and the concluding arc was something of a mess, but nobody can knock out twenty-six cast-iron classics every year, which makes the incredibly strong run from the end of Season 3 to the middle of Season 4 even more impressive. This is a show on which everything is working. Wobbly characters from the first season have bedded in. Strong characters have become deeper and richer. And that incredible supporting cast is now fully established.

- This gave the show the freedom to experiment with form, tone and structure, and gave rise to potentially divisive, but undeniably ambitious, outings like *Take Me Out to the Holosuite*, *Badda-Bing Badda-Bang*, *Little Green Men* and *Looking for par'Mach in All the Wrong Places*. The show that pushed the envelope with serialisation often did its very best work in these purely standalone episodes.

- So **DS9** ends up with a slightly higher overall average than **TNG**, 3.42 instead of 3.30, which I think largely reflects how quickly the new show got its act together. But no one season beats the amazing run of **TNG** Season 6, with its incredible 3.9 average. **DS9**'s best season was its fourth with 3.72 and its last season averaged a still very respectable 3.34.

- What's also slightly odd about **DS9** in the context of the overall **Star Trek** universe is how much it changed and yet how little it influenced. Over seven years, we put the Federation through the kind of bloody conflict only previously glimpsed in horrific alternative universes, we introduced a major new threat made up of three different alien races (Founders, Vorta, Jem'Hadar), rearranged alliances throughout the Federation, eliminated the Maquis as a threat and added vast amounts of lore to the Bajorans, Cardassians, Trill and especially the Ferengi. But the show that continued after **DS9** finished was **Voyager**, which was sealed off from all these changes by design. And the next show was set over 200 years in the past. So nobody else got to pick up these chess pieces from where Ira Steven Behr and company left them (on TV at least).

- As noted, no main characters from this show have been reused in the Kurtzman era, save a couple of very brief cameos, and **DS9** never made it to the big screen either. There was an audience for Picard and Data – until suddenly there wasn't – and although a spin-off movie gathering up some of the cheaper characters from across various series was considered, it never got the green light.

- **Voyager**, meanwhile, quite sensibly, never tried to out-**Deep Space Nine** **Deep Space Nine** and instead was charting its own path. You can't blame it for that, but I'll miss the detailed character work, pointed ethical conundrums and refreshingly bleak outlook that you can only get here.

The TNG Movies – Part One

Starring: Patrick Stewart, Jonathan Frakes, Brent Spiner, LeVar Burton, Michael Dorn, Gates McFadden, Marina Sirtis.

Star Trek: Generations ★★★☆☆

Screenplay by Ronald D. Moore & Brannon Braga, story by Rick Berman & Ronald D. Moore & Brannon Braga. Directed by David Carson. Produced by Rick Berman. Music by Dennis McCarthy. Released: 18 November 1994. Featuring: Malcolm McDowell, William Shatner, James Doohan, Walter Koenig, Alan Ruck, Whoopi Goldberg, Barbara March, Gwynyth Walsh.

A pleasure to see Kirk and Picard sharing the screen, but surely they could have found something more interesting for them to do together than ride horses and make eggs?

When **Deep Space Nine** launched, there was a desire to try to make it seem different from the old show, hence the new, more utilitarian jumpsuit-style uniforms. Throughout the first three years of the spin-off's existence, whenever anyone from Starfleet dropped by, they tended to wear the old **TNG** togs. Somewhere along the way, that thinking changed and on **Voyager**, everyone wore the **DS9** black-with-coloured-shoulders affairs. Now the implication seemed to be that Starfleet was rolling out the new look across all its operations.

Where did that leave *Generations*? Sticking with the old look would leave them behind the times. But the **DS9** uniforms designed to look good for TV wouldn't necessarily work on the big screen. Robert Blackman, who had done such a fine job on the Season 3 redesign for **TNG**, created a whole new set of Starfleet uniforms just for this film, but they didn't work, and there wasn't time to have another go. In the end, the costumes we see are a mishmash of **TNG** and **DS9**-style outfits, including Jonathan Frakes borrowing Avery Brooks's uniform and LeVar Burton borrowing Colm Meaney's, despite which Geordi and Data have several scenes together where Geordi is in the old-style uniform and Data is in one of the new ones. It looks a mess. Quite what was so wrong with the new specially designed clothes isn't clear, but the inconsistency, last-minute making-do, uncertainty and era-confusion evident here is symptomatic of a film that was chaotic to make, searches for an identity without finding one, and ends up pleasing almost nobody, despite the fact that many of the ingredients – and even whole sequences – are excellent.

For the first time arguably since *The Motion Picture*, we're slamming into just what makes these movies so difficult. You begin with a television series featuring an ensemble cast, where you can choose who to focus on, and experiment with different styles, tones and approaches, week by week. Now instead of doing twenty-five-odd stories a year in forty-five minutes each, you've got one chance to tell a two-hour story every two or three years. You need to find a story big enough to make that worthwhile – no wonder the **Trek** movies keep returning to the template of *an alien probe is threatening to end all life on Earth* – and you need to provide some kind of arc for at least some of these characters you're saddled with, who have all been explicitly designed not to grow or change.

Add to this the fact that the production team is stretched incredibly thin right now. The movie was being prepped while **TNG** Season 7 was in production. The main cast barely had a break after *All Good Things* wrapped before returning to Paramount to start work on *Generations*. **Deep Space Nine** is shooting its third season. **Voyager** is about to begin production on its first. No one is focused only on the movie. Everyone's attention is split.

Tasked with writing this were reliable hands Ronald D. Moore and Brannon Braga who, separately and together, had written any number of classic **TNG** episodes (plus a few stinkers). They took months to hammer this screenplay together, under Rick Berman's supervision – with a few weeks out to knock off the television finale before returning to the movie – and they had an almost impossible task. They had to connect the old cast to the new. They had to establish the **TNG** characters for an audience that might not have been watching their syndicated show. They had to tell a brand-new, film-sized story. They had to keep Shatner, Stewart, Berman and Paramount happy. They had to 'service' the other **TNG** regulars. They had to make it work for die-hard fans, general audiences and everyone in between.

Problems start quite early on. Obviously, it should have been Kirk, McCoy and Spock on the *Enterprise-B*. That's why Chekov heads up the medical team and Scotty keeps making scientific assessments of novel phenomena (and Moore and Braga should have rewatched *Relics* before having Scotty witness Kirk's death). On the plus side, there's some wry satire in the press treatment of Kirk when he visits the new ship for its big send-off. You can also glimpse future Vulcan Tim Russ among the bridge crew along with Jenette (*Aliens*) Goldstein and Glenn (*24*) Morshower.

But then we cut from the tension and drama of the death of Captain Kirk to jolly japes with the **TNG** crew all cos-playing *Pirates of the Caribbean* to promote Worf in the silliest way imaginable. Data seems to have regressed considerably in his sophistication (presumably in order to catch up new viewers) and so this is all rather embarrassing, with Picard indulging in some nostalgic but not very believable anti-technology sentiment. When we get down to work, the lighting on the bridge is very dramatic – but it doesn't make the *Enterprise* feel like a very comfortable place to live and work in.

In one of the series' more durable clichés, the senior staff are exploring an abandoned space station littered with corpses. This at least provides something to do for someone who isn't Patrick Stewart or Brent Spiner (now third-billed after Stewart and Frakes) and the reappearance of Malcolm McDowell, eighty-odd years later, is a nifty mystery. But at this stage, it's hard to pin down what the actual story is. We seem to be cutting from point to point at random, lurching from continuity heavy references involving Romulans and the Duras Sisters to beginner's guides for people who've never seen the show before.

Data's emotion chip provides him with some sort of an arc, but it's only very vaguely connected to the theme of the story, such as it is. Spiner is amusing when discovering that he doesn't like what Guinan is pouring, less so when doing Mr Tricorder for Geordi, who of course gets to be Data's-Best-Friend (and is then reduced to unconscious kidnap victim for the remaining run time of the film). But nothing relating to Data's emotion chip will affect the actual plot of the movie in any way at all.

Picard's arc has been badly garbled as well. Troi discovers him looking at family photos (printed out and stuck into albums the way you definitely would in the twenty-fourth century) and he reveals that his brother Robert and nephew René have been killed off-screen – burned to death, which is kind of horrifying. But we don't see them together (unless we took the time to screen *Family* before watching this movie), so – despite manly tears from the Captain – this is something we know about, rather than feel.

Then, at the movie's midpoint, Picard gets swallowed by the Nexus, where a completely generic, very English, Christmas is supposed to tempt him to abandon any sense of duty or purpose. This is only barely connected to the loss of his family members (one of the moppets is identified as René) but Picard sees through the deception almost immediately and, with only the tiniest of pushes from Guinan, he rejects the fantasy. Would this scene have played any differently if we hadn't heard about the fatal fire? I don't see how.

Picard is then told that he can leave the Nexus at will (funny kind of gilded cage, this one) and return to any point in time and space. So rather than being a trap, or a beguilingly convincing fantasy world, it's a place where you can hang out for as long as you please, at absolutely no cost, and at absolutely no risk, and then it becomes a taxi service to the next convenient bit of plot? Thrilling stuff. And where does Picard want to go? Back to France to save Robert and René from the fire? Not only does he reject that option, preferring instead to have another go at stopping Soran (while making life maximally difficult for himself by returning to a point where his devastating plan has almost completely succeeded) it doesn't even occur to him to try to save his brother and nephew. So, why did we spend so much time establishing them? Surely a moral dilemma about whether to do the noble thing and stop Soran, or do the selfish thing and save two people you love, would have some interest to it? Surely, that would make the stop-off in the Nexus mean something? No, Picard immediately knows what the right thing to do is, and does it, without a second's thought, sparing us any of that tedious 'character' or 'drama'.

Also in the Nexus is Kirk – although bafflingly, not Soran – who goes on essentially the same very rapid conversion – with, again, a bit of a push from Picard. How is it that, when exposed to the Nexus, Soran – who seems like a bright enough chap – becomes obsessed with remaining within its synthetic fantasy world, and yet two random Starfleet captains become bored and want to leave inside five minutes? This is a pretty poor honey trap. It certainly fails to understand Picard, who I think is driven by justice and by curiosity, not by family. And, what if Soran had been in there? What if convincing *Soran* was what was required to free him and them? Wouldn't that have been worth watching? Where is Soran while the two captains are playing Martha Stewart? This movie, which was so fixated on the enormous lengths that someone would go to in order to live in paradise, is bafflingly uninterested in what that person's vision of paradise might look like.

So, back we go for round two of Starfleet vs missile, and this would love to be *Yesterday's Enterprise* in which a meaningless death is replaced by a meaningful one. All it actually does is take a heroic death – valiantly saving a ship from imminent destruction – and replace it with a stupid one in which Kirk is brought down by a wonky bridge. From saving the *Enterprise* to done in by shoddy workmanship. Oh my.

Nothing Kirk does at the end of the film is the kind of thing that Kirk and only Kirk could do. Picard could have taken literally anyone else back to Veridian III and the outcome would have been the same. Worf, Troi, Wesley, me, my cat – anyone. And it does make Kirk look rather less than heroic when he only does the right thing *after* it's spelled out for him by Picard. The implication seems to be that even if Kirk had known about the destruction and loss of life that Soran had brought about, he probably would have stuck around making eggs and playing horsey if it hadn't been for Picard pointing out the bleeding obvious. Damn.

That accounts for about an hour and twenty minutes of the film. But someone has taken another **Star Trek** film and cut in forty minutes of scenes from it at random. In this 'rogue' movie, Geordi is kidnapped by Klingons who hack his VISOR and try to blow up the *Enterprise*. Yeah, that does kinda seem like an act of war, doesn't it? Don't worry, nothing comes of it. And we assume Geordi is fine, and they find the bug and take it out. We have to assume that, because we never see Geordi, the VISOR or the bug ever again.

Then the *Enterprise* crashes and – with a full third of the film still to go – every single member of the regular cast of the television show whose name isn't Patrick Stewart is written out of the story, unable to influence events in any way at all. Chekov, Sulu, Uhura and Scotty might not have had much to do in the first three movies but at least you could see them on the bridge in the back of the shot sometimes. In *Generations*, Troi, Crusher, Riker and Worf get about ten lines between them and Geordi only does better because he's in scenes with Data. Was there really no way in which a giant saucer crash-landing on a planet could have had some impact on a plan to launch a rocket from that same planet into an energy ribbon approaching that self-same planet? As it is, the *Enterprise* might as well have been in the Gamma Quadrant.

So, this is a complete mess, far more so than the also structurally flawed *The Motion Picture*, but unlike Robert Wise's film – which feels like a far more self-important and sombre version of the usually fairly breezy TV show – this does feel like **TNG** most of the time. It's fun. The actors are all great. There are individual scenes that work well – some of them work very well. And it moves, unlike *The Motionless Picture*. But, more than anything, this feels like a pile of different story ideas that have been rivetted together at the last minute, and you can really see the joins.

Let's not forget, that's basically how *Wrath of Khan* was written, so it can work, but it's not ideal. And Nicholas Meyer managed to find a meaningful through-line that united all the disparate pieces. Here we have Data facing up to what having emotions means, and then not being in the Nexus where he might have to confront that – instead he just gets his act together off-screen. Then we have Picard thrown by personal grief – which he easily dismisses in order to get on with the running and punching. He's joined by Kirk, who seems happier making lunch than saving the day – just like you remember! And lastly, there's a villain who will go to any lengths to enter his personal paradise, but whose vision of paradise we never even see. It's not exactly precision storytelling. They barely even bother to set up that Data has a cat, so non-fans may have been somewhat baffled at his honey-coloured tears when he rescues Spot from the wreckage of the *Enterprise*.

Last appearance of James Doohan as Scott. Last appearance of Walter Koenig as Chekov. Last appearance of William Shatner as Kirk. Although Shatner's connection with the series would continue throughout his career, he never played the part again, except in video games (this work doesn't consider video games or fan videos). He published a number of **Star Trek** novels, some of which resurrected Kirk after the events of this film, assorted non-fiction books, hosted various **Star Trek** documentaries and of course was a fixture at conventions. He had a big success on television as maverick lawyer Denny Crane in over a hundred episodes of *Boston Legal* from 2004 to 2008 (and a handful of episodes of *The Practice*), and at the age of 90 he became the oldest person to travel into space, courtesy of Jeff Bezos's *Blue Origin* space shuttle. As of this writing, he is one of only three members of **Star Trek**'s original cast who are still alive, along with George Takei, who recently appeared on stage in London in the musical *Allegiance*, and Walter Koenig.

Star Trek: First Contact ★★★★☆

Screenplay by Brannon Braga & Ronald D. Moore. Story by Rick Berman & Brannon Braga & Ronald D. Moore. Directed by Jonathan Frakes. Produced by Rick Berman. Music by Jerry Goldsmith. Released: 22 November 1996. Featuring: Alfre Woodard, James Cromwell, Alice Krige, Neal McDonough, Robert Picardo, Dwight Schultz.

Effortlessly entertaining science fiction adventure story, which never reaches the depths of Khan, *but that rarely seems relevant while it's on.*

Despite the fact that the first movie had been given something of a critical kicking, essentially the same team was reassembled to make the second one. *Generations* had made money, after all, so Paramount was happy to leave them to it. Rick Berman continued as producer, Brannon Braga and Ronald D. Moore wrote the script, Herman Zimmerman designed the sets, but proper movie composer Jerry Goldsmith returned for his first **Star Trek** gig since writing the theme for **Voyager**, and – borrowing a page from *Wrath of Khan*'s book – the *Enterprise*'s first officer became the film's director. With several **Star Trek** television episodes to his name, this was Jonathan Frakes's debut as a movie director and it's pretty impressive, as we'll see.

Whereas that first **TNG** film laboriously set up the old crew, Kirk's death, the new crew on their silly Holodeck sailing ship and so on, this outing wastes no time in sketching in the Borg threat and Picard's relationship to them. In 1982, cinemagoers were either expected to remember who Khan was or to not care, but that won't work here. We need to viscerally understand Picard's experiences if his arc is going to make sense, so we start with bits and pieces of *The Best of Both Worlds*, reshot on a movie budget, putting us right where Picard was.

When we come out of the Captain's assimilation nightmare, we see the new Starfleet uniforms, debuting here a few weeks before they were first seen on TV in the **Deep Space Nine** story *Rapture*. I much prefer these to the jumpsuits we've had for the last few years, and they have a bit of extra texture, which suits the big screen. It's not the only change. Geordi has bionic eyes now, and we're on board the *Enterprise-E*, which has a much more angular, less graceful, but more rugged profile than the TV version and which fills the widescreen frame more effectively. The bridge takes a few design notes from *Voyager* too, moving us even further away from the hotel lobby feel of the *Enterprise-D*.

While plundering the most highly regarded film entry in the series, the second **TNG** film also consults the most profitable film entry in the series and recognises that the story can't really start until the crew goes back in time. It's half an hour into *Star Trek IV* before Kirk's crew begins its slingshot manoeuvre. It's less than ten minutes into this film before the Borg cube is taking lumps out of the *Defiant* and less than two minutes after that before the Borg are seemingly defeated. The *Enterprise* enters the time warp fourteen minutes into a movie that's substantially less than two hours long. That's some efficient storytelling.

This isn't rushed, though. That care taken to educate new viewers as to Picard's history with the Borg extends to Data's quest to be human as well. He's subtly set up as superhuman when he leaps 50 feet into the rocket silo and withstands a hail of bullets from Lily's gun. The contrast when he cradles the injured human flesh that the Borg Queen has given him is very striking.

With three very shiny guest stars – Alfre Woodard, James Cromwell and Alice Krige – it's perhaps no surprise that many of the regular cast are underutilised. The narrative splits into three main components, one for each of the new arrivals: Data captured by the Borg Queen, Picard and Lily fighting the Borg on the *Enterprise* and Riker trying to make sure that Zefram Cochrane's first warp flight happens as the history books say it did. That helps keep everybody occupied, but Crusher gets almost exactly zero, Geordi is only along for the ride and Troi gets her comedy drunk moment and that's it. Worf gets a nifty action scene on the saucer, with new boy 'Hawk' there as backup, but this brutish Klingon in a Starfleet uniform bears scant resemblance to the complex, isolated character who on television has recently embarked on a relationship with a Trill. And putting Hawk in that sequence is a double-edged sword. He's much more killable than Worf or Geordi, which raises the stakes, but we care about him much less than we do about Worf or Geordi.

Overall, this is vastly better than *Generations* in almost every department. Although efficient to the point of breathlessness, the story makes perfect sense on its own slightly ludicrous terms, it's full of engaging sequences, and the stakes feel real. Data's subplot with his emotion chip and the Borg Queen is perfectly on-theme (instead of being grafted on and then discarded as it was in *Generations)* and Alice Krige gets possibly the best entrance of any character in the whole of the franchise. As director, Jonathan Frakes shoots it all with vigour and clarity, and we even get a guest appearance from Robert Picardo as the Doctor (plus Reg Barclay and even Ethan Phillips from **Voyager**, if you look closely). There are good jokes too ('Borg? Sounds Swedish...') and I'll forgive them 'You're astronauts? On some kind of... star trek?' because the whole film has put me in such a good mood.

But as good a time as I had watching this again, and I had a grand old time, this can't quite reach as high as *Wrath of Khan*, even as it helps itself to that Herman Melville iconography once more. The worst you can say about *Khan* is that it's a little smug at times, but the grandly operatic tragedy of the climax washes that almost completely away. *First Contact* is a faultlessly constructed piece of action-adventure storytelling, with suitable breaks for character beats and comedy moments, some appropriate garment-rending and glass-breaking for Patrick Stewart, and it's a story that celebrates **Star Trek** itself. So, every box is ticked. But it doesn't have anything to say beyond the world of the television series that birthed it. The equivalent scene to Spock's death here is the arrival of the Vulcans at the end, which might bring a lump to the throat, but which looks only inwards. And the victory the crew achieves comes at zero cost – unless you count Lieutenant Hawk, and, I mean c'mon.

These are minor quibbles, though, and look, if we got another one of these every two years, I'd be very happy indeed.

Star Trek: Voyager
Season 1

Starring: Kate Mulgrew, Robert Beltran, Roxann Dawson, Jennifer Lien, Robert Duncan McNeill, Ethan Phillips, Robert Picardo, Tim Russ, Garrett Wang. Executive Story Editor: Kenneth Biller. Producers: Brannon Braga, Merri Howard, Peter Lauritson. Co-producer: Wendy Neuss. Supervising producer: Peter Lauritson. Executive producers: Rick Berman, Michael Piller, Jeri Taylor.

VOY S01E01–2 Caretaker ★★☆☆

Teleplay by Michael Piller & Jeri Taylor. Story by Rick Berman & Michael Piller & Jeri Taylor. Directed by Winrich Kolbe. TX: 16 January 1995. Featuring: Armin Shimerman, Richard Poe, Josh Clark, Alicia Coppola, Gavan O'Herlihy, Basil Langton.

To Bujoldly go… (I'll see myself out).

Geneviève Bujold lasted about a day. The idea was kinda nuts. Counting **The Original Series,** three different **Star Trek** shows had established beloved characters by casting experienced TV actors, none of whom were household names. And the actors with the highest profiles prior to their casting (probably LeVar Burton and René Auberjonois) had been rendered pretty much unrecognisable underneath costume and make-up. So there was no need to cast a movie star in the lead of **Voyager,** no matter how much pressure there was to make the third live-action **Star Trek** spin-off a success.

And there was pressure. For many years, American television had been ruled by the Big Three networks: CBS, NBC and ABC. Fox had launched in 1986 but it was still struggling. The way seemed open for another network. Two major media conglomerates – Warners and Paramount – decided to have a go, each seemingly unaware of the plans of the other. Finding an audience for a fifth network seemed plausible. Finding an audience for a fifth and sixth network seemed a lot less likely.

Warner Bros.'s offering, 'The WB', launched in January 1995, with one night of programming per week, and it gradually added more. Flagship shows included *The Wayans Bros.*, *Unhappily Ever After*, and it scored a big hit in 1997 with *Buffy the Vampire Slayer*. The United Paramount Network (UPN) launched only a few days later, and **Star Trek: Voyager** was the first show to be aired. It was the lynchpin of the project and as it turned out, one of the only UPN shows to last more than one season. UPN, alas, was always a bit half-hearted, providing a few hours of programming a week, and only reaching about two-thirds of American homes at launch. UPN and the WB ceased transmitting within days of each other in September 2006, with new channel The CW inheriting programming from both.

But at launch, Paramount had every right to be confident. They had a new **Star Trek** series, which was going to make their network essential viewing. Rick Berman, Michael Piller and Jeri Taylor devised the format and Piller turned **Deep Space Nine** over to Ira Steven Behr so that he could focus on the new show. Ron Moore stayed with **DS9**, but Brannon Braga came over to **Voyager**. **Voyager** took over the stages that **TNG** had been using, and the Berman machine kept on trekking.

The might of that machine should have been enough to guarantee success, but somebody somewhere wanted a film actor, possibly to counterbalance the perceived risk of building a show – in 1994! – around a female leading character. Either way, it didn't work out, and Bujold walked off the set on day two, citing the rapid pace of television production – to the relief of producers who were confounded at her insistence on underplaying everything to the point of inaudibility. The part was offered to the 'first runner-up' and the result is that Kate Mulgrew is still playing Janeway today (lending her voice to **Star Trek: Prodigy**). Bujold would have been Nicole Janeway. Mulgrew is Kathryn. Everything Bujold shot can be seen on the DVD box set. She doesn't look comfortable.

Far more than either **TNG** or **DS9**, the first episode is a 'premise pilot'. *Encounter at Farpoint* and *Emissary* are both mainly 'Here's the world of the show, and these are the people in it'. *Caretaker* instead is chapter one of a longer story – but it has to establish the world and the characters, *as well*, and do it all inside ninety minutes. The world? Well, initially that looks like a done deal – it's the world that Gene Roddenberry and D.C. Fontana and so on established in 1987, which by now is seven years and hundreds of episodes ago. As with *Emissary*, we begin with scrolling text to set the scene for new viewers – the Cardassians, the treaty, the Maquis. Then a whizzy space battle gets underway and we meet some new characters. The captain of the Maquis ship is a Native American named Chakotay. Other officers include half-Klingon B'Elanna Torres, and Vulcan Tuvok. They're heading for 'The Badlands', briefly mentioned in a recent episode of **DS9**. They're a pretty bland bunch, despite their very different backgrounds. Their dialogue is all business. Titles.

After using two classic pieces of **Star Trek** music stapled together for **TNG**, one of that show's small stable of regular composers, Dennis McCarthy, was tasked with coming up for the theme for the first spin-off. The result is that episodes of **Deep Space Nine** open with a slightly constipated march that keeps threatening to develop into a really catchy melody and never quite gets there. So, for the new show, proper movie composer Jerry Goldsmith was engaged to come up with a theme. And he produced a slightly constipated march that keeps threatening to develop into a really catchy melody and never quite gets there. Sigh. The CGI *Voyager* with nacelles that move into position when it goes to warp is cute, though.

Next, and slightly bafflingly, we meet Tom Paris in a Federation penal colony. This is Nicholas Locarno from Season 5 of **TNG** in all but name – he even has basically the same backstory. Possibly he has been renamed to provide greater freedom for the creative team – possibly it's to avoid paying a writer for the copyright – but it's the same actor giving the same performance. We also meet Janeway. While Robert Duncan McNeill is as generically rebellious here as he was in *The First Duty*, Mulgrew makes an instant impression. With her smooth Katharine Hepburn purr, she's as warm as Kirk and as commanding as Picard. I liked her at first sight. Compare Mulgrew and Bujold's versions of the 'clarinet' scene. We got lucky here.

On board the Maquis ship lost in the Badlands was Tuvok, Janeway's chief of security, undercover. Janeway wants Paris to help her retrieve the ship, Vulcan and all, but she makes it clear he will just be there as an observer. *Voyager* is a brand-new ship, with a brand-new crew. Introducing us to lots of new faces and then killing off some pretty major players – including Janeway's first officer, medical officer, and a Betazoid ensign that Paris is sharking after – is a baller move, reminiscent of the first episode of *Red Dwarf*. But it somehow doesn't feel as shocking as maybe it ought. Everybody is so bland that it's hard to spot who's going to survive to episode two and who isn't, but it also doesn't seem to matter all that much. A big deal is made of *Voyager* having 'bio-neural' circuitry. I look forward to that being a major plot point very soon.

Just as Picard was there to give Sisko a send-off, Quark is here to give Harry Kim his introduction to the world of **Star Trek**. He's yet another bland figure whose only defining characterisation appears to be 'young'. Even Bashir managed 'young, cocky, doctor', three entire adjectives to Garrett Wong's one. The bridge is a nice set, halfway between the hotel-in-space of the *Enterprise* and the *Das Boot* aesthetic of the *Defiant*.

The displacement field fries the ship (just after Tom Paris has got through telling Harry Kim he's not exactly a good luck charm) and we get our first sight of the Array. Now stranded on the other side of the galaxy, in a badly damaged ship, *Voyager* needs some friends (and some consoles that don't explode when the ship gets damaged). Shutting down the warp core feels like drama, but doesn't really impact the plot or reveal character. Again, it's all business. However, replacing the deceased doc is one of the show's masterstrokes. Robert Picardo is genius casting, and the character of the Emergency Medical Hologram is genuinely original and will be endlessly fascinating as the series develops. Picardo holds a lot back here – a smart move – but it's already easy to see the potential.

Suddenly, and ridiculously, we're on location in a southern plantation. Thankfully, Janeway figures out immediately that this is an illusion. Given the trauma of the situation, no one seems especially bothered about their crippled ship, the enormous distance they've travelled, or the loss of close colleagues and vital crew. And now the superfluous holography is done away with, and the truth is revealed. After sticking the crew with needles, everyone but Kim (and Torres from the Maquis ship) is returned. Janeway offers Chakotay a truce and Tuvok unmasks himself.

Robert Beltran makes zero impression as Chakotay, snarling at Paris and then curling up with his tail between his legs as soon as possible. Roxann Dawson makes more of an impact as Torres – at least I believe her when she snarls – but, rather like Dax, she's suffering from being a species instead of having a backstory (just as Paris is suffering from having a backstory instead of embodying a characterisation). Familiar face Tim Russ gives a good performance as Tuvok, suggesting tiny flickers of suppressed emotion; it's just that I've seen that performance before when Leonard Nimoy did it on **TOS**.

What happens next is all rather confusing and convoluted. Characters visit the Array, get knocked out, return, get sent back, get experimented on, protest, analyse data, go back, make some new friends, Paris and Chakotay re-enact the end of *Second Chances* with extra racism… Nothing feels like it has much of a purpose, and almost nobody seems to think that any of these problems require anything even approaching urgency. It all builds to Janeway's decision to destroy the Array rather than risk the sector's bad guys, the Kazon, getting their hands on it – a choice that smacks of 'there must have been another alternative'.

Quark has proven that a **TNG**-style drama adventure series can stand a comic relief character, and so Ethan Phillips as Neelix is slotted into this role. The Talaxian rogue is charming enough and I can see why a local guide might be included, but again, it's hard to understand what drives him, compared to Quark or Data or Odo (or even Troi!). Far less necessary and even blander than Kim, Chakotay or Paris is Jennifer Lien as Kes. So, whereas **TNG** started off with at least five very able actors who made instant good impressions (Stewart,

Spiner, Burton, Dorn, Crosby) and **DS9** had one of the strongest casts in the whole franchise, here I'm clinging on to Mulgrew and Picardo and hoping for good things from Russ and Dawson – and the rest are kind of a right-off. It's amazing how, after seven years of doing this, Berman, Piller and Taylor struggle so much to devise, write and cast characters we'll want to follow for multiple seasons.

Some of these characters will develop and grow over the next several years. Some will stall, as we saw happen with Geordi on **TNG** or (for a time) Odo on **Deep Space Nine**. But Chakotay almost never gets anything in terms of character development or even good episodes built around him. **Star Trek**'s prior track record with Native Americans is pretty poor, so it was with some relief that I learned that the production team did at least have the good sense to hire a consultant with a real Native American background to lend some verisimilitude to Mexican–American Robert Beltran's portrayal.

Jamake Highwater was of Cherokee descent, and he had written books and featured in PBS documentaries about Native Americans since the early 1980s. As someone who understood both the Cherokee people and the Hollywood machine, he seemed to be perfectly positioned to flesh out this landmark character. The only problem was that Highwater was a complete and utter fraud, who had already been comprehensively exposed by the *Washington Post* ten years before he found himself in Rick Berman's office. Highwater's real name was Jackie Marks and he was born in Los Angeles to Jewish Eastern European immigrant parents. No wonder that nothing about Chakotay's background, traditions or culture ever has any real specificity or detail.

So, the characters are a bit more woolly than is ideal. That's the first problem. The second problem is that the purpose of this first episode is to establish two main plot engines for the series, and both of them look like they're over and done with almost immediately. Firstly, this crew has been patchworked together from Starfleet officers, Maquis terrorists and Delta Quadrant locals. This is basically unwritten before the episode's end, as everyone puts on a Starfleet uniform and Janeway's authority becomes absolute and unquestioned. Secondly, now they are stranded on the other side of the galaxy, there can be no resupply, no refitting. If they lose a shuttlecraft, it's lost. If they damage something, it can't be replaced. As we'll see, this rarely seems like it's actually an issue, and so what we are left with is: it's **Star Trek**, but we don't have the benefit of building on any existing stories and have to start from scratch. It's all a bit misbegotten – probably my least favourite pilot episode so far.

VOY S01E03 Parallax ★★★☆☆

Story by Jim Trombetta, teleplay by Brannon Braga. Directed by Kim Friedman. TX: 23 January 1995. Featuring: Josh Clark, Martha Hackett, Justin Williams.

Decent origin story for Torres (whose chief character trait is that she throws things) but the quantum singularity feels off-the-shelf.

The *Voyager* crew is at each other's throats (and noses). In an instance of the kind of inter-crew squabbling we were seemingly promised, but which I thought had been taken off the table, B'Elanna Torres has committed what would be a court-martial offence in other circumstances, but Chakotay is clear that they are both no longer Maquis. The dialogue here is pretty clichéd: 'I will make a full report.' 'You do that.' Ugh.

Lip service is also paid to the fact that what was once routine maintenance suddenly isn't without access to a Starbase. Again, if memory serves, you won't hear much of that over the next 170 or so episodes. About the only concession to their self-sufficient status is Neelix in the galley. At this stage, he keeps dragging Kes around like she's a ventriloquist's dummy. Janeway gives her the task of creating a hydroponics lab in cargo bay two, and gets Tom Paris to train with the EMH (who is either 'the embodiment of modern medicine' or has only 'very limited capabilities', depending on whom you ask). She also agrees to try out Torres as chief engineer. There's a decent scene between Chakotay and Janeway regarding Torres, but Beltran is completely outclassed by Mulgrew. I guess that's the right way round, but still…

And it's not all crew rosters and personnel admin this week, it's also gibberish science. *Voyager* encounters a 'type IV quantum singularity', which sounds an awful lot like a black hole to me, except that the description of its event horizon is so off beam that even *Red Dwarf*'s Holly could come up with a more accurate explanation from the *Junior Encyclopaedia of Space*. This turns out to be the Singularity that Jack Built and there's a weird scene where Torres and Janeway aren't sure which is the real ship and which is a ghost image, and Janeway is convinced to give Torres her promotion when Torres picks the wrong ship and Janeway picks the right one. Also, Paris calls their ship 'the Voyager', which sounds completely wrong. But at least we don't keep beaming back and forth at random, and at least some of the plot promises of the pilot are being noticed, if not really fulfilled.

VOY S01E04 Time and Again ★★★✯☆

Story by David Kemper, teleplay by David Kemper and Michael Piller.
Directed by Les Landau. TX: 30 January 1995. Featuring: Nicolas Surovy,
Joel Polis, Brady Bluhm.

Good vehicle for Janeway, and not a bad one for Tom Paris. Another fairly standard-issue moral dilemma and thrilling escape from death, but well-handled.

So, this is the show. It isn't this crew's urgent need to survive long enough to get home. And it isn't how will these two crews manage to work together? It's **The Next Generation** without Starfleet Command. We'll keep turning up to new planets and finding plots there until we're cancelled. While Michael Piller and Rick Berman have oversight of both shows, over the next few years and months, **DS9** becomes the Ira Steven Behr all-pain-no-gain show, while **Voyager** turns into Brannon Braga's wibbly-wobbly-timey-wimey time. So it is here. We arrive at a planet that is a burnt cinder, but when the away team goes to investigate, Janeway and Paris are plunged into the past.

This is the second timey-wimey story in a row, and even has similar dialogue about widening a fracture. Couldn't we at least vary the technobabble we're applying to our science problems? Other than that, this is decent adventure-of-the-week stuff, and Janeway makes a great hero, instantly calling the terrorists' bluff ('I'm a hostage') and then the bluff-caller has her bluff called. This is more interesting and (slightly) more layered than *Parallax* but it's all about situations and actions and barely at all about characters. And of course, it ends with a big ol' reset switch. Still, if you get the lead right, there's time to sort out the rest, and I'd follow Janeway to the end of the universe at this point.

VOY S01E05 Phage ★★☆☆☆

Story by Timothy DeHaas, teleplay by Skye Dent and Brannon Braga.
Directed by Winrich Kolbe. TX: 6 February 1995.
Featuring: Cully Fredricksen, Stephen Rappaport, Martha Hackett.

Someone has half-inched Neelix's lungs, but this episode isn't as much ludicrous fun as that description makes it sound.

Voyager has a power shortage and requires dilithium to keep the lights on (plus a refinery). Janeway seems very cheerful about their desperate situation, stranded seventy years from home – she's chatting happily to Chakotay about breakfast and is then plunged into a sitcom scene with Neelix, who has set up a galley kitchen in the captain's private dining room, and who then invites himself onto the away team.

Down on the rogue planetoid – I know this is going to sound hard to believe – things don't go entirely according to plan. Neelix is zapped and the Doctor determines that his lungs have been removed from his body. Mulgrew and Beltran exchange this information with admirably straight faces. A replicator, which can create any design imaginable, cannot make lungs for Neelix. But the hologram projector can create holographic lungs, which really doesn't make much sense.

This would love to be a really moving and thought-provoking medical ethics drama, but it's far too ridiculous for that and far too strait-laced for the absurdity to be entertaining. Ethan Phillips is remarkable here, and Robert Picardo continues the great work he's been doing ('I'm a doctor, not a decorator'), but Jennifer Lien and Robert Duncan McNeill offer very little, and this has barely enough plot for the running time. Still, better Neelix's lungs than Spock's brain, I suppose.

The away team has nifty wrist-torches, which keep the left hand free. In overly-precise-countdown news, the Doctor has a gizmo that will breathe for Neelix for exactly sixty minutes, following which he will immediately expire – which seems like a manufacturing shortcoming to me. Apart from anything else, does the Doctor not have any more such gizmos? The EMH, which is created and controlled by the ship's computer, still has to give verbal commands to the computer to get things done. Once again, *Voyager* is faced with more than one image of a ship, at most one of which is real.

Cunningly, Martha Hackett's Seska is given two brief lines in Engineering. We barely even see her face clearly.

VOY S01E06 The Cloud ★★☆☆

Story by Brannon Braga, teleplay by Tom Szollosi and Michael Piller. Directed by David Livingston. TX: 13 February 1995. Featuring: Luigi Amodeo, Angela Dohrmann, Judy Geeson, Larry Hankin.

A dull day's nebula-bothering leaving plenty of time for playing pool, meditation and whining about coffee.

A rather slow, undramatic teaser is at least paying lip service to the idea that stranded out here in the Delta Quadrant, some things won't be the same. Janeway's introspection about whether the crew wants her to be an icon or a buddy is rather affecting, but – as Kim puts it – Paris is working from an old rule book. This transitions into a rather less deep motivation: the need for better coffee. Because something else that is still being paid lip service is the idea that there aren't any starbases at which their craft can refuel, which means that replicator power is rationed. A handy nebula may provide some fresh batteries.

Before long, just as happened in three earlier episodes, *Voyager* passes through a weird thing in space and the door closes behind them. And then Kes starts snogging Neelix, leading me to suspect that it's this show's turn to do *The Naked Time*, although in fact nothing comes of this romantic interlude. Meanwhile, both to get in and to get out, Janeway raises shields, fires phasers, and generally burns what must be far more energy than was required to get her a morning cup of Joe. Very wisely, the writers decline to put many easily trackable numbers on any of these issues, but that does mean that the problem we're supposed to be wrestling with is very fuzzy and ill-defined. The Holodeck, it seems, uses triple-A batteries and the rest of the ship uses double-As, so people can go nuts indulging their fantasies without worrying about wasting resources. The lengthy sojourn with Kim and Paris (and the long scene of Janeway meditating under Chakotay's guidance) only adds to the languid feel of the episode.

I imagine that the idea of this story was to establish who these characters are, or were before this catastrophe befell them. But this is a science fiction adventure series and what we're interested in is how these characters will react under the pressure of high stakes situations, not whether they prefer to play pool or drink coffee when off duty. As such, this is a pretty dull outing, despite its emphasis on the life-or-death aspects of the show's premise. Even the big revelation about the 'nebula' is a lift from *Encounter at Farpoint*.

VOY S01E07 Eye of the Needle ★★★★☆

Story by Hilary J. Bader, teleplay by Bill Dial and Jeri Taylor. Directed by Winrich Kolbe. TX: 20 February 1995. Featuring: Vaughn Armstrong, Tom Virtue.

Decent enough exploration of the consequences of the premise, with the destination never in doubt, but the exact route is not without interest.

Voyager stories seem to be one of three main types. 'Oopsie, we're running low on unobtainium', 'Here's something we should investigate' and 'This might be a way to get us home if only we can... wait, no, never mind'. With no friends or enemies in the Delta Quadrant, no visiting dignitaries, no missions from Starfleet Command and no way in which wider political stories can impact them, they're somewhat limited. And all three of these stories have their problems.

'We're running low…' stories contradict one of the unspoken premises of the show, that *Voyager* is a superior ship to pretty much anything else in the area. And they either end with 'We won't have to worry about that for a while', in which case there aren't that many of those stories you can tell, or you actually commit to having the ship fall apart, which breaks the show as well as the vessel.

'Might get us home…' stories tell you the end before they start. Just like breaking the ship, getting home – or even getting substantially closer to home – once again breaks the show. So 'We should investigate…' episodes become the norm, and slowly the political forces in the quadrant become part of the established lore, which does make one wonder what was the benefit of stranding *Voyager* in the Delta Quadrant in the first place, if the most successful kinds of stories are the ones that ignore or seek to progressively minimise the significance of that premise.

This week, it's the second kind of story, and Harry Kim is mournfully fretting about what his family are thinking, and whether anyone is looking for them. He's found a wormhole but it turns out to be only a tiddler, 30cm in diameter, so wherever it leads, it can't accommodate their ship, but they might be able to get a message through – or a transporter beam. The understandably cagey Romulan scientist they contact is able to beam on board, but it turns out he's from twenty years in the past, which is a novel enough way of keeping the show going, and there's some depth of feeling in the plight of the crew and their desire to try to get messages home. However, I don't know how many more times I want to see this story. Threading the needle indeed.

The Doctor requests a name. Don't hold your breath waiting for him to get one.

VOY S01E08 Ex Post Facto ★☆☆☆☆

Story by Evan Carlos Somers, teleplay by Michael Piller and Evan Carlos Somers. Directed by LeVar Burton. TX: 27 February 1995. Featuring: Henry Brown, Francis Guinan, Aaron Lustig, Robin McKee, Ray Reinhardt.

Plodding murder-mystery, which unerringly includes every tired trope it comes near.

As noted, less than ten episodes in and we're already settling into a groove of running through standard **Star Trek** plots with this low-wattage cast instead of Picard's or Sisko's crew. In this case, it's the courtroom drama set in a society with a different kind of justice than ours. Tom Paris is sentenced to relive his crime of murder (in noir-ish black and white) every fourteen hours. It's the kind of thing that a society focused on generating drama rather than delivering justice would do. In flashback, Paris and Kim find themselves in a remarkably twentieth-century Earth society – even by **Star Trek** standards. Their host wears a grey business suit, has people over for dinner, smokes cigarettes, drinks tea, owns a dog, squabbles with his hot wife. It's quite confoundingly familiar.

When we get more flashbacks, it seems as if a team of writers from a dreadful daytime soap has taken over. Paris's interactions with Hot Wife are drenched in clichés and it's hard to take any of it seriously. Plus, the solution to this problem is evidently going to be that the Always-Knows-Best Federation are going to be the first ones to point out the flaw in the system of justice used by this planet for generations. Add to this the fact that Paris appears to be the horny architect of his own misfortune and there's very little to recommend this effort. Plus, it's the damned dog again (see *Aquiel* from **TNG** Season 6). As usual, actors-turned-directors (in this case LeVar Burton) seem to be handed the weakest scripts available. One star for Chakotay's 'Maquis trick' (he has more). Tuvok has been married for sixty-seven years.

VOY S01E09 Emanations ★★☆☆

Written by Brannon Braga. Directed by David Livingston. TX: 13 March 1995. Featuring: Cecile Callan, Jeffrey Alan Chandler, John Cirigliano, Robin Groves, Martha Hackett, Jerry Hardin.

Thin meditation on life after death, with the silly beliefs of the bumpy foreheads quickly set to rights by Auntie Federation. You're welcome.

Everyone on *Voyager* is all-a-tizzy because a stash of unobtainium has been located on an asteroid, but when they beam down, the caves are littered with corpses. Kim and Chakotay disagree about whether they should investigate the bodies or leave them be and there's a diverting discussion about post-mortem rituals. Because this is **Voyager**, they are interrupted by a space-time-anomaly-vacuole and Kim is left behind when everyone else is beamed out. He pops out of a coffin and is told he has returned from the dead.

Meanwhile, the Doctor is able to actually bring one of the aliens back from the dead and once again the stage is set for The Federation Knows Best as generations of wonky beliefs are swept aside by one visit from smug people in colourful space pyjamas. Turns out that encouraging inconvenient family members to off themselves isn't the kindest thing imaginable. Who'dathunkit?

This has echoes of the far superior **TNG** episode *Half a Life* but that was deeply rooted in the characters, and this is all about the concepts. Plus, the

TNG story was saying something about how our society treats the elderly, whereas this is criticising an entirely made-up attitude to death and dying and so it doesn't really resonate. What's most disappointing about all of this is that, a few comments about Native American traditions aside, you can swap the roles of Chakotay, Kim and Torres all you like and nothing much would change. Even given that it's early in the development of the series, that's pretty poor. Jerry ('Mark Twain') Hardin makes a return appearance as Dr Neria.

VOY S01E10 Prime Factors ★★★☆☆

Story by David R. George III and Eric A. Stillwell, teleplay by Michael Perricone and Greg Elliot. Directed by Les Landau. TX: 20 March 1995. Featuring: Josh Clark, Martha Hackett, Ronald Guttman, Andrew Hill Newman, Yvonne Suhor.

That Prime Directive is a bitch, huh, Janeway?

Just as the Federation frequently empires its way around the galaxy studying the primitive natives from a respectful distance, *Voyager* seems to be making a habit of stumbling across rubes who could learn a thing or two from their Alpha Quadrant betters. It's nice therefore to have Janeway's crew encounter their first batch of technologically superior people since the Caretaker. Thrillingly, they have come with offers of a vacation. Their pleasure planet looks like a Manhattan pop-up modern art exhibition and the Sikarians wear decorative audio cables around their heads. It's all a bit low-key and laid back, with the chief interest appearing to be in whether or not poor Harry Kim will get his end away. (Who'd have thought that the major developing plot line of **Voyager** Season 1 would be scurrilous gossip about the Delaney sisters?)

The Sikarians have magical space-folding technology that could whizz the crew home in the twinkling of a video effect, which they cheerfully demonstrate in order to give Harry a change of scene. But when it comes to using it a second time to get our guys back to Federation space, it's no dice. Their own Prime Directive won't let them transport aliens (more than once, I assume) and the irony isn't lost on anyone.

Voyager doesn't have the kind of deep bench of supporting characters that **DS9** was assembling at the same time as this was airing – it doesn't even have its own Ensign Ro, Reg Barclay or Miles O'Brien knocking around the ship. But this Seska keeps cropping up, doesn't she? We know she's Maquis because Janeway, ever eager to integrate the two crews, has given them all their own rank insignia instead of awarding them field commissions into Starfleet. Seska sees Janeway's diplomacy as infatuation and puts pressure on Torres to take matters into her own hands.

Stuck as we are with this the-way-home-that-isn't storyline, having Maquis elements in the crew who oppose the Captain isn't a bad way of making it a bit more interesting. But as with *Caretaker*, the moral dilemma feels a little synthetic. The Sikarians may (or may not) have a principled reason for refusing to help the Federation. But once they're unmasked as hedonistic and selfish bad guys, what ethical reason could there possibly be for not doing an under-the-counter deal? It doesn't hurt them, and it vastly benefits the crew. So, the plot ending of the episode was inevitable, but the character beats with Torres, Tuvok and Seska kick this up a notch.

VOY S01E11 State of Flux ★★★☆☆

Story by Paul Robert Coyle, teleplay by Chris Abbott. Directed by Robert Scheerer. TX: 10 April 1995. Featuring: Martha Hackett, Josh Clark, Anthony De Longis.

For once, we actually engage with the two-warring-crews idea, but nobody seems to know what to do with it, despite the very fun Seska backstory.

The Kazon are back – and remember, the awesome and implacable threat of the Kazon is the whole reason we're in this jam. Nevertheless, when they fire on Chakotay, they are sure to keep their energy weapons on stun. Very considerate warlike alien race! The away mission is oriented around Neelix ferreting out revolting vegetables, but Seska has gone missing just at the moment when everyone needs to beam back. As the sole remaining representative of the two-warring-crews idea, Seska is one of the most fascinating characters in the show, very ably played by Martha Hackett, and we'll be seeing more of her as the series progresses, although on this rewatch, I have to confess that I'd completely forgotten about her.

Even more weird is the fact that we smash into the titles from Chakotay being felled by the Kazon, but then we discover that he and Seska evaded their remaining forces, made it back out into the open, communicated with the ship, beamed back on board safely, got patched up by the Doctor and made soup off-screen, while the carefully cloaked Kazon ship just stood by and watched. It's bafflingly poor.

Today's off-the-shelf ethical dilemma next presents itself: the Kazon themselves are sending out distress calls. The disaster that befell them has apparently been caused by trying to jury-rig Federation technology into a Kazon vessel. Seska seems to be the obvious person to be slipping the baddies

Voyager's tech. So, we trudge through an investigation of this malfeasance, until finally the truth of Seska's identity is revealed. Seska was a Cardassian who infiltrated the Maquis disguised as a Bajoran. That's actually exciting, but she hightails it out of there and it isn't clear when we'll see her again.

Even while trying to seduce him, Seska calls the first officer 'Chakotay'. Doesn't he have a first name? Torres does not exaggerate her repair time estimates.

VOY S01E12 Heroes and Demons ★★☆☆☆

Written by Naren Shankar. Directed by Les Landau. TX: 24 April 1995.
Featuring: Michael Keenan, Marjorie Monaghan, Christopher Neame.

Robert Picardo is fantastic, but he's awash in a sea of incoherent technobabble dressed up in medieval clothes.

As Janeway and Torres are technobothering a protostar, it is noticed that Harry Kim is not on board the ship. He was due some Holodeck time and – look, yes, I know this was covered in a line of dialogue a few episodes ago, but it still strikes me as completely ridiculous to start a story fretting about running out of power and then transition to a plot line about how a very junior officer is burning energy running virtual simulations in his leisure time. Part of the problem is that, as noted, *Voyager* has to be simultaneously the most awesome ship that the Delta Quadrant has ever seen, swatting Kazon cruisers lazily aside, and also a Federation rust bucket, on the brink of falling apart because they can't ever get to a Starbase to make repairs.

As such, it's even more difficult than usual to shrug off the absurdity of the Holodeck, which is usually presented as little more sophisticated than a C.S. Lewis-style dear old magic door, but here is presented as a magic door inside a wardrobe with flat batteries. There can also be no reason at all not to shut the program down. Chakotay even says at one point that doing so would definitely reveal Kim, dead or alive. Instead, the plan is to stick the Doctor in there, because he can't be hurt, and he can't be turned into a hologram. No other way of influencing the computer-controlled environment is even considered.

So, the science fiction here is basically all hand waving and gibberish, but the focus on Robert Picardo makes everything better. His first-night nerves are very touching and he even gets a snog out of it. Theologian, missionary and philosopher (and doctor, to be fair) Albert Schweitzer is a curious person for him to name himself after (and it doesn't stick) but it's hard to feel much when the Holodeck phantoms sacrifice themselves to save him. Plus, it's the *Farpoint* ending again.

VOY S01E13 Cathexis ★★★☆☆

Story by Joe Menosky and Brannon Braga, teleplay by Brannon Braga.
Directed by Kim Friedman. TX: 1 May 1995. Featuring: Michael Cumpsty,
Brian Markinson, Carolyn Seymour.

*'The first officer's brain is missing!' Actually, this isn't too bad, but it could be any
bunch of guys trying to defeat the incorporeal intruder.*

We start with more grinding Holonovel nonsense, and only a week after the
Holodeck damn near killed three crewmembers. Every time we step into
this fantasy world, I can't help thinking, 'Being stranded on the other side of
the galaxy seems like a trivial inconvenience rather than a life-altering crisis.
And lucky our lifeboat is this impregnable pleasure-machine.' Meanwhile,
Chakotay's brain is missing. I dunno, after the theft of Neelix's lungs, you'd
think the crew would have learned to take better care of their vital organs.
In a further mystery, which rather points the way to a solution to the first
problem, the crew are taking actions that they hold no memory of and Kes is
feeling haunted.

  As creeping paranoia takes over the ship, the tension does ramp up quite
effectively, and it's cool to see the crew taking strong clear decisions in a
situation where they have very little information. But this is all plot, all the
time, and nobody's personality is to the fore – even the scene of Torres trying
to help Chakotay by making him a dream blanket, and the Doctor being nice
about it, just feels like it's empty of any actual individual feeling (and lo, it's a
plot point, not a character beat).

  Janeway's Holonovel proves to be nothing more than time-wasting at the
top of the episode, a sin for which a more petty reviewer might have knocked
off half a star.

VOY S01E14 Faces ★★★☆☆

Story by Jonathan Glassner and Kenneth Biller, teleplay by Kenneth Biller.
Directed by Winrich Kolbe. TX: 8 May 1995. Featuring: Rob LaBelle, Brian
Markinson, Barton Tinapp.

*A rematch with the lung-thieves gives us twice our usual ration of Torres, and
Roxann Dawson is excellent, but the show isn't ready to grapple with the issues it
raises.*

Starting an episode of **TNG** was easy, because the *Enterprise* usually had
a thing it needed to be doing. Starting an episode of **DS9** is harder, but

sometimes we benefit from just hanging with our guys for a while until a ship docks, bearing a plot. Starting an episode of **Voyager** is super-hard because there's no one to give them missions, and any sense of 'we're just kicking back for a while and unwinding' kills the premise. This one opens as if they've been given a cartography mission, which they definitely haven't. Why are they messing around charting whoosits and whatsits and looping back to pick up crewmembers so doing, when they should be hauling ass back to the Alpha Quadrant?

We also get a glimpse of some sinister silhouettes operating on B'Elanna. Yep, another day, another plague-ridden planet, another member of the crew transmogrified – this time the Chief Engineer into a full-blown Klingon – and once she has the make-up on, Roxann Dawson starts impersonating Michael Dorn (and doing a fair job). This requires a rescue and since strong regular characters are so thin on the ground, the away team consists of Paris, Torres and good old 'Cannon-Fodder' Durst (I wonder why they call him that?). Kim, Tuvok and Chakotay are needed to form the rescue party.

And here comes the twist! While Klingon Torres is helping the lung-stealers to find a cure for the phage, a human version is locked up with Paris. So, this is *The Enemy Within* but with a character divided along racial lines instead of merely by temperament. And I use the word 'racial' advisedly. This is a show centring a mixed race-looking actor playing a character (with a Hispanic-sounding name) who reveals that she was taunted as a child and so tried to conceal her racial characteristics. Here, rather than being a metaphor for European seafaring explorers, The Federation is coded as white America and the Klingons living among Federation people as pre-civil rights Black Americans, some of whom attempt to 'pass' as white. It's strong stuff. The question is: does this frequently silly primetime science fiction adventure series have the chops to tackle these issues with any depth or finesse? We never really find out, because most of the episode is about gibberish DNA technobabble, viral strains, daring prison escapes, Gamma Quadrant aliens disguised as Starfleet and vice versa. But the episode does give Torres some much-needed depth and Dawson a chance to flex her acting muscles a bit, especially when playing scenes with herself. We also see another Talaxian, which is cool. Speaking of which, Neelix's Plomeek soup is somewhat piquant.

VOY S01E15 Jetrel ★★★☆☆

Story by James Thomton and Scott Nimerfro, teleplay by Jack Klein, Karen Klein and Kenneth Biller. Directed by Kim Friedman. TX: 15 May 1995. Featuring: James Sloyan, Larry Hankin.

The Delta Quadrant seems like a very unsanitary place, as yet another disease visits Voyager, *diagnosed by a **DS9**-style war criminal.*

Tuvok and Neelix are playing a version of pool that I am unfamiliar with, where Neelix is able to play a legal shot without striking a ball. Clearly if this rule was in effect, an immediate stalemate would take place where players would take it in turns to call 'safety' and they barely graze the cue ball with their stick. But, this is the show that brought you 'we sexually reproduce at the rate of one child to every two parents', so I guess I'm not surprised. It turns out to be a metaphor for cowardice or survivor's guilt or some such.

A figure from Neelix's past contacts *Voyager*. Dr Jetrel wants to talk to the Talaxian, despite (or because of) being responsible for the slaughter of 300,000 people. I've moaned in the past about being told things rather than being made to feel things, so it's up to Ethan Phillips to make this more than a story about people we've never met in places we've never visited, and he works very hard to pull that off – arguably too hard.

Turns out that having being near Jetrel's super weapon was enough to give Neelix fatal cooties (this is a riff on miners' dust inhalation, or radioactive testing or some such) so we have yet another **Voyager** degenerative pathogen. Barely a dozen episodes old and this series is already recycling the same ideas over and over again. Still, I'd rather have yet another an episode like this focused on Neelix, than one trying to centre Chakotay or Paris or Kim, all of whom remain stubbornly anonymous.

And whereas Neelix's medical misfortune is pure **Voyager**, the war-criminal backstory feels like a **DS9** cast-off, but without the depth of history we'd get from Cardassia. What helps enormously is guest star James Sloyan (so good in **TNG**'s *The Defector*) who brings detail and empathy to his depiction of the conscience-stricken scientist, under some of Michael Westmore's most haphazard foam latex. And Neelix's confession towards the end is a nice twist. I wonder which of the five credited writers came up with it?

Jetrel's bonkers plan to use the transporters to reverse not just death but total annihilation nearly works but not quite. It is thus completely abandoned, and no one expends any further effort to refine the process.

VOY S01E16 Learning Curve ★★★★☆

Written by Ronald Wilkerson and Jean Louise Matthias. Directed by David Livingston. TX: 22 May 1995. Featuring: Armand Schultz, Derek McGrath, Kenny Morrison, Catherine MacNeal.

'Get the cheese to sickbay.' Actually, this is a rather more thoughtful episode than that line implies, but I pity poor Roxann Dawson, who had to say it with a straight face.

As captain, Janeway has to lead, educate, take responsibility for and be a role model for an entire crew. Naturally, when she needs to unwind, she chooses to cos-play as governess where she has to lead, educate, take responsibility for and be a role model for two obnoxious children – they do say a change is as good as a rest. As noted, I find Holodeck stories in general to be frequently lacking in interest, and totally out of place in the context of the premise of this series. It also – again! – has no further bearing on the plot. Instead, the Vulcan security chief, who has decades of experience of training Starfleet cadets, has to take four particularly obstreperous Maquis crewmembers and try to pummel them into shape. Their unruly disregard for Tuvok's rules and commands raises some interesting questions about the rule of law and where authority comes from.

As well as actually confronting some of the promises of *Caretaker*, this is our first Tuvok-centric episode and there's a fascinating streak of naivety coming through that is helping to differentiate him from Spock (or Data). The question is whether the cadets will learn from the Vulcan or vice versa, and I genuinely couldn't call it. Not only that, but Neelix's cheese has infected the bio-neural circuitry and the ship is falling apart, so a lot of things I confidently said were going to be flatly ignored are being used to generate story. I don't think the show can, will, or even should do stories like this every week, but I was beginning to think we'd never get to it at all.

Voyager Season 1 wrap-up

- A third show was a big ask, and – as I've noted – there's a strong sense in this first small batch of stories (four were held over to kick off Season 2) that we don't really know what makes this series work yet. It's hard to do adventure-of-the-week when there's no one to send us on missions. It's hard to raise the stakes when we can't beat up the ship. No one seems to want to do Maquis-vs-Federation stories very often, and when we try, it's a bit half-hearted. There's nothing so terribly wrong with taking a Federation ship and stranding it halfway across the galaxy, but it seems clear that the idea of making this a part-Federation part-Maquis crew was one that Berman, Piller and Taylor (or some combination thereof) rapidly came to regret, and this aspect is being written out faster than Jennifer Parker in the Doc's DeLorean.

- Out of three aspects of the premise, therefore, we have one that doesn't work – the ship will fall apart and can't be put back together; and one that no one wants to do – the ship is composed of two warring crews with different ideas about the worth of Federation ideals. That leaves us with: Oh no we're seventy years from home – but in itself that doesn't generate any stories, except of course for: I think I've found a shortcut that will, wait, no, never mind.

- So, fine, we're exploring uncharted space just like Kirk used to, and Picard was briefly said to be doing. That means that the interest will lie in who the main characters are and what people and situations they encounter. Sadly, the main characters are a bit of a mixed bag. Janeway and the Doctor are the clear standouts. Thank goodness for Kate Mulgrew, who time and again makes soggy dialogue sound like it means something, and for Robert Picardo, who's such a gift to the writers. Strong performers, working hard to bring their underutilised characters to life are Roxann Dawson and Tim Russ. Having so few stories built around either of them is quite baffling.

- Neelix is permanently sitting in the comic relief spot (when he isn't having his lungs confiscated) and so doesn't tend to make stories happen very often. Kim, Chakotay and Paris are three interchangeable Starfleet guys and Kes is just along for the ride, smiling wanly at the Doctor and rarely displaying anything remotely resembling an inner life. It's a pretty thin collection, and that's going to be a problem.

- The season average is a rather poor 2.77, about the same as **TOS** Season 3 or **TNG** Season 1. But I know there are better things to come.

Star Trek: Voyager
Season 2

Starring: Kate Mulgrew, Robert Beltran, Roxann Dawson, Jennifer Lien, Robert Duncan McNeill, Ethan Phillips, Robert Picardo, Tim Russ, Garrett Wang. Featuring: Majel Barrett. Executive story editor: Kenneth Biller. Producers: Brannon Braga, Merri Howard, Peter Lauritson. Co-producer: Wendy Neuss. Supervising producer: Peter Lauritson. Executive producers: Rick Berman, Michael Piller, Jeri Taylor.

VOY S02E01 The 37s ★★★★☆

Written by Jeri Taylor and Brannon Braga. Directed by James L. Conway. TX: 28 August 1995. Featuring: Sharon Lawrence, John Rubinstein, David Graf, Mel Winkler, James Saito.

If this show is going to be Exploring-We-Will-Go-With-A-Generic-Starfleet-Crew then this a solid example of the type.

'Follow that trail of rust.' In what feels like a real throwback to **TOS**, *Voyager* encounters an old red pickup truck floating in space, and its AM radio picks up an SOS distress signal. Paris has a convenient interest in ancient vehicles, which is what we'll have to make do with until, or if, he develops an actual personality. This is all cheerfully ridiculous and the sight of the senior staff ducking for cover and Tuvok pulling out his phaser when the thing backfires is properly funny.

In another throwback, Janeway decides to land the ship when the transporters are technobabbled to death. It was the impossibility of landing the *Enterprise* every week on a TV budget that led to the invention of the transporter in the first place. And now, here we are, bringing her in to land. The problems of the Maquis crewmembers having apparently been solved at the end of the last season, there's a renewed sense of confidence here, even if the main cast are still all-business-all-the-time, and the sight of USS *Voyager* squatting on an alien world as the crew wanders off is very striking.

The trail leads them to famed navigator Amelia Earhart and various other obstreperous Earth people, whose inability to deal with their situation immediately recalls Ralph Offenhouse and friends from the **TNG** episode *The Neutral Zone*. It's ludicrous enough that the *Enterprise* would stumble across an old capsule from Earth containing three nonentities. It's gigantically preposterous that the hugely famous Earhart would be found by *Voyager* in the Delta Quadrant, but if you can swallow that, then the story skips along quite nicely, aided by some expansive location work and a lovely guest performance from Sharon Lawrence. I rather hoped she'd stay on board.

VOY S02E02 Initiations ★★☆☆☆

Written by Kenneth Biller. Directed by Winrich Kolbe. TX: 4 September 1995. Featuring: Aron Eisenberg, Patrick Kilpatrick, Tim de Zarn.

Decent Federation-pacifists-vs-warlike-aliens story but nothing we haven't seen before and with a very bland leading man.

Chakotay, who still has a backstory where a character is needed, is performing a not-made-up-sounding grieving ritual when the Kazon despatch a kid to take on his shuttlecraft and teach him a lesson. Having bested him in combat, Chakotay beams the lad aboard. Again, I don't quite know why Janeway is indulging this when there are perfectly good Holodecks on *Voyager* (there are even other away teams busy with who knows what). When the first officer tries to drop the sprog off with his parents, the Kazon grab the shuttlecraft in a tractor beam.

'I'm a gentle man, from gentle people,' mumbles freedom fighter and anti-Federation terrorist leader Chakotay. The price for his freedom is to murder the boy, and he naturally declines, so the two of them end up bonding on a booby-trapped moon. Throughout this, Chakotay is nothing more than a Generic Starfleet Officer Who Does Everything By The Book. Swap him with Harry Kim or Tom Paris and nothing much changes. We do learn a bit more about the Kazon, but they largely come across as Diet Coke Klingons, obsessed with dying in battle.

MVP of this episode turns out to be Neelix, who engages in some entertaining brinksmanship with the Kazon, when given the opportunity to spend some time on the bridge. Ethan Phillips finds a quiet authority that is quite a contrast to his usual puppy dog enthusiasm. Oddly, the mini-Kazon is played by Aron Eisenberg, a series regular in all but name over on **Deep Space Nine**, where he plays Nog.

VOY S02E03 Projections ★★☆☆☆

Written by Brannon Braga. Directed by Jonathan Frakes. TX: 11 September 1995. Featuring: Dwight Schultz.

*Typically conceptual **Voyager** episode with a great surprise guest star but a lot of techno-gibberish, which saps a lot of the drama.*

A shipwide red alert summons the Doctor, who turns out to be the only crewmember on board. Janeway's last log entry looks grim, and all escape pods have been launched. It's a strong opening, playing into the extra danger implied by being so far from home. But when Torres shows up and the Doctor's tricorder isn't detecting her, I grow suspicious of her and her cock-and-bull story about Kazon attack fleets and a barely contained warp core breach. For very little reason, Torres tells the Doctor that he's the one who's going to try to solve the problem from the bridge, and that she has been installing remote projectors for the purpose. So it's fairly obvious that this situation is all a fantasy, but I'm still delighted to find an episode centring Robert Picardo and this is a version of one of those cover-of-a-comic-book episodes that were often a highlight of **TNG**.

At the midpoint, Dwight Schultz pops up (in the *Voyager* uniform) and explains that the whole series has been nothing but a Holodeck program. That's more conceptually interesting, but we've moved from the high stakes of a Kazon attack that has crippled the ship to the much lower stakes of there is no ship and nobody is in danger. Eventually, the whole thing degenerates into a Russian doll of holographic let's pretend, which even the Doctor describes as an 'esoteric dilemma'.

The wholly insubstantial Doctor looks terrified when he thinks he is being ambushed in sickbay. Jonathan Frakes directs, and seems immediately at home in the Delta Quadrant, maybe because this is essentially a remake of *Frame of Mind* from **TNG** Season 6.

VOY S02E04 Elogium ★★★☆☆

Story by Jimmy Diggs and Steve J. Kay, teleplay by Kenneth Biller and Jeri Taylor. Directed by Winrich Kolbe. TX: 18 September 1995. Featuring: Nancy Hower, Gary O'Brien, Terry Correll.

Literally everyone has the horn, from anonymous snoggers in the turbolift, to space plankton trying to bone the ship. Neelix and Kes get somewhat lost in the shuffle.

Dashing, rugged Tom Paris is being nice to Kes, which is driving Neelix crazy. Chakotay's conversation with Janeway about intra-crew 'fraternisation' reminds us that she has a husband, Mark, who will give her up for dead if their journey home takes too long. It's a chilling evocation of the reality of their situation, something that this series would too often rather – hey! Look! Kes is putting *bugs* in her mouth. BUGS!

Meanwhile, *Voyager* is studying a swarm of space beetles, and lo! the two events are connected. Jennifer Lien has a rare opportunity to do more than smile wanly as she starts prematurely going through the ~~Pon-Farr~~ Elogium. Quickly, an intense medical drama becomes an academic and theoretical discussion of the benefits and drawbacks of *Voyager* becoming a generational ship, followed by an only slightly more intimate conversation between Neelix and Kes about whether he's ready to be a father. Even Tuvok's personal experience of fatherhood is presented in drily abstract terms.

The emphasis on sex and relationships is at least fresh, and Ethan Phillips does great work, but Jennifer Lien is fighting an uphill battle against a script that gives her rituals and symptoms instead of a personality. It's the Janeway/Chakotay scene that's the biggest disappointment. There should have been a clash of conflicting leadership styles here. Instead, we just get a slightly tedious ethics seminar between two rigorously reasonable adults. But at least it's trying.

VOY S02E05 Non Sequitur ★★☆☆☆

Written by Brannon Braga. Directed by David Livingston.
TX: 25 September 1995. Featuring: Louis Giambalvo, Jennifer Gatti, Jack Shearer, Mark Kiely.

Harry Kim finds himself back on Earth and, for reasons never made clear, opts to go back to the Delta Quadrant instead of being happy.

In another cover-of-a-comic-book high concept opening, Harry Kim is in bed next to his fiancée, back in San Francisco, and like the classic nightmare, he's got a big test and hasn't done his homework. It's refreshing to hear Harry run through the obvious solutions – is he on the Holodeck? Is this a delusion? – but reality persists and in this version of reality it's his old friend Danny who took the assignment on *Voyager* and got lost in the Delta Quadrant instead of him. As is so often the case with this series, the plotting is decent and the concept is fine, but the characterisation is woefully thin. Meanwhile, promising characters like Tuvok and Torres are withering on the vine. It's significant that the reason for Harry's predicament is a random accident. **Deep Space Nine** exists in a world of stories about characters who make moral choices and have to live with the consequences of their actions. **Voyager** exists in a world of people to whom random stuff happens. It's a big difference. Even Harry's dilemma about whether to stay on Earth or go back to *Voyager* is barely given any screen time. Out of his uniform, Tom Paris briefly flickers into life, which is unexpected to say the least.

VOY S02E06 Twisted ★★☆☆☆

Story by Arnold Rudnick and Rich Hosek, teleplay by Kenneth Biller. Directed by Kim Friedman. TX: 2 October 1995. Featuring: Larry Hankin, Judy Geeson, Tom Virtue.

The Delta Quadrant is lousy with spatial anomalies. This one turns Voyager *into an Escher print, which is fun enough, but again the characters suffer.*

The episode opens with yet more Holobollocks as the crew throws Kes a surprise birthday party in that silly French pool room. I really struggle to care about the Kes–Neelix–Paris love triangle. Kes and Paris are so underwritten and Neelix is never more irritating than when he's frustrated. Not invited to the shindig are humourless Tuvok and Kim, who have a blue wibbly thing they need to deal with first. It's a nice moment for Tuvok, who manages to grant Kim's request without breaking the rules.

Kim encounters an officer we've never met before, and they have a long conversation, which is remorselessly just-the-facts-ma'am. It's hard to imagine any other two characters in the franchise having such a meaningless, arid exchange. I swear if I showed that scene to someone who had never seen the show before then they would have no way of knowing who was the series regular and who was the anonymous guest star.

The main thrust of the episode is a riff on *The House That Jack Built* – the corridors of the ship rearrange themselves and the crew find themselves doubling back. Thanks to some creepy music and atmospheric direction, this simple (and delightfully inexpensive) device works reasonably well. So, yet again, we have an episode that is built entirely on its high concept, and which treats its characters as interchangeable pawns. That means we are invited to interrogate the concept and so we are forced to conclude that the ship can be turned into a sort of Möbius Pretzel and suffer no damage to its structural integrity. Uh-huh. Eventually the day is saved when Tuvok comes up with the brilliant stratagem of getting everyone to cross their fingers. There's a flicker of something deeper and richer between him and Chakotay but it soon passes.

The episode ends with the anomaly having deposited a vast store of data into *Voyager*'s databanks. I can't wait to find out what valuable information is there for them. (Spoiler: it's never mentioned again.)

VOY S02E07 Parturition ★★★☆☆

Written by Tom Szollosi. Directed by Jonathan Frakes. TX: 9 October 1995.

Paris and Neelix bury the hatchet and hatch an egg in this slim but focused episode, which makes the most of the show's sometimes meagre-feeling assets.

Paris, at his most punchably smug, is teaching Kes how to pilot a shuttlecraft, but at least he's differentiated from the rest of the crew, which is something. And Paris coming into focus helps with the somewhat tedious Paris–Kes–Neelix triangle, especially as the purpose of this episode is to trap Neelix and Paris together on 'Planet Hell' and have them resolve their differences, just as the problem of the unruly Maquis element was recently solved in *Learning Curve*. It's almost as if the writers see their job as looking for potential elements of drama – and then writing whole episodes designed to iron them flat. I would have been looking for ways to heighten that kind of character conflict, which shows what I know.

But we do at least get an episode that's focused on who Neelix and Paris are, rather than one that picks two characters at random and has them spout nonsense at a blue wibbly thing. (Neelix even says 'Stop trying to impress me with your technobabble' at one point, which made me laugh out loud.) Sure, it's quite a well-worn trope – including in this franchise – to take a pair of characters, trap them in an isolated space and give them a moral dilemma to deal with. Here, even the cave sets look familiar. But it's well-worn because it works, and **Voyager** perhaps should have been doing this kind of story sooner. Neelix's jealousy is something I've struggled to care about, and Tom Paris's rebellious nature was neutered almost immediately. But after a strong showing in an alternative timeline last week, Robert Duncan McNeill is beginning to show what he can do. While he's still a long way from James Dean, Paris has at least got more going for him than Kim and Chakotay, and this plot line even gives Jennifer Lien a chance to act a bit.

Apparently, I'm supposed to hate this episode with its trite moralising and its silly rubber dino-puppet but I found that it gave me a few things that other recent episodes have sorely lacked. Janeway has a new shorter haircut, which is an enormous improvement on the schoolmarm bun she'd been saddled with earlier. Debut of the *Voyager* Country Club and Jazz Concert Musical Appreciation Society, with Harry Kim inheriting Riker's mantle, but on the clarinet instead of the trumpet. Who would choose the clarinet over the trumpet?

VOY S02E08 Persistence of Vision ★★☆☆☆

Written by Jeri Taylor. Directed by James L. Conway. TX: 30 October 1995.
Featuring: Patrick Kerr, Stan Ivar, Michael Cumpsty, Thomas Dekker,
Lindsey Haun, Carolyn Seymour, Warren Munson, Marva Hicks.

The Voyager *crew is haunted by family phantoms, none of which really resonate.*
Poor.

The short haircut on Janeway was temporary, it seems, as we are now back
with The Bun Of Prodigious Complexity. She's also overtired and ratty and,
god help us, the Doctor prescribes an immediate visit to the Holodeck. There
the Captain can lose herself in a Holonovel of such excruciating boredom that
I assume the treatment regimen involves her passing out through aggravated
tedium, which even the luminous Carolyn Seymour can't elevate. Alas, the
ennui can't be contained, and it starts spilling out to other areas of the ship.
There's a crumb of interest in watching Janeway handing over to Chakotay
when she's incapacitated, and there's a little power in the final scene with Kes
and imaginary Neelix, thus the generous-looking star rating. But then the
Chakotay/Torres clinch manages to weaken both characters. The Doctor has
to watch a YouTube tutorial before he can help Kes reprogram the console.

VOY S02E09 Tattoo ★☆☆☆☆

Story by Larry Brody, teleplay by Michael Piller. Directed by Alexander
Singer. TX: 6 November 1995. Featuring: Henry Darrow, Richard Fancy,
Douglas Spain, Nancy Hower, Richard Chaves.

Chakotay stumbles across his ancestors, in a gallopingly stupid quirk of fate, which
also fails to meaningfully develop his character.

A scrawl on a desolate moon sends Chakotay into a flashback where his dad
is teaching him about sacred lands. Although Janeway hangs a lantern on
it, this is another ludicrous coincidence, where one of a handful of people
stranded thousands of light years away from home comes into contact
with something that is meaningful to them personally. Chakotay is such a
resolutely dull character that even this enthusiastic burrowing into his past life
and family culture does nothing whatsoever to bring him into sharper focus.
And as tiresome as I found Kira bleating about 'the Emissary' over on **Deep
Space Nine**, this super-generic-sounding 'ancient tribe' business is even more
grating. In the B-plot, Kes teaches the Doctor about compassion by giving
him COVID, which is... fine. Everyone else is firmly in **TNG** Season 1 all-
business all-the-time mode. Even Janeway gets nothing to do.

VOY S02E10 Cold Fire ★★★☆☆

Story by Anthony Williams, teleplay by Brannon Braga. Directed by Cliff Bole. TX: 13 November 1995. Featuring: Gary Graham, Lindsay Ridgeway, Norman Large.

Decent example of the I think we've found a way home oh wait never mind type of **Voyager** *story, with all the predictability that implies.*

This isn't a two-parter, but it's picking up story threads that go all the way back to the pilot, so we get a 'previously on…' recap in any case. The remains of the Caretaker are doing the shimmy shimmy shake, raising the possibility that the other like being might be nearby. Once again, *Voyager*'s straight-line path home seems littered with familiar-looking treasures. Meanwhile, despite his patient psi tutelage, no amount of Tuvok digging into Kes's mind can succeed in dredging up an actual character. Her education continues once a second array comes into view as Ocampan Morpheus shows her that there is no spoon. Eventually, 'Suspiria' manifests as a meek blonde-haired little girl and, in a *Twilight Zone*-style gag, appears to murder both Tuvok and B'Elanna, but don't worry, they're fine. None of this is bad, exactly, but it's all hugely 'so what?', the television equivalent of a big shrug.

VOY S02E11 Maneuvers ★★★★☆

Written by Kenneth Biller. Directed by David Livingston. TX: 20 November 1995. Featuring: Martha Hackett, Anthony De Longis, Terry Lester, John Gegenhuber.

Seska returns, in league with the Kazon, in a thrilling space adventure that is as good as anything this show has done so far.

A Federation beacon lures the ship into a hydrogen cloud, whereupon they are set upon by a particularly crafty Kazon gang that ends up boarding *Voyager*. The raiding party makes off with a transporter module, whatever that may be, which they think they'll be able to integrate now that they have help from Martha Hackett's deliciously evil Seska. I'd completely forgotten about this entire storyline – if I ever saw these episodes – and the turncoat Cardassian is rapidly becoming my third favourite character after Janeway and the Doctor.

Her wild-card energy raises the game of many around her. The business of the Kazon sects seems a bit more interesting this time round, a handy way of differentiating them from other more monolithic races, and a source of additional complexity, instead of simply allowing the Kazon to be whatever we need them to be this week. There's even a bit of not-entirely-colourless off-duty banter from B'Elanna and Chakotay (Chakotay!) Despite the rapid pace of shooting a new episode every seven or so days, director David Livingston finds the time to turn an ordinary seeming walk-and-talk into a dramatic hand-held shot, showing off the extensive interconnected *Voyager* sets.

When Chakotay heads off on his own, in a vainglorious attempt to destroy the stolen tech, he seems a tiny bit more like the proudly rebellious Maquis leader we met in the pilot, and less like the blandly stiff career Starfleet woodblock we've been watching for thirty-odd episodes. He leaves a message telling Janeway not to come rescue him, but of course she does, on B'Elanna's urging. The climax features some rather ropey plotting, as B'Elanna boasts that her unique Maquis skills will allow her to beam Chakotay off the Kazon ship as they whizz past at warp – following which they slow down before they attempt the rescue, and then bargain for the Commander's return rather than using the transporter in any case. It's Martha Hackett's show, though, and she's fantastic.

VOY S02E12 Resistance ★★★★☆

Story by Michael Jan Friedman and Kevin J. Ryan, teleplay by Lisa Klink. Directed by Winrich Kolbe. TX: 27 November 1995. Featuring: Alan Scarfe, Tom Todoroff, Joel Grey, Glenn Morshower.

Cabaret star Joel Grey elevates this otherwise fairly ordinary stew of routine science fiction adventure tropes.

Neelix, Janeway, Tuvok and Torres are undercover in an attention-grabbing teaser. Janeway is shot and they are all arrested in pursuit of this week's supply of unobtainium, the absence of which requires *Voyager* to drop its shields (briefly). Bafflingly, junior ensign Harry Kim is the one tasked with repairing the warp drive, whereas chief engineer Torres is part of the team on the planet below.

Janeway's absence on the bridge means that Chakotay is in the centre seat, running things with his usual bland efficiency. Held prisoner by the invading Zagbars, Tuvok and Torres make a more interesting pairing, but Tuvok has yet to reveal anything beyond standard-issue Vulcan detachment. Speaking of which, Janeway finds herself seemingly adopted by Very Fancy Guest Star Joel Grey, one of the native Zoobles who mistakes *Voyager*'s captain for his missing daughter. This is all perfectly decent adventure hijinks, with purring villains interrogating our captive heroes, political manoeuvring from orbit and so on. Joel Grey's subplot feels a bit fresher, a bit more meaningful, but can't transcend the overall feeling of familiarity, despite the excellent performance from a Broadway legend.

VOY S02E13 Prototype ★★☆☆☆

Written by Nicholas Corea. Directed by Jonathan Frakes. TX: 15 January 1996.
Featuring: Rick Worthy, Hugh Hodgin.

Wonderful showcase for Roxann Dawson, but the story she's doing such good work in is both silly and overfamiliar.

Prior to the episode's start, *Voyager* has picked up a silver mannequin, which looks alarmingly like the shapeshifting Kamelion robot from 1980s *Doctor Who*. Unable to determine its power source, Torres pulls an all-nighter. We actually get some glimmers of personality as she spars with first Kim and then Neelix, and Roxann Dawson is better than ever. Repairing the machine is really only act one busywork, however. It perks up and its unsettling politeness now causes it to remind me of Legion from the *Red Dwarf* episode of the same name. V'Ger-like, it wants to find that which created it. It is – like so many things in science fiction stories – supposedly the last of its kind and it kidnaps Torres so she can make it new double-A batteries and revive its fellows.

As director, Jonathan Frakes shoots the teaser from the automated unit's point of view, *RoboCop*-style, which adds a little interest, but this fairly routine outing is only really worth watching for Roxann Dawson, and the Cybernaut-style costumes are particularly silly and unconvincing. Did Frakes really learn nothing from the Exocomps? The final reveal that the war between the Zagbars and the Zoobles only continued because the robots wanted to keep fighting is a nicely savage twist, but I could have done without Torres literally saying, 'My god, what have I done?'

Torres asserts that there is only one sentient artificial life form serving in Starfleet – Data. That will change before this series is over.

VOY S02E14 Alliances ★☆☆☆☆

Written by Jeri Taylor. Directed by Les Landau. TX: 22 January 1996.
Featuring: Martha Hackett, Anthony De Longis, Charles O. Lucia, Raphael Sbarge, John Gegenhuber, Simon Billig, Larry Cedar.

Lurches clumsily from one supposed status quo to the next, but nothing really seems like it matters, except of course that the Federation is never to be questioned. Ugh.

The Kazon, least impressive season Big Bad candidates since the Ferengi first showed up, have *Voyager* pinned down, but mysteriously depart before dealing the final blow. In engineering, some poor boob has been badly burned when his console exploded in his face – they really should do something about that

– and the Doctor pronounces that he can't be saved. There's often a feeling on **Voyager** that – despite all the complex reality-bending plot lines – nothing much matters because it's always reset city. Bumping off a character who's never been heard to speak before doesn't change that, whether or not Roxann Dawson looks grief-stricken, whether or not Robert Beltran tells bland stories about first meeting the guy. So when Chakotay pitches a change in tactics to Janeway, making *Voyager* more Maquis and less Starfleet, it's not so much that I don't want that to happen, or I don't believe any of the changes will be lasting (although both are true), it's that I don't much care. It feels cosmetic.

Since Chakotay is a walking charisma bypass, when Tuvok makes all the same points, in a well-acted but rather laborious scene, Janeway does an abrupt about-face and decides to forge an alliance with Seska – yay, more Martha Hackett. But I'm increasingly dismayed at the extent to which Tuvok is becoming Just Another Vulcan. His relationship with Janeway is similar to that between Spock and Kirk, but where is the McCoy character to round out the triad? **Voyager**'s most significant on-ship relationship is turning out to be a two-legged stool.

Eventually, circumstances solve Janeway's dilemma for her when a more palatable alliance presents itself. Her attitude to the Prime Directive (which I thought only applied to pre-warp civilisations) switches from 'We are forbidden from involving ourselves in local affairs' to 'If there's a chance to bring stability to this region, I can't pass it up'. There are interesting ideas here, but there are so many different plot beats packed into forty-five minutes that none of them really has a chance to register. We go from we're Starfleet, to we need to be more Maquis, to we need an alliance with Seska, to we need an alliance with the Kazon's enemies, to our enemy's enemy can't be trusted, to the one thing we don't need is to be more Maquis. So, on the one hand, Starfleet's supremacy on board *Voyager* is assured, and on the other, there aren't any real consequences for the ship, which has plenty of food and anti-matter, despite the dire circumstances of the teaser. They don't even make good use of Martha Hackett. I'm incredibly disappointed.

VOY S02E15 Threshold ★★☆☆☆

Story by Michael De Luca, teleplay by Brannon Braga. Directed by Alexander Singer. TX: 29 January 1996. Featuring: Raphael Sbarge, Mirron E. Willis.

Even more scientific gibberish than usual in which being in a hurry turns Paris into Brundlefly. He got better.

Paris and Torres are working on a new trans-warp drive. I note that Torres seems to be able to recruit whichever regular character seems convenient to help her with engineering problems – Janeway, Paris, Kim, the Doctor, even Neelix. Similarly, if Starfleet's best pilot, Lieutenant Tom Paris, isn't medically fit for the record-breaking, epoch-defining test flight, Junior Ensign Kim can take over. These people not only don't have much in the way of interiority, they don't even have clearly defined areas of expertise we can rely on.

The warp 10 conversation is pretty much gibberish. If that's the theoretical limit, tending to infinity, then why do they need to cross it? Wouldn't getting 99 per cent of the way there still be incredibly useful? And once Paris does get the shuttle to warp 10, nothing we see looks anything like infinite velocity. It just brings Paris back as a rapidly decaying, pan-allergic, chlorine-breather. But as a vehicle (sorry) for examining the main characters, it's serviceable – at least to begin with. Paris getting more character stuff than he's had all season, and I'm really warming to Torres – I loved her acid-tongued 'fill him in' as she leaves the table to get snacks, while Paris and Kim attempt to sum up years of warp theory in two minutes to an eager Neelix. The Doctor's sarcastic quips struck me as a little overdone this week, though.

It all goes spectacularly awry in the finale, however, which sees Paris and Janeway transformed into corpulent whiskery seal creatures that have sired rubbery offspring. Big news, you say? Nah, they're restored to full health and sanity moments later. Phew. It's often said that **DS9** was far more interested in the consequences of its characters' actions, and had no need to return to the status quo at the end of each episode, whereas **Voyager** always had its finger hovering over the reset button. If so, this is **Voyager**'s 'hold my beer' moment, as the last act is practically made of reset button, taking mere seconds to reverse the biological calamity visited on the Captain minutes earlier, and all off-screen. This is a famously terrible episode, many peoples' least favourite, but I thought the first twenty minutes weren't that bad, whereas *Crossfire* – although nothing in it is quite as terrible as Paris and Janeway fish-fornicating – was basically nonsense all the way through.

Also, since the trans-warp drive did work, kinda, after only a month of trying, and based on what seemed like a fairly minor insight, it does suggest that generations of Federation engineers simply didn't want to create this, as opposed to weren't able to. Despite their partial success, *Voyager*'s crew doesn't seem to want the gift of infinite velocity much either, because they never return to the project. On the other hand, threads with disloyal crewmembers, begun last episode, continue to pay off, which is heartening.

VOY S02E16 Meld ★★★★☆

Story by Mike Sussman, teleplay by Michael Piller. Directed by Cliff Bole. TX: 5 February 1996. Featuring: Brad Dourif, Angela Dohrmann, Simon Billig.

Voyager holds its own Darwin Awards. I wouldn't want this darker tone every week, but this makes effective and unexpected use of the show's premise, which is something of a rarity.

In an unusually grim teaser, the burned remains of a murdered crewmember are found in engineering. Since it turns out there's a weirdo on board and since Brad Dourif is available, he's played by Brad Dourif. In fact, Suder's more than a weirdo. He's a stone-cold psychopath who killed a man just because. This is something that Tuvok cannot accept. But the bigger problem is: adrift decades from home, with no higher authorities to refer to, what is to be done with an irredeemable danger to others? Tim Russ is as good as ever, and for once manages to become something a bit more than just Spock Lite when the Doctor therapeutically removes Tuvok's emotional control. It's some of the best character work we've seen so far on this show.

VOY S02E17 Dreadnought ★★★★☆

Written by Gary Holland. Directed by LeVar Burton. TX: 12 February 1996. Featuring: Raphael Sbarge, Nancy Hower, Michael Spound.

Doomsday Machine Redux *with great material for* Voyager's *chief engineer.*

Torres is coming into focus now. Roxann Dawson has been impressive from the start, but initially her only character trait was 'shouts and throws things'. This is, to be fair, a significant improvement on Harry Kim ('young') and Chakotay ('vaguely Native American-ish') but not much to build a character on. More recently, something more detailed, conflicted and interesting has emerged, and this storyline is a great vehicle for those traits, as Torres has to disarm a deadly self-aware missile that she created (and creepily programmed with her own voice). You have to swallow a lot of coincidences to make this one work – it's basically a square **DS9** storyline, hammered into a round **Voyager** hole – but once you get past that, you get a foe that rivals Nomad or the Doomsday Machine for its implacable cunning, and personal stakes that actually feel like they mean something. LeVar Burton directs and makes the most of the tense script. That creepy lieutenant is still writing fan mail to Seska, but she's got her assistant to fend off his advances now.

VOY S02E18 Death Wish ★★★☆☆

Story by Shawn Piller, teleplay by Michael Piller. Directed by James L. Conway. TX: 19 February 1996. Featuring: Raphael Sbarge, Peter Dennis, Maury Ginsberg, John de Lancie, Jonathan Frakes, Gerrit Graham.

What is it about playful godlike beings that tends towards legal wrangling? Janeway plays judge in the case of Q vs Q and it's amusing enough.

While I'm waiting for Seven of Nine to turn up, I dimly remember that the pairing of Q and Janeway is meant to be rather good fun, especially as Q's visit to *Deep Space Nine* was the rather soggy *Q-Less*. Alas, it's not John de Lancie who materialises on the transporter pad, but rather Gerrit 'The Critic' Graham, whose impersonation doesn't have the bite and fizz of the original and who badly overdoes the hand gestures. Thankfully, the OG isn't far behind, patronising Janeway and smarming around the bridge, whereupon the Q who wants only to die seeks asylum on board *Voyager*. That hearing takes up the rest of the episode, which seems a bit low stakes given that either party could whisk everyone home in an instant. Flowing in to fill the gap is a Jonathan Frakes as Riker – in the old costume (plus, rather less interestingly, Maury Ginsberg and Isaac Newton). Excitingly, Janeway offers the mortal Q the chance to join the crew. Predictably, he goes ahead with his plan to take his own life.

VOY S02E19 Lifesigns ★☆☆☆☆

Written by Kenneth Biller. Directed by Cliff Bole. TX: 26 February 1996. Featuring: Susan Diol, Raphael Sbarge, Martha Hackett, Michael Spound.

*Desperately tedious the-Doctor-in-love story with all of **Voyager**'s worst habits on full display.*

For reasons that pass understanding, the Doctor creates a holo-puppet of a patient before trying to cure her. Most people on this ship end up simply announcing facts that relate to their job. Now, Kes is reduced to a bland Nurse Chapel, which seems an odd use of a character who looks on paper to be so unusual and exotic. The patient is the latest guest on board to be suffering from the phage. The Doc and his new patient wander around and pass the time of day until he decides to fall in love with her. It's criminally uninteresting. Even worse is the dire management training film enacted by Paris and Chakotay, which is so boring that even Janeway refuses to participate – and then the writers bail on it too, as it isn't resolved. I almost didn't make it to the end of this one. Dr McCoy gets a shout-out. Seska is wasted again.

VOY S02E20 Investigations ★★★☆☆

Story by Jeff Schnaufer and Ed Bond, teleplay by Jeri Taylor. Directed by Les Landau. TX: 13 March 1996. Featuring: Raphael Sbarge, Martha Hackett, Jerry Sroka, Simon Billig.

Tom Paris leaves, except no he doesn't. Various plot lines are resolved, but the script consistently finds the least interesting way to tell the story.

Oh god, Neelix has a podcast. His disreputable Talaxian friend is legitimate now and has come to pick up Tom Paris. Although this storyline has been brewing for a few episodes, it's frustrating that we have to hear about his reaction to being stood down, his decision to leave, Janeway's response and so on – all second-hand. It makes for a strong(-ish) out of the teaser, but I'm not sure it's a price worth paying. Making Paris's story all about Neelix is not the way I would have gone. And nor is making Neelix's reaction to Tom's departure all about the Doctor's sudden and mysterious desire to be television star.

Similarly, Janeway's plan to get Tom kicked off *Voyager* and thus unmask the spy makes a certain amount of TV-show sense, but denying us access to all of this decision-making in the hope of catching us unawares means we trade understanding of our characters for surprise. Sound familiar? And of course, if it isn't even that much of a surprise, then that's simply weakening the fabric of the story, with no upside, especially given that the surprise is that Tom Paris is on a less interesting journey than we were briefly led to believe. On the other hand, Neelix's laborious detective work plods its way towards a conclusion that we've known about for many episodes now. In fact, almost nothing that Neelix does really impacts the outcome – he's just a mechanism to dole out the actual story slowly enough that it lasts forty-five minutes. And why was Jonas so keen to give up *Voyager* to Seska and the Kazon anyway? Does he think he'll get home quicker on a Kazon ship? Why?

During these shenanigans, the warp drive is out of action and once again, *Voyager* needs supplies in order to make repairs. Visiting a nearby star system on impulse power seems to present no problems, which makes interstellar distances seem very small (or impulse speeds very fast). Torres waits for Jonas's console to explode in his face before giving the computer verbal instructions. It's been almost a year since the Caretaker. Martha Hackett is wasted yet again.

VOY S02E21 Deadlock ★★☆☆☆

Written by Brannon Braga. Directed by David Livingston. TX: 18 March 1996.
Featuring: Nancy Hower, Simon Billig.

Some bad stuff happens. But then again, maybe it doesn't. Mulgrew's never been
better but this can't escape that nothing-really-matters feeling so typical of early
Voyager.

After all this time heading out of the Delta Quadrant, we're still in Vidiian
space (they're the organ-botherers and phage sufferers). I understand the
show's reluctance to give us any clear idea of how far we've gone or how far
through our journey we are, but c'mon. When they take a detour, suddenly
photon blasts start taking the ship apart. It's all fairly bewildering, but it is at
least dramatic, culminating in the death of Ensign Wildman's newborn baby.
That's clue number one that a big ol' timey-wimey reset button is marching
in the direction of this story – and that suspicion becomes a racing certainty
when Harry Kim is sucked out into space.

Suddenly we're on a different version of *Voyager*. Essentially this is
adventure-series-as-video-game. If you get killed on this attempt, switch to
another saved game and have another go. So on the one hand – hurrah! we
get to blow up the ship. But on the other hand – boo! nothing really matters
any more. Once again, the characters are reduced to cardboard cut-outs who
just announce facts at each other. What if the *Voyager* that solved the problem
correctly the first time was more like the Mirror Universe, where their success
was due to selfish decision-making that prioritised only their own safety? Now
which ship do you want to survive? Better, isn't it? Instead, we get drenched in
technobabble during which the two ships 'merge' (complete with profoundly
weak double-exposure visual effects) and then the Vidiians storm on board
the 'good' ship, but by that time, it doesn't matter who lives or dies – we can
restore anyone we lose from the backup. Still, it is at least fun and exciting and
it's always cool to have two versions of this (or any) captain sharing the screen,
even if the effects work isn't always 100 per cent convincing.

Ludicrously, the Doctor's solution to Ensign Wildman's excruciating labour
is to use the transporters to beam the horny-foreheaded infant out of her only
after she's pushed for several hours. Moments later, when engineering is hit, all
casualties have to walk themselves over to sickbay.

VOY S02E22 Innocence ★★☆☆☆

Story by Anthony Williams, teleplay by Lisa Klink. Directed by James L. Conway. TX: 8 April 1996. Featuring: Marnie McPhail, Tiffany Taubman, Sarah Rayne, Tahj D. Mowry, Richard Garon.

Tuvok struggles to keep three little tykes alive, while Janeway tries to make friends with the grown-ups. Routine, anodyne stuff for the most part.

We might be in a hurry to make it home, but there's always time to stop and smell the flowers, even if such olfactory investigations cost the life of a crewmember. Having failed to protect his comrade, Tuvok now has three moppets to keep alive. This is basically a rerun of *The Galileo Seven*, but with kids, and once again, Tuvok's – sadly never seen – family life turns out to be the most interesting thing about him. His Vulcan approach to life is regarded as odd by the very human-seeming moppets, who contrast strongly with their isolationist, philosophical parents. They also bear no resemblance whatsoever to long-lived pensioners with juvenile bodies, which renders the would-be clever twist completely ridiculous. *Voyager* can run for four years without refuelling. No sign of the absolute paddywacking that the ship received last week. Everything looks as good as new. ('That'll buff right out.') Lucky that, as a tour party of drab locals are being shown around and sneering at most things.

VOY S02E23 The Thaw ★☆☆☆☆

Story by Richard Gadas, teleplay by Joe Menosky. Directed by Marvin V. Rush. TX: 29 April 1996. Featuring: Michael McKean, Thomas Kopache, Carel Struycken.

Torres and Kim are plunged into a cheapskate dreamscape, which looks like a bad episode of Batman *unaccountably made thirty years too late.*

A message from a dead planet includes strict instructions to stay the hell away, so of course Janeway puts their journey home on pause and rapidly beams up their stasis pods and begins trying to defrost them. Examining alien machinery from the other side of the galaxy, Kim begins confidently pressing buttons and announcing what the people in the pods are experiencing. In fact, most of what's said about the pods is nonsense. Why bother going into stasis if you're going to be conscious the whole damned time? You might as well just build a bunker and make some sandwiches. Surely, the point is that your consciousness skips the intervening years?

Kim and Torres enter the dreamscape, which looks like some kind of hideous children's television version of a sex party, redolent of some of the more embarrassing episodes of **TOS** like *Catspaw* or *The Empath*. It's ghastly and even the frequently brilliant Michael McKean can't save it – the grey romper suit doesn't help, but it's a doomed enterprise in any case. There's a glimmer of that handy ethical dilemma about saving the lives of artificial persons, but the one-dimensional moustache-twirling of the Clown makes it all thoroughly unconvincing. Once more, all of the dialogue is blandly functional. McKean reels off facts about Kim and Torres but that doesn't amount to them registering as people. You could swap pretty much all of their dialogue and it would sound the same. They are also dumber than usual. 'It's almost as if he can read our minds,' announces Harry at one point, seemingly having not understood a word of what's been said to him for the last fifteen minutes. The plot is resolved only when the Clown acts decisively against his own interests and lets Torres go virtually on a whim. Including a little person as a dose of added weirdness is pretty nasty as well, considering we've never seen a little person on the crew of this or any starship. Half a star for the quietly effective closing seconds, but this was very close to being a one-star clunker.

VOY S02E24 Tuvix ★★★★☆

Story by Andrew Shepard Price and Mark Gaberman, teleplay by Kenneth Biller. Directed by Cliff Bole. TX: 6 May 1996. Featuring: Tom Wright, Simon Billig, Bahni Turpin.

Tom Wright is superb, in this ultimate version of the Space Trolley Problem, but Janeway's course of action is clear once you remember she's the captain of the good ship Reset Button.

I remember this one. And I remember the stink about it from those who criticised every decision Janeway made from blowing up the Array onwards. Apparently, the ethical thing to do was to let Tuvix live. But, let's not get ahead of ourselves. From the first season of **TOS**, a malfunctioning transporter has been a handy plot-generating mechanism. It's best not to ask exactly how it works. Just as no physical principle exists that could split Kirk into good and evil, no physical principle exists that could combine a Vulcan and a Talaxian into a single living entity with a blended personality. And it's notable that the transporter functions as a body-backup whenever there's a debilitating disease doing the rounds and at no other time. (The Doctor also asserts that he has none of Tuvok or Neelix's DNA on hand, which seems profoundly unlikely. There would be skin cells on their pillows for a start.)

Anyway, this is really about Tom Wright's performance as 'Tuvix' and it's a testament not just to him, but to Tim Russ and Ethan Phillips that this works at all. You couldn't do this with, say, Harry Kim and Chakotay because bland plus bland still equals bland. But Tuvok and Neelix are distinct and they are well-defined enough by now for this to be attempted. Sadly, the rest of the bridge crew are their usual dry professional selves for the most part. Only Kes shows a flicker of emotion at this extraordinary turn of events, although she tries not to show it – and that further saps the drama. The episode's best scene uses Kes's loss to shine a light on how Janeway is dealing with being stranded in the Delta Quadrant. And after that, I can accept any decision the Captain makes.

I am surprised that the script doesn't rustle up a medical emergency that forces the decision to separate, but I think it is a more interesting story when it doesn't let Janeway off the hook, even if the outcome is never really in doubt – of course she'll kill one person to save two (especially when those two are in the opening titles). That makes all the brow-furrowing and anxious standing around doing nothing from the rest of the crew feel a bit synthetic and half-assed. This storyline was originally pitched as a goofy comedy, and I admire the decision to try to play it more seriously, but the last five minutes of the script feels as helpless in the face of this dilemma as all of Tuvix's crewmates. It is a nice scene with Janeway, though.

VOY S02E25 Resolutions ★★☆☆☆

Written by Jeri Taylor. Directed by Alexander Singer. TX: 13 May 1996.
Featuring: Simon Billig, Susan Diol, Bahni Turpin.

Leaving the Captain behind feels bold, but a big swing like this exposes the weaknesses in the characterisation, and it may be too late to fix that now.

Another day, another virus. Infected before the story began, Janeway and Chakotay have been in stasis on the planet below for two and a half weeks and the Doctor's best idea is to contact the lung-stealers, which the Captain vetoes. I dunno, it might have been better to stick with plan a) and just haul ass back to the Alpha Quadrant rather than doing whatever it was that got the two most senior bridges officers this dose of space dropsy in the first place. Speaking of plan a), half an episode later, after endless handwringing and debating, *Voyager* does contact the lung-stealers, notably the Doctor's ex, and they are only too happy to help (kinda). Good thing we went on this massive detour then. All told, this little stop-off must have added three or four months to their journey.

The fate of Tuvix is never mentioned, naturally, but third-in-command Tuvok now takes over the centre seat (although he sticks with the gold shoulders). He beams down his erstwhile boss some picnic blankets and a Gameboy and leaves her to play with 'protein cofactors', whatever they may be, while Chakotay just sticks to colour-coding their campsite and refuses to call Janeway 'Kathryn' (he finds it easier when she's in the hot tub in the nuddy). As *Voyager* cruises away, naturally, it's do-gooding by-the-book Harry Kim who foments rebellion and questions Tuvok's orders, while wildcard Tom Paris keeps his head down and tries to quietly get on with his work. Meanwhile, on the plague planet, Maquis terrorist leader Chakotay is all 'Some things you just can't change – more soup?' Very few Starfleet officers we've ever seen would be so defeatist, but this makes no sense at all for someone who was prepared to throw away his whole career for the sake of a cause he believed in. That's a huge problem for a show at the end of its second year. It's very late in the day for the characters to still be getting randomly assigned motivations according to the needs of this week's plot. It's a good showing for Tuvok and Janeway, at least, even if the Janeway/Chakotay pairing has even less flirty crackle than the fish-fornicating in *Threshold*.

We're down another photon torpedo, this one used like a video game smart bomb to take out three Vidiian ships at once. Is anyone keeping count of how many they have left?

VOY S02E26 Basics, Part I ★★★☆☆

Written by Michael Piller. Directed by Winrich Kolbe. TX: 20 May 1996. Featuring: Martha Hackett, Anthony De Longis, Brad Dourif, Henry Darrow, John Gegenhuber, Nancy Hower, Simon Billig.

Barely adequate season finale, which laboriously strands our crew on a hostile planet but doesn't leave me in much doubt that they will survive, thrive and eventually triumph over their foes.

Hey – Brad Dourif's Suder is still on board. And is playing with orchids, always the plant of choice for the psychopath, for reasons that are beyond my horticultural ken. Rather more dramatically, Seska is reaching out to Chakotay for help when their son is seized by her Kazon allies. So now, instead of continuing with their first and most important mission – hauling ass back to the Alpha Quadrant – they're going to turn back again and return to Kazon space.

Chakotay's dream ghost dad has some spooky words of wisdom to impart, but Janeway needs no such encouragement to commit *Voyager* to this rescue mission. They scoop up a wounded Kazon, who relates the unlikely news that Seska has been killed off-screen. All I'm saying is, she'd better not have been. Knowing that the episode has to be forty-five minutes long, the Kazon make brief attacks, one at a time, picking away at *Voyager*'s belly, until the unguarded Kazon they brought on board detonates the bomb in his bloodstream, crippling the ship. More talk of low power reserves but Janeway still thinks using a couple of spare batteries to conjure up some holographic decoy ships is a good idea. When they try this, the Doctor briefly appears outside the ship in a bafflingly stupid gag, which undercuts the tension at precisely the wrong time and is the least funny thing Robert Picardo has ever said or done on this show. They later go (in the heat of battle!) and get real Talaxian ships to provide actual support, which seems like it might have been a better idea in the first place.

Janeway calls for evacuation, but the self-destruct system has been hit and blown itself up. That leads to the actual point of this slackly plotted and rather slow-moving season finale. The Kazon take control of *Voyager* (very, very easily, even given that Seska has been able to give them a few pointers about how to operate Federation ships) and strand Janeway and her crew on a volcanic planet with no food, water or shelter. It's not a bad end-of-season cliffhanger, but there are plenty of threads to pull on for part two (the Doctor, Suder, Paris, Seska herself) and one wonders why the ruthless Kazon didn't just kill them all when they had the chance.

Part of the problem is that a lot of the major developments feel familiar from very recent episodes. The ship was messed up just as badly if not worse in *Deadlock* and Janeway was abandoned on a remote planet with no hope of rescue just last week. And the effects work frequently falls short of what the script requires, with ropey shots of *Voyager* taking off and *One Million Years BC*-style local wildlife, which I assume were the work of Ray Harryhausen on an off day. 'Command codes', a gimmick from *The Wrath of Khan*, is still going strong as a method by which any ship may gain access to the systems of any other ship, even one from the other side of the galaxy.

Voyager Season 2 wrap-up

- Looking back on this season, it feels like an improvement, as you might expect. The first episode out of the gate was confident and fun, promising characters like Tuvok and Torres have been given more room to grow, strong characters like Janeway and the Doctor continue to impress, and we kept Martha Hackett around as Seska.
- But this is not reflected in the season average, which is pretty much the same as Season 1, 2.73 compared to 2.77 – about the same as the first two seasons of **TNG**.

- That's not only due to another absence of five-star classics, but the disappointing number of absolute clunkers like *Tattoo*, *Lifesigns*, *Alliances* and *The Thaw* – and that's after I dredged up two whole stars for *Threshold*, which for some people is the worst episode of **Star Trek** ever made.
- Best of this lacklustre bunch were *Maneuvers*, *Dreadnought* and the excellent *Meld*, which not only had a strong science fiction adventure plot, and managed to ask some pertinent questions about justice and morality, it also deepened the characterisation of what should have been one of the major assets of the show – Tim Russ as Tuvok, who too often has been written as Just Another Vulcan, but who here shows a reckless, almost naïve streak, which is (sorry) fascinating.
- As well as the format fighting itself – Too serialised or not serialised enough? *Voyager* can't pop into a starbase for repairs but always starts each episode looking brand new. Maquis and Starfleet are at each other's throats or get along great? – the big problem continues to be the characters. Chakotay is little more than a bundle of vaguely First Nation stereotypes with no specificity at all, and shows nothing of what drove him to join the Maquis. Paris and Kim are interchangeable placeholders. I have no interest in Kes whatsoever.
- Also stalled is Neelix, who began to show a bit more depth in *Initiations*, but whose character has not developed at all since then. Even his relationship with Kes and the love triangle with Paris, as tiresome as that was, seems to have been neatly resolved and put away. But resolving these conflicts makes the characters less interesting, not more.
- Maybe nothing exposes what went wrong with Season 2 more clearly than Tom Paris And The Arc That Never Was. We spend half a dozen or more episodes setting up first the traitor on board *Voyager* who is secretly working with the Kazon, and then three or four setting up Paris's reluctance to continue serving on this Federation ship – only to chuck all of that character development away and substitute a ludicrous spy mission instead, following which our onboard traitor obediently chucks himself off a gantry.
- Still, we are finally out of Kazon space now, so perhaps the next batch of adversaries will prove more interesting.

Afterword

Leaving the audience on a cliffhanger is a well-worn **Star Trek** tradition, one that reignited the franchise back in 1990. And while the end of *Basics, Part I* might not have had quite the same impact as the end of *The Best of Both Worlds*, and I certainly don't imagine that the gap between *Volume II* and *Volume III* will cause my readership to lose their collective minds, I nevertheless fondly imagine that I'm continuing a long-established principle by interrupting the narrative in this way.

As I write these words, my journey is complete. I watched the last episode of **Enterprise** a few days ago and have been working on getting this volume ready for the publishers since then, feeling a vague sense of loss. Sure, there's a lot more **Star Trek** out there, with no fewer than six new series hitting our screens since 2017, but as well as being a personal rewatch, part of the remit for this exercise was seeing these episodes in their historical context. That's harder to do when new episodes are dropping all the time, so there's currently no plan for *Volume IV*.

But, never say never…

In the meantime, if you'd care to join me for the rest of Janeway's adventures in the Delta Quadrant, for Picard's final two big screen missions and for Jonathan Archer's escapades in the pre-Federation days, I would be honoured.

Tom Salinsky
December 2023

Appendix: Episodes by Rating

Episodes with the same star rating can be assumed to be equally good.

DS9	S05E15	By Inferno's Light	★★★★★
DS9	S02E23	Crossover	★★★★★
DS9	S06E13	Far Beyond the Stars	★★★★★
DS9	S05E14	In Purgatory's Shadow	★★★★★
DS9	S06E19	In the Pale Moonlight	★★★★★
DS9	S04E10	Our Man Bashir	★★★★★
DS9	S06E06	Sacrifice of Angels	★★★★★
DS9	S05E06	Trials and Tribble-ations	★★★★★
DS9	S04E03	The Visitor	★★★★★
DS9	S04E01	The Way of the Warrior	★★★★★
DS9	S03E26	The Adversary	★★★★☆
DS9	S02E05	Cardassians	★★★★☆
DS9	S05E22	Children of Time	★★★★☆
DS9	S03E07	Civil Defense	★★★★☆
DS9	S01E19	Duet	★★★★☆
DS9	S05E24	Empok Nor	★★★★☆
TNG	MO002	First Contact	★★★★☆
DS9	S05E13	For the Uniform	★★★★☆
DS9	S04E19	Hard Time	★★★★☆
DS9	S04E04	Hippocratic Oath	★★★★☆
DS9	S03E03	The House of Quark	★★★★☆
DS9	S02E26	The Jem'Hadar	★★★★☆
DS9	S04E08	Little Green Men	★★★★☆
DS9	S02E20	The Maquis, Part I	★★★★☆
VOY	S02E16	Meld	★★★★☆
DS9	S06E02	Rocks and Shoals	★★★★☆
DS9	S03E05	Second Skin	★★★★☆
DS9	S05E02	The Ship	★★★★☆
DS9	S02E03	The Siege	★★★★☆
DS9	S07E08	The Siege of AR-558	★★★★☆

DS9	S04E07	Starship Down	★★★★☆
DS9	S05E19	Ties of Blood and Water	★★★★☆
DS9	S04E23	To the Death	★★★★☆
DS9	S06E11	Waltz	★★★★☆
DS9	S07E25	What You Leave Behind	★★★★☆
DS9	S02E22	The Wire	★★★★☆
VOY	S02E01	The 37s	★★★★☆
DS9	S05E09	The Ascent	★★★★☆
DS9	S05E01	Apocalypse Rising	★★★★☆
DS9	S02E13	Armageddon Game	★★★★☆
DS9	S07E15	Badda-Bing Badda-Bang	★★★★☆
DS9	S06E04	Behind the Lines	★★★★☆
DS9	S05E26	Call to Arms	★★★★☆
DS9	S07E14	Chimera	★★★★☆
DS9	S02E02	The Circle	★★★★☆
DS9	S04E13	Crossfire	★★★★☆
DS9	S03E09	Defiant	★★★★☆
DS9	S03E21	The Die is Cast	★★★★☆
VOY	S02E17	Dreadnought	★★★★☆
DS9	S07E23	Extreme Measures	★★★★☆
DS9	S03E23	Family Business	★★★★☆
DS9	S06E05	Favor the Bold	★★★★☆
DS9	S04E22	For the Cause	★★★★☆
DS9	S03E14	Heart of Stone	★★★★☆
DS9	S02E01	The Homecoming	★★★★☆
DS9	S04E11	Homefront	★★★★☆
DS9	S04E05	Indiscretion	★★★★☆
DS9	S06E18	Inquisition	★★★★☆
DS9	S07E16	Inter Arma Enim Silent Leges	★★★★☆
DS9	S07E10	It's Only a Paper Moon	★★★★☆
VOY	S01E16	Learning Curve	★★★★☆
DS9	S05E03	Looking for par'Mach…	★★★★☆
VOY	S02E11	Maneuvers	★★★★☆
DS9	S02E21	The Maquis, Part II	★★★★☆
DS9	S02E08	Necessary Evil	★★★★☆
DS9	S05E04	…Nor the Battle to the Strong	★★★★☆
DS9	S04E12	Paradise Lost	★★★★☆
DS9	S03E11	Past Tense, Part I	★★★★☆
DS9	S02E18	Profit and Loss	★★★★☆
DS9	S04E06	Rejoined	★★★★☆

DS9	S04E14	Return to Grace	★★★★☆
DS9	S03E01	The Search, Part I	★★★★☆
DS9	S07E02	Shadows and Symbols	★★★★☆
DS9	S05E21	Soldiers of the Empire	★★★★☆
DS9	S06E26	Tears of the Prophets	★★★★☆
DS9	S06E01	A Time to Stand	★★★★☆
DS9	S05E08	Things Past	★★★★☆
DS9	S07E06	Treachery, Faith, and the Great River	★★★★☆
DS9	S02E25	Tribunal	★★★★☆
DS9	S03E06	The Abandoned	★★★☆☆
DS9	S05E05	The Assignment	★★★☆☆
VOY	S02E26	Basics, Part I	★★★☆☆
DS9	S05E23	Blaze of Glory	★★★☆☆
DS9	S04E26	Broken Link	★★★☆☆
DS9	S01E06	Captive Pursuit	★★★☆☆
DS9	S06E16	Change of Heart	★★★☆☆
DS9	S07E20	The Changing Face of Evil	★★★☆☆
DS9	S07E09	Covenant	★★★☆☆
DS9	S01E08	Dax	★★★☆☆
VOY	S02E21	Deadlock	★★★☆☆
DS9	S03E15	Destiny	★★★☆☆
DS9	S05E16	Doctor Bashir, I Presume?	★★★☆☆
VOY	S01E07	Eye of the Needle	★★★☆☆
DS9	S03E25	Facets	★★★☆☆
DS9	S07E01	Image in the Sand	★★★☆☆
DS9	S03E20	Improbable Cause	★★★☆☆
DS9	S01E20	In the Hands of the Prophets	★★★☆☆
DS9	S02E04	Invasive Procedures	★★★☆☆
VOY	S01E15	Jetrel	★★★☆☆
DS9	S03E13	Life Support	★★★☆☆
DS9	S01E11	The Nagus	★★★☆☆
VOY	S02E07	Parturition	★★★☆☆
DS9	S03E12	Past Tense, Part II	★★★☆☆
DS9	S02E17	Playing God	★★★☆☆
VOY	S01E10	Prime Factors	★★★☆☆
DS9	S01E15	Progress	★★★☆☆
DS9	S06E21	The Reckoning	★★★☆☆
VOY	S02E12	Resistance	★★★☆☆
DS9	S04E18	Rules of Engagement	★★★☆☆
DS9	S03E02	The Search, Part II	★★★☆☆

DS9	S02E09	Second Sight	★★★★☆
DS9	S02E16	Shadowplay	★★★★☆
DS9	S06E25	The Sound of Her Voice	★★★★☆
DS9	S06E09	Statistical Probabilities	★★★★☆
DS9	S07E22	Tacking Into the Wind	★★★★☆
DS9	S07E04	Take Me Out to the Holosuite	★★★★☆
DS9	S03E19	Through the Looking Glass	★★★★☆
DS9	S07E18	'Til Death Do Us Part	★★★★☆
VOY	S01E04	Time and Again	★★★★☆
VOY	S02E24	Tuvix	★★★★☆
DS9	S01E12	Vortex	★★★★☆
DS9	S07E21	When It Rains…	★★★★☆
DS9	S02E14	Whispers	★★★★☆
DS9	S04E17	Accession	★★★☆☆
DS9	S07E03	Afterimage	★★★☆☆
DS9	S02E12	The Alternate	★★★☆☆
DS9	S01E05	Babel	★★★☆☆
VOY	S03E01	Basics, Part II	★★★☆☆
DS9	S05E12	The Begotten	★★★☆☆
VOY	S01E13	Cathexis	★★★☆☆
VOY	S02E10	Cold Fire	★★★☆☆
DS9	S02E24	The Collaborator	★★★☆☆
VOY	S02E18	Death Wish	★★★☆☆
DS9	S07E24	The Dogs of War	★★★☆☆
VOY	S02E04	Elogium	★★★☆☆
DS9	S01E01	Emissary	★★★☆☆
DS9	S03E04	Equilibrium	★★★☆☆
DS9	S03E22	Explorers	★★★☆☆
VOY	S01E14	Faces	★★★☆☆
DS9	S07E13	Field of Fire	★★★☆☆
DS9	S01E17	The Forsaken	★★★☆☆
TNG	MO03	Generations	★★★☆☆
DS9	S07E07	Once More Unto the Breach	★★★☆☆
DS9	S06E14	One Little Ship	★★★☆☆
DS9	S02E15	Paradise	★★★☆☆
VOY	S01E03	Parallax	★★★☆☆
DS9	S01E03	Past Prologue	★★★☆☆
DS9	S07E17	Penumbra	★★★☆☆
DS9	S05E10	Rapture	★★★☆☆
DS9	S04E24	The Quickening	★★★☆☆

DS9	S02E07	Rules of Acquisition	★★★☆☆
DS9	S04E20	Shattered Mirror	★★★☆☆
DS9	S06E03	Sons and Daughters	★★★☆☆
VOY	S01E11	State of Flux	★★★☆☆
DS9	S06E24	Time's Orphan	★★★☆☆
DS9	S06E22	Valiant	★★★☆☆
DS9	S06E17	Wrongs Darker Than Death or Night	★★★☆☆
DS9	S04E16	Bar Association	★★⯪☆☆
DS9	S02E19	Blood Oath	★★⯪☆☆
DS9	S05E18	Business as Usual	★★⯪☆☆
DS9	S05E11	The Darkness and the Light	★★⯪☆☆
DS9	S01E18	Dramatis Personae	★★⯪☆☆
VOY	S01E12	Heroes and Demons	★★⯪☆☆
VOY	S02E02	Initiations	★★⯪☆☆
VOY	S02E22	Innocence	★★⯪☆☆
VOY	S02E20	Investigations	★★⯪☆☆
DS9	S01E04	A Man Alone	★★⯪☆☆
DS9	S02E06	Melora	★★⯪☆☆
VOY	S02E08	Persistence of Vision	★★⯪☆☆
VOY	S02E03	Projections	★★⯪☆☆
DS9	S03E16	Prophet Motive	★★⯪☆☆
VOY	S02E13	Prototype	★★⯪☆☆
DS9	S02E10	Sanctuary	★★⯪☆☆
DS9	S03E24	Shakaar	★★⯪☆☆
DS9	S05E17	A Simple Investigation	★★⯪☆☆
DS9	S04E15	Sons of Mogh	★★⯪☆☆
DS9	S07E19	Strange Bedfellows	★★⯪☆☆
DS9	S04E09	The Sword of Kahless	★★⯪☆☆
DS9	S03E17	Visionary	★★⯪☆☆
DS9	S06E07	You are Cordially Invited…	★★⯪☆☆
DS9	S01E13	Battle Lines	★★☆☆☆
DS9	S04E25	Body Parts	★★☆☆☆
VOY	S01E01	Caretaker	★★☆☆☆
DS9	S07E05	Chrysalis	★★☆☆☆
VOY	S01E06	The Cloud	★★☆☆☆
DS9	S03E18	Distant Voices	★★☆☆☆
VOY	S01E09	Emanations	★★☆☆☆
DS9	S05E20	Ferengi Love Songs	★★☆☆☆
DS9	S06E20	His Way	★★☆☆☆

DS9	S05E25	In the Cards	★★☆☆
DS9	S05E07	Let He Who Is Without Sin...	★★☆☆
DS9	S06E10	The Magnificent Ferengi	★★☆☆
DS9	S04E21	The Muse	★★☆☆
VOY	S02E05	Non Sequitur	★★☆☆
DS9	S01E09	The Passenger	★★☆☆
VOY	S01E05	Phage	★★☆☆
DS9	S01E07	Q-Less	★★☆☆
VOY	S02E25	Resolutions	★★☆☆
DS9	S06E08	Resurrection	★★☆☆
VOY	S02E15	Threshold	★★☆☆
VOY	S02E06	Twisted	★★☆☆
DS9	S06E12	Who Mourns for Morn?	★★☆☆
VOY	S02E14	Alliances	★☆☆☆
DS9	S06E15	Honor Among Thieves	★☆☆☆
DS9	S01E16	If Wishes Were Horses	★☆☆☆
DS9	S07E11	Prodigal Daughter	★☆☆☆
DS9	S02E11	Rivals	★☆☆☆
DS9	S01E14	The Storyteller	★☆☆☆
VOY	S02E23	The Thaw	★☆☆☆
DS9	S07E12	The Emperor's New Cloak	★☆☆☆
VOY	S01E08	Ex Post Facto	★☆☆☆
DS9	S03E10	Fascination	★☆☆☆
VOY	S02E19	Lifesigns	★☆☆☆
DS9	S03E08	Meridian	★☆☆☆
DS9	S01E10	Move Along Home	★☆☆☆
DS9	S06E23	Profit and Lace	★☆☆☆
VOY	S02E09	Tattoo	★☆☆☆

Index

NOTE: Titles of episodes are not included in this index when they appear as their own section, only if they are mentioned elsewhere in the text. Contributors are not indexed when they appear at the top of an episode review, only if they are mentioned elsewhere in the text.

12 Monkeys (1995 movie), 119
2001: A Space Odyssey (1968 movie), 119
24 (US TV show), 111, 125, 153, 160
35mm film, 2, 3

ABC (US TV network), 109, 167
Academy Award, 17
action figures, 102
Adams, Cecily, 102, 120
Adams, Mary Kay, 88
admiral, 20, 36, 45, 59, 74–5, 77, 93, 115, 137, 140, 148
adoption, 22–3
Adversary, The (**DS9** episode), 64
advert, 82, 112, 156
ageing to death, 57
Ahab, Captain, 96
airlock, 40, 143
Alaimo, Marc, 4, 16, 25, 36, 48, 64, 68, 97, 120, 143
Alamo, The (battle), 147, 151
Albino, The, 34
Alien (1979 movie), 105
alien-of-the-week, 7, 9
Aliens (1986 movie), 160
Alixus, 31
All Good Things (**TNG** episode), 66, 155, 160
All Our Yesterdays (**Star Trek** episode), 81
All Quiet on the Western Front (novel), 89
Allegiance (musical), 164
Alliance, The (Mirror Universe), 144
Alliances (**Voyager** episode), 207
Alpha Quadrant, 112, 123, 129, 132, 149, 178, 182, 204, 205

Alternate, The (**DS9** episode), 30
AM radio, 186
ambassador(s), 15, 64, 142, 156
America, 14, 26, 51, 60, 68, 70, 122, 139, 153, 182
Amok Time (**Star Trek** episode), 127
anomaly, 87, 88, 177, 190
Anslem (fictional novel), 80
anti-technology sentiment, 15, 31, 161
Apollo 13 (1995 movie), 72
Aquiel (**TNG** episode), 177
Arandis, 91
arc vs non-arc, 45–6, 49, 51, 59, 61, 122, 128–9
see also serialisation
Archer, Captain Jonathan, ix
Arena (**Star Trek** episode), 127
Arissa, 100
Arjin, 33
arms dealing, 35, 40
army (American), 70
array (Dominion), 115, 142
Array, The, 170, 193, 203
artificial life form, 195
Ashbrook, Daphne, 24
Asimov, Isaac, 119
assassination, 74, 92, 148
Assignment, The (**DS9** episode), 130
Atlantis (Bajoran), 94
Auberjonois, René, 2, 3, 8, 11, 15, 18, 25, 44, 54, 59, 74, 79, 84, 92, 93, 95, 104, 115, 121, 146, 167
as director, 55
audience, 18, 28, 45, 147, 158, 160, 208
for **Deep Space Nine**, ready-made, 17

movie, 105
studio, sitcom, 102
television:
    for a fifth network, 167
    for ongoing storylines, 109
    trained by the story, 126
Austin Powers (1997 movie), 72
autopsy, 52
Avery, Tex, 21
Awakenings (1990 movie), 139
award, 55, 133, 198
    see also prize

Babylon 5 (US TV show), 10, 45–6,
    134–5, 142
Back to the Future (1985 movie), 70
Back to the Future, Part II (1989 movie),
    90, 185
backlot, 89
backstory, 4, 12, 28, 37, 41, 68, 73, 95, 118,
    137, 169, 170, 179, 183, 187
Badda-Bing Badda-Bang (**DS9**
    episode), 158
Badlands, 53, 95, 124, 168, 169
Bajor, 20, 21, 27, 39, 62, 76, 85, 94, 107,
    117, 129, 134, 157
    joining Federation, 39, 94
    moon, 137
    sun, 98
Bajoran(s), 2, 5, 12, 16, 22–3, 38, 39, 44, 48,
    52, 59–60, 62, 68, 75, 76–7, 83, 92, 95,
    114, 116, 117, 125, 129, 139, 143, 155,
    156, 158
    conflict with Cardassians, 47, 81, 85, 110
    Dukat disguised as, 149
    government, 19, 61–2
    religion, 3, 17, 38, 50, 55, 76, 118, 125,
        129, 133–4, 138, 143, 151
    Seska disguised as, 180
Ba'ku, 144
Balance of Terror (**Star Trek** episode), 127
baldric, 65, 82
Band-Aid, 52
Banks, Jonathan, 12
Bar Association (**DS9** episode), 85
bar mitzvah (Ferengi), 54
Barbeau, Adrienne, 148

Barclay, Reginald, 166, 178
Bareil Antos, 20, 32, 38–9, 50, 52–3,
    64, 118
Barrett, Majel, 15, 80
Barry, John, 72
baseball, 105, 108, 134, 139
Bashir, Dr Julian, 3–4, 6, 7, 8, 9, 12–13, 15,
    20, 22, 23, 24, 26, 33, 35, 36, 37, 38, 39, 44,
    46, 49, 51, 52–3, 55, 56–7, 59, 60, 63, 64,
    67, 68, 70, 72, 73, 77, 78, 82, 83, 85, 88, 89,
    91, 93, 97, 98, 99, 100, 101, 102, 106, 112,
    116, 118–19, 121, 123, 124, 126, 136, 139,
    140, 144, 147, 148, 150, 153, 157, 169
    duplicate, 97–8, 157
    genetic backstory, 99, 113, 118–19, 126
    not a botanist, 37
    relationship with Dax, 8, 9, 14, 18, 130,
        138, 145, 151, 152, 154, 155
    relationship with Garak, 23, 36–7, 56,
        58, 72
    relationship with O'Brien, 13, 27–8,
        29, 58, 67, 73, 77, 116, 120, 125, 138,
        141, 152
    underused, 39, 119, 133, 149, 151, 156
bat'leth, 71
Batman (superhero franchise), 119
Battle of Britain, The, 77
Battlestar Galactica (2004 TV show), 77
Bauer, Jack, 153
Bauer, Teri, 125–6
BBC, 2
beaming *see* transporter
beard, 19, 59, 65, 79
Becker (US TV show), 135
beer (hold my), 197
Behr, Ira Steven, 110–11, 142, 147, 157,
    158, 168, 173
Beimler, Hans, 68, 142, 147, 157
Bell, David, 101, 139
Bell, Felecia M., 58, 79
Bell, Gabriel, 71, 51–2
Beltran, Robert, 170, 171, 172, 174, 196
Bennett, Tony, 128
Benteen, Captain Erika, 73
Benzar, 129
Berkoff, Steven, 100
Berman, Rick, 1, 12, 18, 23, 27, 69, 108,
    109–10, 160, 164, 168, 171, 173, 184

Best of Both Worlds, The (**TNG** episode), 3, 127, 164

Betazed, 127, 129

Beymer, Richard, 19

Bezos, Jeff, 164

Bill and Ted's Bogus Journey (1991 movie), 126

bio-memetic gel, 56, 127

bio-neural circuitry, 169, 184

Bird of Prey, 75, 103

birth, 77, 143

birthday, 56, 190

Blackadder (UK TV show), 152

Blackman, Robert, 159

Blade Runner (1982 movie), 32

Blake, Geoffrey, 33

blockade, 137

blog, 77

blood, 92, 124, 146, 206
  Klingon, colour of, 66

blood test, 86, 98

blood wine, 88

'Blue Danube, The' (waltz), 119

Blue Origin (space shuttle), 164

Blu-ray, 3

board game, 9–10, 105

Bochco, Steven, 111, 109–10

Body Parts (**DS9** episode), 85

body swap, 8–9, 39, 46–7, 62

bomb, 43, 58, 72, 92, 98, 205, 206

Bonsall, Brian, 114

Book of the Dead (Bajoran), 151, 152, 155

bookkeeping, 45, 88, 144

Boot, Das (1981 movie), 70, 169

Borg, 3, 41, 43, 110, 111, 164

Borg Queen, 165–6

Boston Legal (US TV show), 164

Bottomley, Nathan, 106

Boy's Own, 81, 142

Braga, Brannon, 160, 164, 168, 173

Brahms, Leah, 73, 110

brain:
  broken, 122
  missing, 174, 181
  part missing, 53

Breaking Bad (US TV show), 12

Breen, 98, 149, 150, 151, 153, 154, 155, 156

Briar Patch, 144

Bridge on the River Kwai, The (1957 movie), 31

Brigadoon (musical), 48

Broadway, 194

Brocksmith, Roy, 68

Brooks, Avery, 2, 18, 51, 52, 57, 59, 77, 80, 94, 113, 120, 128, 130, 139, 159
  as director, 40, 48, 59, 122,

Brown, Doc, 185

Brunt, Liquidator, 61, 76, 83, 85, 120, 131

budget, 3, 6, 35, 74, 81, 107, 153, 164, 186

Buffy the Vampire Slayer (US TV show), 77, 168

Bugsy Malone (1976 movie), 130

Bujold, Geneviève, 167, 168

Burton, LeVar, 68, 77, 159, 167, 171
  as director, 177, 198

By Inferno's Light (**DS9** episode), 108

Byrd, Danny, 189

Cabaret (musical), 194

Cage, The (**Star Trek** pilot), 3

Cagney and Lacey (US TV show), 80, 110

camping trip, 40

captain's log, 25, 112, 127, 188

card game, 13, 25, 46, 92

Cardassia (Prime), 23, 49, 52, 54–5, 60, 66, 80, 85, 96, 98, 104, 134, 137, 156, 183

Cardassian(s), 4, 17, 21, 22–3, 33, 35, 38, 40, 41, 45, 46–7, 48, 54, 56, 59, 61, 68, 74, 75, 79, 80, 83, 91–2, 96, 97, 98, 101, 104, 105, 107, 113, 114, 115, 116–17, 119, 125, 127, 134, 140, 143, 150, 151, 152, 154, 155, 156, 158, 168, 180, 193
  conflict with Bajorans, 47, 81, 85, 110
  government, 36, 68, 99, 101
  occupation of *Deep Space Nine*, 25, 91–2, 113

Caretaker (**Voyager** episode), 168, 179, 184

Caretaker, the, 193, 200

Carpenter, John, 63

Carrington Award, 55

Carry On (movie series), 130

cartoon character, 21

Casablanca (1943 movie), 34

Casey, Bernie, 35–6

casino, 9, 72, 147

caste system, 76

cat:
  belonging to Data, 163
  mine, able to assist Picard as well as
    Kirk, 162
  white, owned by gangster, 124
Catspaw (**Star Trek** episode), 203
caves, 53, 118, 156, 177
  all looking the same, 71, 191
CBS (network), 109, 167
CGI *see* visual effects
Chain of Command (**TNG** episode), 2,
  40, 127
Chakotay, Cmdr, 168, 170, 171, 172, 173,
  175, 177, 179, 180, 182, 183, 187, 188,
  189, 190, 191, 192, 194, 196, 199, 204,
  205, 207
  brain missing, 181
  interchangeable, 178, 185, 187
  Native American background, 171, 178,
    181, 192, 198, 205, 207
Chandler, Raymond, 100, 146
Changeling(s), 2, 44, 45, 65, 72, 73, 81, 84,
  86, 89, 93, 95, 97, 98, 100, 108, 115, 116,
  129, 136, 140, 141, 146, 152
  see also Founders, Great Link, Odo, TFC
Chao, Rosalind, 89
Chapel, Nurse Christine, 199
ChatGPT, 99
Chattaway, Jay, 72
Cheers (US TV show), 110
cheese:
  component of Vic Fontaine, 128
  get this to sickbay, 184
Chekote, Admiral, 20
Chekov, Pavel, 59, 109, 160, 163
Cherokee, 171
child(ren), 2, 10, 17, 22–3, 25, 27, 35, 40,
  44, 47, 48, 66, 68, 71, 73, 75, 76, 81, 91,
  95, 97, 99, 107, 114, 120, 130–1, 132,
  143, 182, 183, 184, 187, 202, 205
Children of Time (**DS9** episode), 132
chlorine, 197
Christian, Claudia, 135
Christmas, 2, 161
Chronicles of Narnia see Narnia
chronoton particles, 51
Circle, The (splinter group), 20

City on the Edge of Forever, The (**Star Trek**
  episode), 127
Civil Defense (**DS9** episode), 64
clarinet:
  early **Voyager** scene involving, 169
  played by Harry Kim, 191
cliché(s), 6, 10, 13, 14, 16, 18, 28, 29, 50,
  57, 58, 68, 71, 77, 82, 94, 100, 101, 106,
  123, 124, 125, 143, 146, 161, 172, 176,
  177, 183, 191, 194, 195
cliffhanger, 44, 84, 110, 113, 206, 208
cloaking device, 43, 104, 145, 179
clone(s), 49, 102, 141, 156
Close Encounters of the Third Kind (1977
  movie), 94
Clown, The, 203
Coburn, James, 72
Cochrane, Zefram, 165
coffee, 49, 174–5
coincidence, 106, 192, 193, 198
Cold War, 70, 140
Colicos, John, 71, 141
colonist(s), 13, 35, 96, 98, 169
Columbo (US TV show), 25, 109
combadge, 45, 49, 70, 93
Combs, Jeffrey, 49, 61, 81, 83, 102, 120,
  141, 154
comic relief, 40, 117, 170, 185
Coming of Age (**TNG** episode), 126
command codes, 206
commercial *see* advert
competitive dad, 28
computer (fictional), 48, 128, 139, 174,
  180, 200
  Cardassian, fussy, 15
  transporter operated by, 29, 32, 38, 96
conference, 72, 119, 126, 127, 148
conflict (between regulars), 5, 18, 63, 87,
  95, 191, 207
conjuring trick *see* sleight of hand
console, 192
  exploding, 156, 170, 195, 200
Conspiracy (**TNG** episode), 73, 110
conspiracy theory, 91
cookery, 46
Coronation Street (UK TV show), 109
coronavirus *see* COVID-19

corpse(s), 12, 38, 87, 89, 94, 101, 117, 133, 161, 177
cos-play, 13, 73, 76, 141, 160, 184
costume(s), 2, 8, 12, 72, 73, 90, 121, 138, 159, 167, 195, 199
see also uniform
countdown (overly precise), 48, 174
courtroom drama, 7, 40, 77
cover-of-a-comic book, 188, 189
COVID-19, 23, 192
Crane, Denny, 164
creationism, 17
credit, not given, 19
credits (opening/closing), viii, 3, 10, 19, 25, 26, 35, 36, 45, 51, 55, 62, 64, 65, 94, 99, 101, 107, 112, 113, 116, 132, 133, 150, 151, 152, 169, 179, 183, 204
credits (transporter), 60
criminal(s), 16–17, 110, 183
see also war criminal
Critic, The (US TV show), 199
Crockett, Davy, 141
Cromwell, James, 69, 165
Crosby, Denise, 33, 171
Crosby, Mary, 33
cross-dressing, 24–5, 131
Crossover (**DS9** episode), 57, 58, 64, 78
Crusher, Dr Beverly, 49, 74, 134, 163, 165
relationship with Picard, 74
Crusher, Wesley, 134, 162
Crystal, Lola, 129
cure, 6, 149, 154, 182, 199
for death, 106, 177, 183
Curry, Dan, 116
Cusack, Lisa, 132–3
CW, The (network), 168
Cybernaut(s) (*The Avengers*), 195
Cyrano de Bergerac (play), 88

Dabo (game), 25
Dabo girl, 27, 48
see also Leeta
Daley, Arthur, 27, 101
Dallas (US TV show), 109
Damar, Gul, 117, 119, 120, 149, 150, 151, 152, 153, 154, 156, 157
Dambusters, the, 73
Danson, Ted, 135
Dark Page (**TNG** episode), 46

Darmok (**TNG** episode), 127
Darren, James, 128
darts (game), 56
Darwin Awards, 198
Data, Lt Cmdr, 28, 53, 158, 159, 160–1, 163, 165, 170, 184, 195
date (calendar), 97
date (romantic), 53, 118
dated (old-fashioned), 55, 61, 99, 131
Dawson, Roxann, 170, 171, 181–2, 184, 185, 195, 196, 198
Dax, Curzon, 8, 34, 63, 91, 136, 143
Dax, Ezri, 136, 137, 138, 139, 141, 142, 143, 144, 145–6, 148–9, 150, 151, 153, 157
absent, 153, 154, 155
is not Jadzia, 143, 150
lusted after by Quark, 144
relationship with Bashir, 151–2, 154, 155
Dax, Jadzia, 3–4, 6, 7, 9, 14, 21, 22, 26, 30, 31, 32–3, 43, 44, 46, 50, 51, 57, 62–3, 64, 66, 68, 69, 70, 71, 72, 81, 82, 85, 87, 92, 94, 97, 103, 113, 115, 117, 119, 121, 123, 124–5, 127, 129, 136, 138, 139, 142, 143, 144, 148–9, 150
absent, 23, 39, 127
biology, 3, 8, 22, 46, 136
compared to B'Elanna Torres, 170
death of, 133–4, 137
lusted after, 9, 14, 18, 24, 49, 130
relationship with Bashir, 151–2
relationship with Worf, 76, 88, 91, 97, 99, 107, 112, 115, 124, 125
Dax, Joran, 63, 145–6
Dax, Lela, 63
Dax, Tobin, 63, 143
de Boer, Nicole, 136, 138, 145, 146, 149
de Lancie, John, 41, 199
Dead Ringers (1988 movie), 52
Deadlock (**Voyager** episode), 206
Dean, James, 191
death, 12, 21, 36, 38, 51, 66, 71, 73, 82, 83, 87, 89, 91, 95, 97, 102, 105, 117, 118, 120, 121, 133, 134, 141, 146, 147, 149, 160, 161, 162, 164, 166, 196, 201
cure for, 106, 177, 183
foreshadowed, 146
good, 97, 141, 162

personified, 126
right to, 199
rituals relating to, 29, 68, 177–8
Death Star, 81
Deep Space Nine (space station) 10, 25, 27, 31, 36, 37, 41, 48, 53, 65, 75, 79, 81, 92, 96, 98, 105, 106, 115, 117, 122, 129, 130, 132, 133, 134, 138, 153, 199
evacuated, 21, 22, 107, 108
in opening titles, 3
rebuilt by O'Brien, 54
defection, 140
Defector, The (**TNG** episode), 183
Defiant (spaceship), 43, 47, 49, 51, 59, 63, 70, 72, 74, 77, 79, 80, 81, 84, 90, 95, 103, 107, 112, 115, 117, 123, 132, 142, 151, 155, 165, 169
presumed destroyed, 44
Worf sleeping on, 76
Defiant-class ship(s), 130
Delaney sisters, 178
DeLorean (car), 70, 185
Delta Quadrant, ix, 93, 171, 174, 175–6, 183, 187, 188, 189, 190, 201, 204
Deral, 49
deus ex machina, 48
Devil in the Dark, The (**Star Trek** episode), 127
DeYoung, Cliff, 11
dilemma *see* ethical dilemma
dinosaur, 191
disability, 24
Disaster (**TNG** episode), 77
disguise, 16, 24, 52, 86, 90, 131, 148, 149, 180, 182
Distant Voices (**DS9** episode), 72
diversity, 2, 14, 75
Divine Treasury, 71
DNA, 8, 182, 203
Doctor Who (UK TV show), ix, 9, 17, 24, 106, 195
Doctor, The (EMH), 166, 170, 172, 174, 179, 185, 188, 192, 193, 196, 197, 198, 199, 200, 201, 203, 204, 206
name for, 176, 180
documentary (**Star Trek**), 164
dog, 177
Doman, John, 62

Dominion, The, 25, 27, 41, 45, 49, 51, 56, 61, 66, 67, 73, 82, 84, 97, 98, 99, 104, 105, 107, 113, 115, 119, 126, 128, 129, 130, 133, 140, 141, 142, 148, 152, 154, 156
alliance with Cardassians, 45, 99, 101, 152, 156
Dominion War, 2, 45, 84, 85, 108, 112, 123, 127–8, 129, 131, 132, 136, 140, 148, 158, 155–6
Dom-jot, 93
Donnie Brasco (1997 movie), 123
Doohan, James, 163
doohickey(s):
agricultural, 62
for blood testing, 86
for operating transporter, 96
Dooley, Paul, 37, 97
Doomsday Machine, The (**Star Trek** episode), 198
Dorn, Michael, 1, 65, 88, 122, 124, 171, 182
as director, 126
Douglas, Kirk, 62
Dourif, Brad, 198
Dr Seuss, 102
Dr Strangelove (1964 movie), 206
drama school, 37
Dreadnought (**Voyager** episode), 207
dream, 26, 38, 45, 46, 62, 78, 92, 101, 146, 153, 202–203, 205
dream blanket, 181
Dream Team, The (1989 movie), 119
Drebin, Frank, 89
Dreyfus, Richard, 94
Driscoll, Scott, 90
drugs (narcotics), 37
drugs (therapeutic), 130
drugs (truth), 40
Duet (**DS9** episode), 18, 19, 127, 158
Dukat, Gul, 4, 16, 19, 22–3, 25, 26, 35, 36, 40, 42, 48, 49, 60, 68, 81, 85, 86, 92, 94, 97, 98, 99, 101, 107, 108, 112, 113, 114–15, 116, 117, 119, 120–1, 125–6, 134, 143–4, 149, 150, 151, 152, 153, 154, 156, 157
absent, 81, 133
Duras Sisters, 5, 161
Durst, Lt Pete, 182

DVD box set, 168
Dynasty (US TV show), 109

Earhart, Amelia, 187
earring, 19
Earth, 49, 51, 66, 70, 72–3, 137, 160
    attacked by Breen, 150
    Harry Kim suddenly returned
        to, 189–90
    literature of, 58
    people from, 38, 187
    twentieth-century fashion sense, 177
Eddington, Lt Michael, 44, 63, 72,
    95–6, 104
    revealed as traitor, 80
Ehrmantraut, Mike (*Breaking Bad*), 12
Eisenberg, Aron, 144, 187
El Guindi, Fadwa, 99
Elogium, 189
Emergency Medical Hologram, 53, 99
    see also Doctor, The
Emissary (**DS9** episode), 116, 168
Emissary of the Prophets, The, 3, 76, 129,
    149, 192
emotion chip, 161, 165
emotion(s), 30, 66, 118, 132, 153, 163, 170,
    198, 204
Empath, The (**Star Trek** episode), 203
Encounter at Farpoint (**TNG** episode), 3, 4,
    175, 180
Enemy Within, The (**Star Trek**
    episode), 182
energy weapon, 179
    see also phaser(s)
engineer(s), 26, 32, 105, 130, 142, 172, 182,
    194, 196, 197, 198
engineering (main), 174, 195, 198, 201
English (language), 37, 70, 103
Enigma novels *see* novel, Cardassian
Enterprise, USS, 2, 3, 8, 9, 16, 26, 28, 31,
    40, 77, 89, 90, 110, 164
    impossibility of landing, 186
Enterprise, USS (B), 160, 162
Enterprise, USS (D), 161, 162, 169, 187
    crash of, 163
Enterprise, USS (E), 165
ER (US TV show), 18
escape pod(s), 151

escape room, 147
Escher, M.C., 190
Espenson, Jane, 77
ethical dilemma, 6, 53, 55, 82, 103, 119,
    126, 128, 140, 153, 158, 162–4, 170, 174,
    179, 189, 190, 191, 196, 203–204
exams, 57
Exocomp(s), 195
exposition, 7, 33, 38, 53, 124
eyepatch, 38

Face of the Enemy (**TNG** episode), 46–7
Family (**TNG** episode), 137, 161
family, 40, 43, 45, 46, 60, 66, 68, 73, 75, 77,
    89, 131, 133, 145, 153, 157, 161, 162,
    176, 177, 192, 202
Family Business (**DS9** episode), 64, 76
fan (devotee), 1, 2, 64, 76, 90, 108, 145, 198
    of facts, 20
    service, 90
    works created by, 23, 163
fangirl, 24
Far Beyond the Stars (**DS9** episode), 124,
    127, 135, 157–8
farce, 25
farmer(s), 31
Farrell, Terry, 2, 3, 18, 22, 33, 34, 69, 88,
    102, 117, 124–5, 130, 138
    compared to Nicole de Boer, 137
    departure from **DS9**, 134–5, 136
Fascination (**DS9** episode), 64
fascism, 51
Fawcett, Farrah, 65
Federal Communications Commission, 69
Federation *see* United Federation
    of Planets
Female Changeling, The *see* TFC
feminism, 24
Ferengi, 2, 16, 24, 60, 62, 67, 70–1, 76,
    85, 93, 114, 131, 139, 141, 144, 157,
    158, 195
    death rituals, 29
    falling-over episodes, 147
    in Starfleet, 54
Ferengi Love Songs (**DS9** episode), 108, 121
Ferenginar, 10, 61, 83, 102, 120, 131
'Fever' (song), 129
Fields, Peter Allan, 8, 96

fifth network, 167
film noir, 25, 177
Finn, Dr Claire, 61
Finnegan's Wake (novel), 5
First Duty, The (**TNG** episode), 169
fish-fornicating, 197
flagship, 28
flashback, 25, 192
flashback box *see* Orb(s) of the Prophets
Fleming, Ian, 72, 100
Fletcher, Louise, 17, 39, 93, 130
flute, 27
Fly, The (1986 movie), 196
Fontaine, Vic, 128, 133, 137, 142, 144, 147, 156, 157
Fontana, D.C., 8, 168
food, 23, 53, 84, 92, 94, 196, 206
For the Cause (**DS9** episode), 96
For the Uniform (**DS9** episode), 108, 157
Forbes, Michelle, 1, 3, 16
Force of Nature (**TNG** episode), 50
Foster, Meg, 80
Foundation (book series), 119
Founder(s), 45, 58, 59, 61, 63, 92, 113, 115, 117, 146, 151, 158
Fox (network), 167
Frakes, Jonathan, 1, 159, 161, 195, 199
    as director, 45, 49, 164, 165, 188
Frame of Mind (**TNG** episode), 188
framing sequence, 30
Frasier (US TV show), 18
fraud, 171
fridge logic, 104
Friends (US TV show), 110
fringe (hairstyle), 20
frontier town, 31
Fuller, Bryan, 94

gadget, 24, 31, 37, 143
    see also doohickey, gizmo
Gagh, 145
galaxy-class ship, 41
Galaxy Quest (1999 movie), 96
Galileo Seven, The (**Star Trek** episode), 202
Gambit (**TNG** episode), 123
Game of Thrones (US TV show), 108
Gameboy, 205
Gamma Quadrant, 25, 31, 33, 40, 49, 84, 97, 98, 123, 156, 163, 182

gangster movie, 124
Garak, Elim, 4, 22–3, 34, 36–7, 40, 42, 45, 47, 56, 58, 65–6, 72, 79, 81, 83, 84, 85, 92, 97, 98, 105, 107, 112, 113, 116, 127–8, 138, 148, 152–3, 154, 156, 157
    absent, 16, 32, 133
    relationship with Kira, 48
gay *see* homosexual
Geisel, Theodor *see* Dr Suess, 102
generator, 89
genetic engineering, 99
George, Brian, 99
gewgaw, 12, 134
Ghemor, Tekeny, 47, 101
ghost, 74, 89
Gibney, Susan, 73
Gibson, Henry, 131
Giger, Dr, 106
Gilora Rejal, 55
Gimli (dwarf), 10, 93
Ginsberg, Maury, 199
gizmo, 14, 24, 31, 174
    failed, unable to be replicated, 105
    mind-mashing, Romulan, 153
    see also doohickey, gadget
G'Kar, 10
Gless, Sharon, 80
Glover, John, 22
goatee, 38, 59, 65, 79, 118
gold, 70
    belt buckle, 115
    braid, 77
    colour of uniform, 59, 205
gold-pressed latinum *see* latinum (gold-pressed)
Goldsmith, Jerry, 164, 169
Goldstein, Jenette, 160
Goodfellas (1990 movie), 77
Google, 118
gossip, 32
Gowron, Chancellor, 84, 86, 98, 148, 152
Grable, Betty, 43
Graham, Gerrit, 199
grammar, 39
Grand Guignol, 94
grand jury, 92
Grand Nagus *see* Zek
Gray, Bruce, 20
Great Link, The, 84, 141, 149

Great River, The, 141
Grey, Joel, 194
Grilka, 88
Grodénchik, Max, 61
grunts, 67
guerrilla warfare, 62, 151
Guinan, 161
gun, 12, 57, 123, 143, 150, 165
   see also phaser
gunrunning *see* arms dealing

Hackett, Martha, 43, 174, 179, 193–4, 206
   wasted, 196, 200
hairstyle, 27, 43, 53, 59, 65, 82, 113, 137,
   191, 192
Half a Life (**TNG** episode), 177–8
hallucination, 122, 126, 137, 170
Haney, Anne, 8
Hard Time (**DS9** episode), 85
Hardin, Jerry, 178
Harry Potter (book series), ix, 21
Harry Potter (character), 53
Harryhausen, Ray, 206
hat (tinfoil), 91, 116
Hawk, Lt, 165–6
H-bomb, 43
Heart of Stone (**DS9** episode), 64
Hepburn, Katharine, 169
Hertzler, J.G., 102, 146
Higgins, Henry, 67
high priest *see* priest
Highwater, Jamake *see* Marks, Jackie
Hill Street Blues (US TV show), 110
Hippocratic Oath (**DS9** episode), 81, 85
hippy (movement), 52
His Way (**DS9** episode), 135
Hitchhiker's Guide to the Galaxy, The, ix
Hoffman, Dustin, 119
Holly (*Red Dwarf*), 172
Hollywood, 171
Holodeck, 180, 181, 184, 187, 188, 189,
   190, 192
   power source of, 175
hologram, 49, 53, 96, 99, 100, 121, 128,
   139, 142, 144, 170, 174, 199
   decoy ships, 206
Holonovel, 181, 192
holosuite, 25, 49, 56, 72, 77, 93, 94, 100,
   129, 139, 144, 147, 157

homophobia, 69
homosexual anxiety, 25
homosexuality, 23, 69
Honey I Shrunk the Kids (1989 movie), 123
Honor Among Thieves (**DS9** episode), 145
Hope, Leslie, 125
Hopkins, Kaitlin, 87
horse, 162
Host, The (**TNG** episode), 3
Hot Wife, 177
House of Quark, The (**DS9** episode), 88
'House that Jack Built, The' (*Avengers*
   episode), 172, 190
hoverball, 91
Hudson, Cal, 35–6
human(s), 2, 10, 14, 30, 38, 44, 53, 57, 60,
   68, 71, 73, 83, 87, 88, 91, 93, 103, 117,
   125, 127, 139, 165, 182, 202
   assessed by Quark, 142
hydroponics, 172

I, Borg (**TNG** episode), 67
idiom, 37
If Wishes Were Horses (**DS9** episode), 41
illusion, 189
I'm All Right Jack (1959 movie), 76
Image in the Sand (**DS9** episode), 137
Immunity Syndrome, The (**Star Trek**
   episode), 70
imprisonment, 31
impulse power, 200
In Purgatory's Shadow (**DS9** episode),
   108
In the Cards (**DS9** episode), 108
In the Hands of the Prophets (**DS9**
   episode), 18
In the Pale Moonlight (**DS9** episode),
   135, 157
Incredible Shrinking Man, The (1957
   movie), 123
India(n), 27, 99
Indiscretion (**DS9** episode), 75
Initiations (**Voyager** episode), 207
in-joke, 27
Inner Light, The (**TNG** episode), 78, 127
Inquisition (**DS9** episode), 135
insanity *see* madness, 15
insurance, 83
internet, 90

Internet Movie Database, x
Invasion of the Body Snatchers (1956
    movie), 30
Ironside (US TV show), 109
Ishka, 61, 102, 114, 120, 131
It's A Wonderful Life (1946 movie), 66
Itzin, Gregory, 8

Jack (genetically enhanced), 119
Jackson, Peter (director), 10
jail *see* prison
James Bond (media franchise), 27, 35, 72
Janeway, Captain Kathryn, 60, 93, 111,
    128, 168, 169, 170, 171, 172, 173–4, 175,
    178–9, 180, 181, 184, 185, 186, 187, 188,
    191, 192, 193, 194, 196, 197, 199, 200,
    202, 203, 204–205, 205–206
    husband, 188–9
Janeway, Captain Nicole, 168
Janeway, Mark, 188–9
Jaro Essa, 20–1
Javert (*Les Miserables*), 96
Jem'Hadar, 41, 43, 45, 47–8, 67, 69, 81, 82,
    84, 87, 97, 98, 104, 107, 112, 113, 114,
    115, 117, 124, 130, 134, 142, 154, 158
    factions, 123
Jenner, Barry, 115
Jens, Salome, 84, 115, 141
Jetrel, Dr, 183
Johnson, Penny, 61, 80
Jonas, Michael, 200
Jones, Indiana, 71
Jonestown Massacre, 143–4
Joseph (SS *Santa Maria*), 31
journalism, 89
Joyce, James, 5
Julius Caesar (Shakespeare play), 58
Junior Encyclopaedia of Space, The, 172
justice system, 39

K'Ehleyr, 88
K7 (space station), 90
Kafka, Franz, 40, 148
Kahn, Lenara, 69
Kakapo, 89
Kamelion, 195
kamikaze *see* suicide run
Kamin, 78
Kazon, 170, 179, 180, 187, 188, 193–4,
    195, 196, 200, 205, 206, 207

K-E, Elmie, 23
Keaton, Michael, 119
Kendra Massacre, 39
Keogh, Captain Declan, 41
Kes, 134, 170, 172, 175, 181, 185, 188–9,
    191, 193, 199, 204, 207
    relationship with Neelix, 190, 191
Ketracel White, 113, 115
Khan Noonien Singh *see* Noonien
    Singh, Khan
Khan, Razka, 68
Kilana, 87
Kiley, Richard, 26
Kim, Ensign Harry, 169, 170, 174, 175,
    176, 177, 178, 180, 182, 183, 185, 187,
    189–190, 190, 191, 194, 195, 197, 198,
    201, 202, 204, 207, 202–203
    in love, 178
    returned from the dead, 177
Kira Meru, 125
Kira Nerys, Intendant, 57, 79, 118
Kira Nerys, Major, 3, 4, 5, 8, 9, 12, 13, 14,
    16–17, 19, 20, 21, 25, 26, 30, 31, 32,
    33, 35, 36, 37, 38, 44, 46–7, 50, 51, 52,
    53–4, 62, 65, 68, 70, 72, 75, 77, 81, 84,
    85, 86, 88, 95, 97, 98, 101, 106, 107, 108,
    112, 113, 115, 116, 117, 119, 120, 121,
    123, 124, 125, 129, 130, 136, 138, 140,
    142, 143–4, 146, 151, 152–3, 154, 155,
    156, 157
    absent, 23
    carrying Keiko's baby, 83, 94, 99
    hologram of, 49
    promoted to colonel, 137
    relationship with Garak, 48
    relationship with Odo, 74, 103–104,
        116, 117, 118, 129
    sidelined, 81–2, 91
Kirk, Captain James T., ix, 38, 74, 90, 101,
    110, 159–60, 162, 169, 185, 196, 203
    death of, 164–6
kiss, 69, 175, 180, 188
Kite, Fred, 76
Kleavage Sisters *see* Duras Sisters
Klingon(s), 5, 22, 28, 34, 38, 45, 56, 65–6,
    66, 71, 75–6, 79, 80, 83, 84, 85, 86, 89,
    90, 98, 102–103, 104, 114, 124, 134, 138,
    139, 141–2, 151, 162, 168, 182, 187
    food, 53

gods, 73
language, 103
opera, 97, 129
religion, 73, 75, 117, 137
rituals, 75
Klingon Empire, 77, 98, 103
Koenig, Andrew, 27
Koenig, Walter, 27, 163, 164
Kor (Klingon), 71, 141
Krige, Alice, 165
Krim Aldos, General, 20, 21
Krusiec, Michelle, 131
Kryptonite (metaphorical), 150
Kubus Oak, 39
Kurn (Klingon), 75
Kurosawa, Akira, 120
Kurtzman, Alex, 158

La Forge, Geordi, 7, 10, 23, 30, 60, 72, 159,
    161, 162–3, 165, 171
LA Law (US TV show), 18, 110
labour camp, 16, 19
Langella, Frank, 19–20
language, 6, 47
Las Vegas, 129
latinum (gold-pressed), 22, 34, 119, 121
    first mention of, 5
Lawrence, Sharon, 187
Leanne (Jake's girlfriend), 53
Learning Curve (Voyager episode), 191
Lecter, Hannibal, 145
Leeta (Dabo girl), 91, 99, 102, 107, 117
legend, 60
Legion (Red Dwarf), 195
Legolas, 10, 93
Leiter, Felix, 35–6
Lennier, Ambassador, 142
Let Who is Without Sin (DS9 episode), 108
Lethean(s), 56
Lewis, C.S., 180
Leyton, Admiral, 73
Li Nalas, 19, 21
Liebkind, Franz, 32
Lien, Jennifer, 170, 174, 189, 191
Life Support (DS9 episode), 118
Lifesigns (Voyager episode), 207
Line of Duty (UK TV show), 126
Liotta, Ray, 77
literature, 58, 92

'Little Achievements' (fan fiction), 23
Little Green Men (DS9 episode), 85,
    121, 158
little person, 203
Lloyd, Rob, 147
Locarno, Nicholas, 169
location (filming on), 93, 170
lockdown, 6, 22, 23
Lofton, Cirroc, 2, 10, 18, 26, 32, 64, 65, 66,
    88–9, 106
log see captain's log
Londo, 10
Looking for par'Mach in All the Wrong Places
    (DS9 episode), 108, 158
Lord of the Rings, The (movie series), 10
Lord of the Rings, The (novel series), 93
Lore (TNG character), 110
Lost (US TV show), 111
Lost in Space (US TV show), 142
love see romance
love potion, 50
Luddite, 30–1
lungs (stolen), 181
lungstealers see Vidiian(s)
Luvsitt, Mona, 72

MacGuffin, 3, 19, 21, 100, 124
Macht, Stephen, 20, 21
Mad Max (film series), 12
Madison, Lt Tawny, 96
madness, 15
Madred, Gul, 40
MAGA, 91
magic door (dear old), 180
magic see sleight of hand
Magnificent Ferengi, The (DS9
    episode), 135
make-up (prosthetic), 10, 11, 20, 22, 23, 24,
    25, 31, 34, 74, 97, 100, 122, 123, 183
Man Called Hawk, A (TV show), 59
Man in the Glass Booth, The (play), 17
Mandalorian, 98
Mandan, Robert, 23
Maneuvers (Voyager episode), 207
Manning, Richard, 68
mansplaining, 37
Maquis, the, 35, 36, 49, 53, 80, 95–6,
    104, 110, 158, 168, 169, 170, 171, 172,

177, 179–80, 184, 187, 191, 194, 196,
    205, 207
    rank insignia, 178
Mardah (Dabo girl), 48
Markham, Monte, 91
Marks, Jackie (aka Jamake Highwater),
    171
Marlowe, Philip, 100
Marritza, Aamin, 16, 17
Mars, Kenneth, 32
Marshall, Kenneth, 96, 104
martial law, 73
Martin, Andrea, 61, 102
Martok, General, 97, 102–103, 104, 114,
    117, 141–2, 146, 152, 154, 157
    absent, 133
Marx, Harpo, 139
MASH (US TV show), 18
mask (costume), 46
matriarchy, 27
Matrix, The (1999 movie), 193
Matter of Honor, A (**TNG** episode), 103
Mays, Willie, 106
McCarthy, Dennis, 169
McCormack, Una, 128
McCoy, Dr 'Bones', 90, 160, 196, 199
McDowell, Malcolm, 161
McFadden, Gates, 1, 40
McFly, Marty, 70, 90
McGivers, Lt Marla, 55
McGoohan, Patrick, 47
McKean, Michael, 203
McMillan & Wife (US TV show), 109
McNeill, Robert Duncan, 169, 174, 191
Meaney, Colm, 1, 2, 18, 28, 29, 32, 33, 40,
    63, 78, 89, 105, 124, 131, 153, 159
medal(s), 139
medical emergency, 26, 37, 46, 204
medical ethics, 52–3, 55, 83, 88, 174, 189
medical procedure, 57, 78, 132, 139–40,
    144, 160, 183, 197
medicine, surprising innovations in, 24, 140
meditation, 175
Meld (**Voyager** episode), 207
Melora Pazlar, 24
Melville, Herman, 166
memory, 9, 18, 47, 52, 53, 63, 64, 66, 70, 73,
    76, 78, 89, 90, 102, 108, 109, 119, 141,
    144, 151, 163, 164, 172, 181, 199, 203

mental health issues, 119
mentor, 33
Meridian (**DS9** episode), 64
Metaphor, Key **Star Trek**, 60
Meyer, Nicholas, 163
Midsummer Night's Dream, A (Shakespeare
    play), 50
Miller, Dick, 51
Minbari, 142
mind control, 71, 89
Minder (UK TV show), 27, 101, 121
minefield (figurative), 119
minefield (literal), 107, 116
miniaturisation (of people), 123
Miradorn twins, 11
Mirror Mirror (**Star Trek** episode), 38, 90
Mirror Universe, 37–8, 57, 64, 78–9, 118,
    145, 201
Miserables, Les (novel), 96
mismatched pair, 13, 29, 68, 75, 88, 93, 97,
    120, 191, 194, 205
Miss America, winner of, 91
missile(s), 104, 162
Möbius loop, 190
Moby Dick (novel), 96, 166
Moffat, Steven, 133
monologue(s), 128
Monty Python and the Holy Grail (1974
    movie), 196
Monty Python's Life of Brian (1978
    movie), 125
Moogie *see* Ishka
moon, 53, 187, 192
    Bajor's, 137
    inhabitant of, 130
Moore, Ronald D., 45, 59, 117, 139, 160,
    164, 168
moppet(s), 161, 202
Mora Pol, Dr, 28, 44, 95
moral dilemma *see* ethical dilemma
Morn, 70, 91, 121
    introduction of, 6
    sharking after Dax, 14
morphogenic virus, 141, 149, 150, 152,
    154, 156
Morshower, Glenn, 160
Moses (Jem'Hadar), 47
moustache (twirled), 39, 94, 157

Move Along Home (**DS9** episode), 18, 40, 41
movie(s) (**Star Trek**), x
Mr Mom (1983 movie), 132
Mr Tricorder, 161
Mudd, Harry, 110
Mulgrew, Kate, 157, 168, 169, 171, 172, 174, 185, 201
Mumy, Bill, 142
Muniz, Enrique, 87
Murder One (US TV show), 111
murder-mystery, 5, 176
Muse, The (**DS9** episode), 85
music, 27, 191
    incidental, 72, 101, 112, 139, 164, 169, 190
    absent, 37
    see also theme music
My Fair Lady (musical), 67

Nagus *see* Zek
Naked Time, The (**Star Trek** episode), 7, 15, 175
Nanook of the North, 129
Narnia (book series), 108
Natima Lang, 33–4
Native American, 168, 171, 178, 207
NATO, 60
navy, 60
Nazi(s), 16
NBC (network), 110, 167
nebula, 174
Nechayev, Admiral Alynna, 36
Neelix, 170, 172, 175, 179, 183, 183, 187, 188–9, 192, 194, 195, 197, 200, 203–204, 207
    cooking, 182
    lungs missing, 173–4, 181, 185
    relationship with Kes, 190, 191
Neria, Dr, 178
Neutral Zone, The (**TNG** episode), 187
Neverending Sacrifice, The (Cardassian novel), 37
New Orleans, 73
New York, 122, 178
New York Times, 128
New Zealand, 89
Newton, Sir Isaac, 199

Nexus, 161, 163
Nimoy, Leonard, 170
nitpickers, 90
Nixon, President Richard M., 19, 21
Noah, Dr, 72
Nog (Ferengi), 3, 13, 10–11, 26, 40, 41, 53, 54, 62, 64, 66, 70, 73, 76, 78–9, 92–3, 96, 99, 104, 105, 106, 113, 116, 119, 124, 130-1, 141, 142, 144, 157, 187
    absent, 133
    friendship with Jake, 5, 12–13, 41, 106
Nomad, 198
Noonien Singh, Khan, 55, 99, 164
novel(s), 80, 146
    Cardassian, 37, 56–7, 58
    Star Trek, 17, 163
    see also Holonovel
NTSC (video standard), 2
nuclear weapon, 43, 70
nudity, 40, 205
nurse, 52, 95, 199

O'Brien, Chief Miles, 1, 3, 4, 6, 10, 12–13, 14, 15, 17, 19, 22–3, 28, 29, 30, 31, 32, 33, 38, 39, 48, 51, 52, 54, 56, 57, 58, 60, 62, 67, 72, 73, 75, 77, 79, 85, 86, 87, 88, 89, 96, 99, 105, 107, 116, 120, 121, 123, 125, 126, 136, 138, 140, 141, 144, 146, 147, 149, 150, 151, 152, 155, 157, 178
    absent, 39
    must suffer, 40, 41, 78, 101, 108, 132
    undercover, 123–4
O'Brien, Keiko, 5, 17, 23, 29, 30, 67, 77, 78, 83, 88, 89, 95, 99, 130, 132, 157
O'Brien, Kirayoshi, 132
O'Brien, Molly, 30, 132
Obsidian Order, the, 37, 58
Ocampan(s), 193
Ocean's 11 (1960 movie), 146
Octopussy (1983 movie), 27
Oculus Quest, 150
Odan, 3
Odd Couple, The (play), 29, 55, 93, 120
Odo, Constable, ix, 3, 4, 5, 6, 8, 9, 15, 16, 21, 22, 25, 28, 30, 32, 36, 38, 39, 43, 44, 45, 46, 47, 51, 52, 53–4, 56, 58–9, 62, 63, 64, 65–6, 67, 70, 72, 79, 80, 81, 84, 85, 92–3, 100, 107, 113, 114, 115, 119, 126,

128, 130, 132, 133, 136, 140, 146, 149, 151, 152, 153, 154, 155, 156, 170, 171
absent, 23
as a solid, 86, 89, 95, 108
origins of, 11
relationship with Kira, 74, 103–104, 116, 117, 118, 129
relationship with Quark, 10, 20, 24, 48
Odyssey, USS, 41
Offenhouse, Ralph, 187
On the Buses (UK TV show), 130
One Flew Over the Cuckoo's Nest (1975 movie), 118, 140
One Million Years BC (1966 movie), 206
one thing I don't understand, 54
Only Fools and Horses (UK TV show), 13
Opaka, Kai, 3, 12
opening titles *see* credits
opera (Klingon), 29, 97, 129
optimism, 12, 30, 35, 41
Orb(s) of the Prophets, 3, 12, 38, 118, 125, 138
orchid(s), 205
Original Series, The *see* **Star Trek**, 31
Orion Syndicate, 123, 144
Orpheus (*The Matrix*), 193
Orville, The (US TV show), 61
Oscar *see* Academy Award
Our Man Bashir (**DS9** episode), 85, 100, 129
Our Man Flint (1966 movie), 72

Pa'Dar, Kotan, 23
Pa'Dar, Rugal *see* Rugal
PADD, 10, 21, 125
Pah-wraith(s), 130, 132, 134, 143, 149, 150, 155, 156
Pais, Josh, 101, 120
pantomime, 15
Paradas, 30
Paradise Syndrome, The (**Star Trek** episode), 31
Parallax (**Voyager** episode), 173
Paramount (studio), 1, 3, 85, 89, 110–11, 160, 164, 167, 168
parenthood, 95, 97, 99, 101, 114, 120, 189, 202, 205

Paris, Lt Tom, 169, 170, 172, 173, 174, 175, 176–7, 182, 183, 185, 187, 188, 196–7, 199, 200, 205, 206, 207
interest in ancient vehicles, 186
out of uniform, 190
relationship with Kes, 190, 191
Parker, Jennifer, 185
Parn, Legate, 36
passing (as white), 182
Past Tense (**DS9** episode), 64, 71
peace conference, 52, 72
Peel, John, 17
Pel, 25
penal system, 39, 78, 169
Penumbra (**DS9** episode), 153, 155, 156
perspective, story told from an unusual, 30
Peters, Brock, 73
Peyton Place (US TV show), 109
phage, 199, 201
phaser(s), 36, 54, 118, 175, 186
Philips, Gina, 12–13
Phillips, Ethan, 166, 170, 174, 183, 187, 189, 204
phone, people playing on, 23
photon torpedo, 205
Picard, Captain Jean-Luc, 1, 2, 3, 7, 20, 23, 30, 35, 40, 60, 67, 73, 110, 128, 139, 158, 159, 161–3, 164–6, 169, 176, 185
compared to Sisko, 12
relationship with Dr Crusher, 74
Picard, René, 161
Picard, Robert, 161
Picardo, Robert, 99, 166, 170, 171, 174, 180, 185, 206
Pike, Captain Christopher, 3, 46, 133–4
Piller, Michael, 27, 68, 168, 171, 173, 184
pilot, 197
Pink Panther (movie franchise), 83
pips (rank), 59, 65
Pirates of the Caribbean (movie franchise), 160
Piscopo, Joe, 128, 142
Pitt, Brad, 119
plague, 182, 183
Plakson, Suzie, 1
Planet Hell, 191
plastic surgery, 16, 75
Plomeek Soup, 182

plot device, 21
plot hole, 63, 126
    see also fridge logic
podcast
    Neelix's, 200
    Star Trek related, 106
poet, 76
poison, 96
politics, 21, 36, 38
Pon Farr, 189
pool (cue sport), 183, 190
Pop, Iggy, 120
positronic(s), 53
Potter, Harry see Harry Potter
power shortage, 73, 173, 175, 206
pox see morphogenic virus, 141
Practice, The (US TV show), 164
pregnancy, 79, 83, 84, 85, 86, 88, 94, 155,
    157, 201
Press Gang (UK TV show), 133
Pressman, Lawrence, 47
pre-Warp civilisation(s), 20
priest (Bajoran), 3
Prime Directive, 6, 20, 178, 196
Primmin, Lt, 9
Prin, Silaran, 94
Princess Bride, The (1987 movie), 131
prison, 19, 67, 98, 120, 149, 182, 194
Prisoner, The (UK TV show), 46, 148
prize, 55, 86, 106, 151
Producers, The (1967 movie), 32
profit, 5, 9, 55, 120, 165
Profit and Lace (DS9 episode), 135, 158
Progress (DS9 episode), 16, 18
promenade, 26, 56, 147
promotion, 59, 63, 131, 138, 160, 172
prophecy, 54–5, 76, 94, 129
Prophet Motive (DS9 episode), 64
prophet(s), 39, 54, 76, 130, 134, 149, 150
    see also wormhole aliens
protein cofactors, 205
psychopathy, 37, 62, 198, 205
pun, 106
puppet, 88, 191
puzzle, 9
'Pyramids of Mars' (Doctor Who serial), 9

Q (Star Trek character), 7, 110, 199
Q Who (TNG episode), 41

Q-Less (DS9 episode), 18, 199
Quantum Leap (US TV show), 109
quantum singularity (type IV), 172
Quark (Ferengi), 3, 4, 6, 10, 16, 21, 22,
    24–5, 27, 30, 33, 36, 40–1, 44, 45, 47, 49,
    55, 56, 69, 70, 74, 82, 83, 84, 85, 88, 91,
    92–3, 94, 95, 100–10, 112, 117, 119–20,
    121, 125, 127, 130, 131, 132, 137, 138,
    142, 144, 149, 151, 152, 153, 154, 155,
    157, 169, 170
    absent, 23, 39
    in love, 33–4
    objectifiying Dax, 9, 18
    pronunciation of name, 5, 9, 67
    relationship with Odo, 11, 20, 48
Quark's Bar, 19, 27, 34, 56, 73, 76, 86, 102,
    121, 138, 145
Quark's Treasure (spaceship), 70
quicksand, 31, 53

Rached, Nurse Mildred, 21
racism, 23, 51, 119, 122, 170, 182
Radcliffe, Daniel, 65
radiation, 56, 133
Raiders of the Lost Ark (1981 movie), 71
Rain Man (1988 movie), 119
raktajino, 26
Rand, Yeoman Janice, 109
Ransom, Tim, 119
Rapture (DS9 episode), 97, 164
Ratatouille (2007 movie), 88
ratings see viewing figures
Ravinok (spaceship), 68
Red Dwarf (UK TV show), 28, 57, 109,
    169, 172, 195
Red Squad, 73, 130
redshirt(s), 87, 105, 196
Reilly, Bobby, 148
Rejoined (DS9 episode), 85
Relics (TNG episode), 160
religion, 129, 143
    Bajoran, 3, 12, 17, 114, 118
Remmick, Lt Cmdr Dexter, 126
remote projectors (hologram), 188
replication, 62, 80, 92, 105, 117
    biomolecular, 55
replicator(s), 10, 80, 92, 174, 175
reset button, 20, 37, 66, 82, 85, 108, 140,
    196, 197, 201, 203

Resolutions (**Voyager** episode), 82
'Rest of My Life, The' (*Press Gang* episode), 133
restoration (of **Star Trek** episodes), 93
ret-con, 44
Reunion (**TNG** episode), 114
Rick and Morty (US TV show), 56
Riker, Cmdr William T., 49, 103, 163, 165, 191
Riker, Thomas, 38, 49–50
riots, 51
Risa, 91
Rix, Brian, 25
Ro Laren, Ensign, 1, 178
Robinson, Andrew, 4, 23, 34, 36, 37, 58, 59, 64, 97, 105, 122, 128, 156
Robocop (1987 movie), 92, 195
Rocks and Shoals (**DS9** episode), 135
Roddenberry, Gene, 20, 35, 122, 168
    no conflict rule, 5
Rom (Ferengi), 11, 24, 25, 26, 44, 55, 70, 72, 76, 85, 102, 107, 116, 117, 120, 136, 142, 144, 157
    absent, 133
romance, 7, 23, 26, 32, 33, 34, 50, 52, 53, 61, 68, 69, 74, 79, 88, 91, 96, 99, 102, 104, 115, 116, 124, 125, 130, 140, 151, 153, 156, 175, 190, 199, 207
Romeo and Juliet (play), 129
Romulan(s), 37, 43, 45, 56, 59, 83, 97, 127–8, 129, 134, 148, 153, 161, 176
    weapons, 137
Roseanne (US TV show), 110
Ross, Admiral William, 137, 148, 157
Rostand, Edmond, 87
Roswell, New Mexico, 70
Rotarran (spaceship), 115
Rozhenko, Alexander, 114
Rugal, 23
Rule(s) of Acquisition, 11, 35
    rewritten by Grand Nagus, 55
Rules of Acquisition (**DS9** episode), 61
Rumpole of the Bailey (UK TV show), 39
runabout, 12, 30, 31, 41, 43, 54, 67, 92, 97, 98, 104, 107, 123, 137, 157
running gag, 14, 70
Rusot, Gul, 152
Russ, Tim, 22, 57, 160, 170, 171, 185, 198, 204, 207

Russell, Benny, 122, 137
Russia, 60
Russian doll, 188

Sadler, William, 126, 148, 153
sailing ship (solar), 59
Salinsky, Tom, 162
San Francisco, 189
Sanctuary District, 51
Sao Paulo, USS, 154
Sarandon, Chris, 27
Sarina (mental patient), 140
satire, 72, 76, 120, 160
saucer-separation, 4
sauna, 81
scanner screen, 35
Schuck, John, 36
Schultz, Dwight, 188
Schweitzer, Albert, 180
science fiction, 26, 71, 89, 122–3, 137, 175, 207
scientist(s), 26, 54–5, 69, 72, 176, 183
Scoggins, Tracy, 55
Scotch (whisky), 125
Scott, Captain Montgomery, 160, 163
screwball comedy, 7
seafaring explorers, 59–60, 164, 182
Second Chances (**TNG** episode), 170
Second Skin (**DS9** episode), 64, 101
Second World War, 16
Section 31, 148, 153, 155
security (Starfleet), 9
self-destruct, 48, 206
self-sealing stem bolts, 13–14, 55, 106
serialisation, 19–20, 22, 61, 76, 85, 97, 109–11, 155, 207
    lack of, 25
Seska, 174, 178–9, 179–80, 193, 196, 198, 199, 200, 205–206
Seskal, 155
Seven of Nine, 199
Seven Samurai (1954 movie), 120
sexism, 13, 14, 18, 27, 55, 61, 131
Seymour, Carolyn, 192
Shakaar, 62, 74, 84, 95, 103, 107, 108
    absent, 102
Shakespeare, William, 11, 50
Shane (1953 movie), 144

shapeshifter(s), 11, 59, 74, 84, 95, 146
  see also Changeling, Odo, TFC
shapeshifting, physics of, 5, 11
Shatner, William, 160, 163–4
shaving, 71
Shawn, Wallace, 10, 24–5, 32, 55, 102, 131
Shepherd, Mark Allen, 121
shields, 107, 175, 194
Shimerman, Armin, 2, 8, 10, 18, 25, 34, 41,
  61, 67, 83, 88, 93, 102, 116, 121
Ship, The (**DS9** episode), 108, 157
Shore Leave (**Star Trek** episode), 14
short cut, 175, 185
shuttle(craft), 7, 21, 22, 26, 44, 53, 72, 104,
  153, 171, 187
shuttlepod, 133
Shyamalan, M. Night, 30
sickbay, 188, 201
Siddig, Alexander, 2, 8, 9, 18, 22, 29, 37, 52,
  53, 79, 97, 113, 118, 119, 122, 126, 148,
  153, 157
  as director, 101, 131
Siege of AR-558, The (**DS9** episode), 157
Sikarians, 178–9
Silence of the Lambs, The (1991 movie),
  121, 145
Simple Investigation, A (**DS9** episode), 108
Sinatra, Frank, 128
Sirella, 117
Sirtis, Marina, 1
Sisko, Benjamin, ix, 3–4, 5, 9, 10, 11, 12,
  16, 17, 21, 23, 25, 26, 30, 31, 35, 36, 41,
  42, 44, 45, 46, 47, 48, 49, 51–2, 54, 57–8,
  59–60, 61, 62, 64, 65, 66, 67, 68, 70, 71,
  72, 73, 74, 75, 76–7, 79, 80–1, 85, 86, 87,
  90, 92, 93, 94, 95–6, 97, 98, 101, 103,
  104, 105–106, 107, 108, 114–15, 116,
  117, 120, 121, 122, 123, 125, 127–8, 129,
  132, 133, 136, 137, 139, 140, 142, 147,
  149, 151, 152, 154, 155, 156, 157, 176
  absent, 39
  badly cut uniform, 11
  bonding with son, 19
  compared to Picard, 7
  perspective of, 3
Sisko, Jake, 10–11, 13, 20, 27, 29, 41, 44,
  48, 50, 53, 60, 63, 64, 66, 73, 78, 79, 85,
  88–9, 92–3, 104, 105, 107, 112, 113, 117,
  129, 130–1, 133, 151, 154, 155, 157
  absent, 25, 39
  academic career, 31, 32, 40
  mother, 26
  relationship with father, 19
  relationship with Nog, 5, 11, 12, 53,
    73, 92–3
Sisko, Jennifer, 3, 57–8, 78–9
Sisko, Joseph, 73, 122
sitcom, 27–8, 32, 91, 99, 102, 106, 110,
  125, 173
Skrreean(s), 27
Sky (television network), 2
sleight of hand, 69
Sloan (Internal Affairs), 126, 148, 153
Sloane, Lily, 165
Sloyan, James, 28, 183
smart bomb, 205
Smith, Kurtwood, 92
Smith, Melanie, 97
smuggling, 70
snitch (golden), 21
soap opera (daytime, dreadful, writers of),
  109, 177
softie (pillow-sniffing), 80
Son'a, 144
Soran, 162
Sorcerer's Apprentice, The, (folktale) 54
soup, 179, 182, 205
South Park (US TV show), 119
Space Jesus, 3, 93, 157
Space Seed (**Star Trek** episode), 55
space squash, 28
space station (abandoned, corpse-ridden),
  7, 9, 161
space:
  long career in, 24
  real-life journey to, 164
space-sickness, 137, 138
speed limit, 50
Spenser for Hire (US TV show), 59
Spiner, Brent, 1, 161, 171
Spitting Image (UK TV show), 181
Spock, Mr, 38, 90, 101, 160, 170, 184,
  196, 198
  death of, 166
Spock's Brain (**Star Trek** episode), 174
sports movies, 139
spreadsheet, ix
spy, 200

spy film, 94
St Elsewhere (US TV show), 110
stand-up comedy, 142
star rating, x, 14, 32, 47, 54, 72, 89, 105, 122, 177, 192, 203, 207
Star Trek (1966 TV show), ix, 14, 15, 29, 31, 34, 37–8, 55, 60, 85, 89, 93, 108, 126, 127, 163, 164, 170, 186, 203
  compared to **Deep Space Nine**, 18, 42
Star Trek (franchise), 36, 40, 70, 77, 94, 122, 128, 155, 158, 160, 166, 167, 168, 169, 171
  best ever episodes, 127
Star Trek (movies), 36
Star Trek: Discovering the Television Series Volume I, ix
Star Trek: Discovering the Television Series Volume II, ix
Star Trek: Discovering the Television Series Volume III, ix
Star Trek II: The Wrath of Khan, 163, 164, 206
  compared to *First Contact*, 166
Star Trek IV: The Voyage Home, 165
Star Trek VI: The Undiscovered Country, 66
Star Trek: Deep Space Nine, ix, 159, 160, 168, 169, 171, 173, 178, 183, 187, 189, 192
  compared to **Voyager**, 171, 181, 197, 168
Star Trek: Discovery, 14, 38, 69, 94
Star Trek: Enterprise, ix
Star Trek: First Contact, 2, 51, 92, 93, 122
Star Trek: Generations, 2, 45, 49, 164
  compared to *First Contact*, 165
Star Trek: Insurrection, 144, 148
Star Trek: Lower Decks, 157
Star Trek: Nemesis, x, 157
Star Trek: Picard, 51, 157
Star Trek: Strange New Worlds, 46, 111
Star Trek: The Animated Series, 18
Star Trek: The Motion Picture, 115, 160
  compared to *Generations*, 163
Star Trek: The Next Generation, ix, 1, 2, 15, 28, 38, 45, 50, 59, 63, 64, 71, 73, 81, 85, 104, 108, 109–10, 114, 126, 134, 137, 159, 160, 170, 173, 177–8, 187, 192
  best ever episodes, 127

compared to **Deep Space Nine**, 4, 8, 9, 10, 17–18, 21, 23, 26, 29, 30, 31, 41, 46, 66, 74, 157
compared to **Voyager**, 168, 171, 181
end of run, 42
episode remade for **Voyager**, 188
ratings, 111
remastered, 3
role of the Maquis in, 35
stages used by, 168
uniforms, 9, 65
writing staff, 68
Star Trek: Voyager, ix, 2, 42, 43, 48, 50, 53, 64, 99, 103, 108, 111, 134, 158, 159, 160, 164, 165
  compared to **Deep Space Nine**, 18, 65, 74, 82, 85, 90–1, 120, 147
costumes, 9, 73, 93
role of the Maquis in, 35
uniforms, 9, 73
Star Wars (1977 movie), 81
starbase, 115, 172
Starfleet, 2, 9, 16, 26, 31, 35, 36, 37, 41, 44, 45, 49, 54, 60, 62, 64, 66, 67, 74, 78, 86, 87, 96, 99, 103, 107, 114, 116, 126, 132, 140, 142, 144, 145, 148, 152, 162, 171, 173, 175, 178, 184, 185, 187, 194, 195, 196, 197, 205, 207
Starfleet Academy, 51, 70, 73, 146
Starfleet Intelligence, 124, 138
Starship Down (**DS9** episode), 85
stasis, 53, 202, 204
Steuer, Jon Paul, 114
Stewart, Martha, 162
Stewart, Patrick, 1, 2, 161, 166, 170
Sting (pop music artist), 47
stories (all true, especially the lies), 37
Storyteller, The (**DS9** episode), 18
Sto'Vo'Kor, 137
Straczynski, J. Michael, 134
streaming (TV), 111
Strickland, Gail, 31
stun (phasers set to), 36, 179
Sturges, John, 120
submarine, 69
subspace seaweed, 33
Suder, Lon, 205
suffragette(s), 60

suicide, 41, 52, 131, 134, 156, 199, 207
Sulu, Hikaru, 163
sunblock, 41
surgery *see* plastic surgery
surrender, 96, 107, 119, 140, 156
survival suit, 92
Suspicions (**TNG** episode), 29
Suspiria (**Voyager** character), 193
swearing, 132
Swit, Loretta, 80
symbiont, 8, 22, 69
Symbiosis (**TNG** episode), 67
syndication (television), 4, 5, 42, 85, 157
synergy (corporate, cross-franchise), 49–50, 57, 99

Tain, Enabran, 59, 97
Take Me Out to the Holosuite (**DS9** episode), 158
Takei, George, 164
Tal Shiar, 37, 59
Talaxian(s), 170, 182, 200, 203, 206
Tarzan (character), 132
taser, 189
Tattoo (**Voyager** episode), 207
taxation, 69
Taylor, Jeri, 111, 168, 171, 184
tchotchke, 143
teaser, 5, 14, 24, 33, 57, 74, 79, 98, 104, 115, 120, 123, 174, 188, 194, 195, 196, 198, 200
Technicolor, 93
technobabble, 173, 180, 182, 186, 188, 191, 201
tennis, 57
Terok Nor, 79, 92
terrorism, 35, 152, 171, 173, 187, 205
text scroll, 168
TFC (The Female Changeling), 116, 141, 149, 150, 154, 156, 157
Thames TV (UK production company), 27
Thaw, The (**Voyager** episode), 207
theme music, 27, 65, 164, 169
thing (blue, wibbly), 190, 191
Thing, The (1982 movie), 105
Third Man, The (1949 movie), 101
this-is-the-story-we-tell-with-this-character, 15, 21, 24
Thompson, Susanna, 69

Thomson, Spike, 133
Thrax, 92
Threshold (**Voyager** episode), 205, 207
Through the Looking Glass (**DS9** episode), 64, 78
Tigan, Ezri, 144
Time to Stand, A (**DS9** episode), 116
time travel, 50–2, 56, 66, 70, 92, 103, 122, 131–2, 165, 173, 176, 187
T'Lara, Admiral, 77
To the Death (**DS9** episode), 85
Todd, Tony, 66, 75
Toddman, Admiral, 59
Tongo (game), 25, 125
Tootsie (1982 movie), 131
Torchwood (UK TV show), 77
Torres, Lt B'Elanna, 168, 170, 172, 178, 179, 180, 181, 182, 188, 189, 192, 193–4, 196–7, 198, 200, 202–203, 206
    repair time estimates (not exaggerated), 180
torture, 20, 37, 59, 125, 148, 149, 153
Total Recall (1990 movie), 100
trade union, 76
Trainspotting (1996 movie), 36
Trakor (Bajoran prophet), 55
transgender, 69
translator *see* universal translator
transporter, 31, 51, 57, 60, 72, 126, 133, 142, 146, 155, 179, 183, 186, 193, 201, 202, 205
    automatic, 29, 32, 38, 96
    malfunctioning, 203
trans-warp drive, 197
treasure map, 71
Treasure of the Sierra Madre, The (1948 movie), 71
Trial, The (novel), 148
Trials and Tribble-ations (**DS9** episode), 108, 122, 127
trick *see* sleight of hand
tricorder, 57, 161, 188
Trill(s), 3, 7, 22, 33, 46, 62, 69, 117, 130, 136, 139, 158
Troi, Counsellor Deanna, 30, 88, 161, 162, 163, 170
    relationship with Worf, 74
Troi, Lwaxana, 15, 46, 50, 79–80
Trotter, Del Boy and Rodney, 13

Trouble with Tribbles, The (**Star Trek**
    episode), 90
T'Rul, 43
Trump, Donald, 91
turbolift, 188
Tuvix (individual), 203–204, 205
Tuvok, Lt, 168, 169, 170, 179, 182, 183,
    184, 186, 189, 190, 193, 194, 196, 198,
    202, 204, 205, 206, 207
    marriage, 177
    on **DS9**, 57
Twain, Mark, 178
Twilight Zone, The (US TV show), 91, 193
Twitter, 54
Two Ronnies, The (UK TV show), 27

Uhura, Lt Nyota, 109, 163
Unhappily Ever After (US TV show), 168
uniform(s), ix, 2, 19, 21, 26, 31, 35, 41, 43,
    47, 59, 63, 65, 73, 93, 97, 99, 115, 148,
    159, 164–5, 188, 199, 205
    bonkers admirals', 77
    floppy necklines, 9, 11
    Odo, 84
    painted on, 38
    unreplicatable, 10
union *see* trade union
United Federation of Planets, ix, 5, 12, 27,
    28, 29, 30, 36, 39, 41, 45, 48, 51, 58, 60,
    62, 63, 66, 70, 73, 80, 84, 85, 89, 91, 92,
    94, 96, 98, 103, 105, 107, 110, 112, 115,
    116, 119, 131, 134, 141, 142, 151, 154,
    155, 158, 169, 178, 179, 180, 184, 185,
    187, 197, 206
    always-knows-best, 177, 195
    territory controlled by, 50
universal translator, 27, 70
unobtainium, 175, 177, 194
UPN (network), 85, 108, 111, 168
utopia, 12

valet, 72
Valiant, USS, 130–1
Vantika, Rao, 9
Varis Sul, 13
Vash, 7
VCR(s), 109
vegetables (revolting, ferreted out by
    Neelix), 179

Verad Kalon, 22
Veridian III, 162
V'Ger, 195
VHS *see* VCR(s)
video game, 5, 163, 201, 205
Vidiian(s), 201, 205
viewing figures, 4, 109, 110–11
virtual reality, 149, 150
virus, word-scrambling, 6, 204
vision quest, 94
Visitor, Nana, 1, 2, 3, 8, 12, 16–17, 18, 20,
    33, 34, 38, 46–7, 54, 63, 74, 83, 92, 94,
    104, 115, 118, 126, 129, 146
Visitor, The (**DS9** episode), 80, 85, 127
VISOR, 162–3
visual effects, 3, 11, 90, 99, 116, 130, 132,
    134, 156, 169, 178, 201, 206
    shoddy, 67
vole(s), 33
Vorta, 87, 102, 107, 113, 117, 120, 141, 158
Voyager, USS, 165, 169, 173, 177, 178, 183,
    187, 190, 192, 194, 195, 196, 198, 199,
    200, 201, 202, 204, 207
    best ship in the Quadrant, 176, 180
    crew of, 172
    evacuated, 205–206
    landing on planet, 186
Vulcan (planet), 129
Vulcan(s), 35, 36, 10, 139, 160, 184, 194,
    196, 203, 207
    first contact with, 166

Wadi, The, 9
'Wagon Train to the Stars', 1
waiter, 7
Waltz (**DS9** episode), 135
war, 12, 64, 163
    is hell, 88, 142–3
    see also Dominion War
war criminal, 16, 183
war games, 75
Warner Bros. (studio), 167–8
Warner, David, 4
warp core, 130, 170
    breach, 66, 188
warp drive, 31, 43, 50, 169, 194, 197, 200
    historic first flight, 165
Washington Post, 171
Wayans Bros., The (US TV show), 168

WB, The (network), 167–8
weapon(s), 5, 29, 43, 64, 84, 100–101, 134, 137, 143, 151, 153, 179, 183
wedding, 107, 112, 117, 149
Weekend at Bernie's (1989 movie), 120
weightlessness, 24
Welles, Orson, 101
West Side Story (1961 movie), 19
West Wing, The (US TV show), 111
Westmore, Michael, 11, 22, 25, 97, 100, 123, 183
Weyoun, 81, 83, 85, 102, 106, 107, 113, 115, 116, 120, 126, 140–1, 149, 150, 151, 154, 156, 157
    absent, 133
wheelchair, 24
White *see* Ketracel White
wig, 15
Wikipedia, x
Wildman, Ensign Samantha, 201
Williams, Vanessa, 91
Winn Adami, 17, 21, 39, 42, 52–3, 61–2, 64, 85, 94, 105–106, 116, 129–30, 149, 150, 151, 152, 153, 154, 155, 156, 157
    absent, 133
Wire, The (**DS9** episode), 58
Wire, The (US TV show), 62
Wise, Robert, 163
Wizard of Oz, The (1937 movie), 137
Wizard of Oz, The (novel), 106
woke, 69, 75
wolf (cartoon), 21
Wolf 359, 3
Wolfe, Robert Hewitt, 135
Wong, Garrett, 169
Woodard, Alfre, 165
Worden Marc, 114, 117
Worf, Lt Cmdr, 28, 65, 67, 69, 70, 71, 72, 74, 75, 76, 77, 79, 81, 82, 85, 86, 91, 93, 94, 97, 98, 101, 103, 106, 107, 112, 114,
115, 117, 118, 121, 124, 125, 127, 129, 132, 134, 136, 137, 141–2, 146, 150, 151, 152, 154, 155, 160, 162, 163, 165
    absent, 144
    in love, 88
    relationship with Dax, 99, 138
    relationship with Troi, 74
    thought dead, 148–9
World War II *see* Second World War
'Worm That Turned, The' (*Two Ronnies* sketch), 27
Wormhole
    artificial, 69
    Bajoran, 3, 4, 6, 7, 11, 12, 31, 41, 61, 72, 97, 129, 134
    Barzan, 114
    tiddler, 176
wormhole aliens, 4, 117, 134
Wounded, The (**TNG** episode), 23
Wright, Tom, 203–204

Yar, Lt Tasha, 82, 134
Yarka, Vedek, 54
Yates, Kasidy, 61, 66, 68, 80, 94, 122, 133, 147, 149, 155, 157
Yesterday's Enterprise (**TNG** episode), 127, 162
Yojimbo (1961 movie), 151
YouTube, 192
Yulin, Harris, 16–17

Zagbars vs Zoobles, 12, 29, 31, 78, 194, 195
Zek, Grand Nagus, 10, 24, 42, 55, 64, 102, 120, 130, 131, 142, 144, 154
Zimmerman, Dr Lewis, 99
Zimmerman, Herman, 164
Ziyal, 81, 97, 98, 114, 117, 120
zone (in the), 62
Zoom (software platform), 23, 47, 96